On Antisemitism

On
Antisemitism

A Word
in History

Mark
Mazower

Penguin Press   New York   2025

PENGUIN PRESS
An imprint of Penguin Random House LLC
1745 Broadway, New York, NY 10019
penguinrandomhouse.com

LIBRARY OF CONGRESS CATALOGING-IN-PUBLICATION DATA
Names: Mazower, Mark, author
Title: On antisemitism : a word in history / Mark Mazower.
Description: New York : Penguin Press, 2025. |
    Includes bibliographical references and index.
Identifiers: LCCN 2025019238 (print) | LCCN 2025019239 (ebook) |
    ISBN 9780593833797 hardcover | ISBN 9780593833803 ebook
Subjects: LCSH: Antisemitism—History
Classification: LCC DS145 .M378 2025 (print) | LCC DS145 (ebook) |
    DDC 305.892/4—dc23/eng/20250620
LC record available at https://lccn.loc.gov/2025019238
LC ebook record available at https://lccn.loc.gov/2025019239

Printed in the United States of America
1st Printing

The authorized representative in the EU for product safety and compliance is
Penguin Random House Ireland, Morrison Chambers, 32 Nassau Street,
Dublin D02 YH68, Ireland, https://eu-contact.penguin.ie.

in memory of

Michael Davies
(1959–2024)

CONTENTS

Part 1: Europe in the Age of the Antisemites

Part 2: On the Battlefield of Ideas

ACKNOWLEDGMENTS

This book owes a great deal to my intellectual home of the past two decades, Columbia University. In particular, it would not have been possible without the resources of its great library, and the work, friendship, and helpfulness of fellow scholars. The Department of History has offered an environment of pedagogic vitality, collegiality, and care: For me it has epitomized academia at its best. Seth Anziska and Zvi Ben-Dor Benite have been my guides from the outset: I cannot thank them enough for their insights and encouragement. For their willingness to read the manuscript in draft and for their intellectual generosity, I owe an immense debt of gratitude to Lee Bollinger, Saul Dubow, David Feldman, Carol Gluck, Gil Hochberg, Kostis Karpozilos, Ira Katznelson, Rashid Khalidi, Rebecca Kobrin, Peter Mandler, David Pozen, Camille Robcis, Adam Shatz, Maria Stepanova, and Alan Tansman. Elisheva Carlebach, Seth Schwartz, and Michael Stanislawski provided not only reading lists but also a reminder through their own scholarship of Columbia University's uniquely rich tradition in Jewish history. My thanks too to Tareq

Baconi, Leonard Benardo, Dan Bouk, Florent Brayard, Betsy, Ed, and Daniel Cohen, Molly Crabapple, Zohar Elmakias, Katherine Fleming, Sarah Gensburger, Isabella Hammad, Lorien Kite, Paul LeClerc, Geoffrey Levin, Jason Ludwig, Alexis Papahelas, Gerry Rosberg, Robert Rubin, Victoria Sanger, Yasmine Seale, Adam Tooze, and Alexandre Toumarkine for helpful conversations. My brother David Mazower, with his encyclopedic knowledge of Yiddish culture, has been a unique resource for me as for so many others. Several chats with Fred Wiseman opened up new avenues: He has been an inspiration. None of the above is responsible in any way for what follows. I am especially indebted to my students for the many conversations we had together, interrupted only occasionally by the sound of police helicopters overhead, during a memorable couple of years in the university's history. In Paris, Marie d'Origny, Brune Biebuyck, Sari Castro, and Meredith Hunter-Mason tolerated my distraction and have been the best of colleagues.

It has been a pleasure and a privilege to work with Scott Moyers and Simon Winder for more than two decades now. They embraced the idea for this book right at the start and I have benefited from their thoughtfulness, experience, and practiced editorial eye. Helen Rouner and the Penguin Press team have been a joy to work with. And I owe thanks as always to James Pullen, Sarah Chalfant, and Andrew Wylie for their support. Hiya Jain provided me with indispensable research assistance and feedback that helped remind me just how odd much of this story really is: I look forward to seeing where her own path takes her.

Sir Arthur Conan Doyle, the creator of Sherlock Holmes, once confided to his private journal: "One should put one's shoulder to the door and keep out the insanity all one can." In the course of tackling this topic, I have sometimes felt the same way and would like to thank my family for their support, especially my mother, Miriam Mazower, Jed and Selma Mazower, and above all Julie Fry, who has not only heard more than anyone could ever want to about antisemitism but been the best antidote imaginable to the lunacy of the world and a reminder of its beauties. A different kind of support was provided by the memory of my father and my grandparents, whose attitude to the matters discussed here has served as a kind of inspiration.

I started writing this book during the final months in the life of Michael Davies, an old and dear friend. He was a charismatic and fearless teacher of history, and after leading a school trip to Israel and the West Bank, he developed a pedagogy to bring the study of the world's most intractable conflicts into the classroom, founding a charity called Parallel Histories that now helps educators around the world. The courage with which he faced his own death made an ineradicable impression on everyone who knew him. This book is dedicated to his memory and to his wife, Carys Davies, a writer of wondrous gifts.

On Antisemitism

Confusion

"That's a great deal to make one word mean," Alice said in a thoughtful
tone.

LEWIS CARROLL, *ALICE'S ADVENTURES IN WONDERLAND*
AND *THROUGH THE LOOKING-GLASS* [1]

One of our most vivid glimpses of life in the Third Reich started out
as a set of jottings by Victor Klemperer, a professor of literature who
wanted to record the ways in which words were changing and terms
that once had helped to clarify the world were coming to befuddle it.
Klemperer was trying to understand how the Nazi dictatorship had
turned language into an instrument of power, but the truth is that words
themselves are mutable things. That is why good dictionaries track
shifts in their usage, the variations in meaning that appear or vanish
as some emerge and others become obsolete. Such changes may catch
us by surprise, and when they do they can cause confusion and argument. Which brings us to the word at the heart of this book.[2]

It was in 1879 that a rabble-rousing German pamphleteer called
Wilhelm Marr announced the formation of a League of Antisemites
to oppose the granting of full legal equality to the Jews. In the blink
of an eye there was an abstract noun: *antisemitism*. It entered the
Encyclopaedia Britannica in 1910 and spread globally once Adolf Hitler
made an extremist version of the creed the ideological core of Germany's war to dominate Europe. "Antisemitism," the historian Salo
Baron remarked in 1942, "has become a world power."[3]

Today dozens of countries have pledged to combat it, envoys

monitor it, and there are task forces and working groups dedicated to eradicating it. Yet with those accused of antisemitism ranging from white supremacists to the UN secretary-general, never has there been less consensus on what it actually means: "When it comes to antisemitism many of us literally don't know what we're talking about and are happy to admit it," the historian David Feldman has noted. "As for the rest of us who think we *do* know . . . we are congenitally unable to agree among ourselves." There are arguments about the hyphen: anti-semitism versus antisemitism. There is anti-antisemitism and now there is anti-anti-antisemitism too.[4]

Things were not always so complicated. Antony Lerman, the long-time editor of the *Antisemitism World Report*, reminds us that only half a century ago the foe was by common consent the far Right, whose racist stereotyping, conspiracy theories, and Holocaust denialism had done so much harm and caused such unspeakable suffering. The muddle we find ourselves in started once the fight against these extremists came to be entangled with a question that used to occur to almost no one: When is criticism of Israel antisemitic? How essential a Jewish state (a political entity) is to being Jewish (an ethnic or religious identity) is a vital but unsettled issue that has been and is to this day passionately debated among Jews themselves, as well as forming part of the wider debate on the question of Israel and Palestine. The result is now general uncertainty over what one may say about Israel without being accused of antisemitism. How we came to find ourselves in such a quandary is the question this book tries to answer.

The shadow of the Nazi genocide unavoidably hangs over any discussion of this subject, for it was only after 1945 that the study of antisemitism really became systematic. A survey of attitudes toward Jews in London's East End had been undertaken in 1939 without making much impact. Ten years later, however, when a group of émigré social scientists based at Columbia University published their findings on the roots of hatred, the result was a series of bestselling studies that spurred further investigation. "The history of antisemitism, which before the war had been the preserve of a couple of bold pioneers, [is] now attracting the attention of many scholars," one observed two decades later. Since then, academic research has flourished across many disciplines, and it has provided insights without which this book could not have been written. But the Holocaust looms over the subject in a second sense too, as a major cultural phenomenon of our times. For as an influence shaping the ways antisemitism is now generally understood, academic scholarship takes second place to something that we might call Holocaust consciousness. The nineteenth century has been described as a time when people thought with History; so far as antisemitism is concerned, we think these days with the Holocaust.[5]

Widespread public awareness of the Final Solution did not emerge immediately. When discussion really got going in the 1960s and 1970s in Europe, it involved a generational reckoning with the past on the very terrain where wartime persecution, deportations, and killings had taken place. But as Holocaust memorialization spread around the globe, it turned history into a source of general moral and political lessons: to bear witness rather than to remain silent; to act, not to stand by and watch; to combat hate and prejudice. By the end of the century, dozens of films were appearing each decade. Forty-plus governments have now created remembrance ceremonies, and visitor numbers to Auschwitz have quadrupled in recent years to more than two million annually. Not everyone has seen this as entirely good. "For the sake of our collective sanity as Jews, we should all stop for a moment," wrote the Israeli state archivist Evyatar Friesel, who had himself fled Nazi Germany as a boy, "and try to bring ourselves under control."[6]

Alongside the evident benefits, one of the consequences has been what one critic called "exaggerated and wrong-headed Holocaust and Nazi analogies." Familiarization with the catastrophe seems to have made some people more inclined to draw alarming parallels between present and past than to register the significant differences. In Israel, where the country's first leaders had once actually discouraged reminders of Jewish weakness, the 1970s saw the Holocaust turned into an inescapable rhetorical trope, especially after Prime Minister Menachem Begin, whose parents had been killed in the war, repeatedly likened Israel's predicament to that of the Jews under the Nazis. In the United States, where American Jews generally were enjoying conditions of prosperity and security, a paradoxical sense of insecurity increased as the century ended. Asked in 1960 what they thought the future held, American rabbis had been optimistic that antisemitism would continue to decline, and the Middle East conflict would be settled by the century's end. A survey of the American Jewish community around the same time found that both Israel and the Holocaust had had "remarkably slight effects on the inner life of American Jewry." By the century's end they were central to its self-definition, and impressive material success was accompanied by a growing sense of anxiety and victimhood. Many commentators were puzzled. While "the American Jewish community has become the model for what an ethnic group can accomplish," noted the writer Leon Wieseltier in 2002, "imprecise and inflammatory analogies abound. Holocaust imagery is everywhere."[7]

Polling data on social attitudes in the United States indicated that the marked drop in anti-Jewish discrimination that had taken place over half a century showed no signs of being significantly reversed in the new millennium: Before the longtime head of the Anti-Defamation League retired in 2015, a headline spoke of the "declining face of antisemitism."[8] It is true that there was a resurgence of prejudice in Europe after the Cold War ended, as right-wing nationalism reentered the mainstream, and in western Europe, especially in France, synagogues, cemeteries, and other Jewish communal centers were attacked, often as proxies for Israel: The perpetrators tended to be either right-wing extremists or young Muslims.[9] The constant invocation of the Holocaust, however, gave the past misleading weight. For one thing, in many places other groups were more affected by rising xenophobia than Jews; for another, neither Muslims nor Arabs were Nazis any more than Israelis were. "[Arab antisemitism] is directed first and foremost against Israel and not necessarily against world Jewry," noted Yehoshafat Harkabi, a former chief of Israeli military intelligence. "Or more precisely, because of Israel it is directed also against the Jews."[10]

Yet the ghosts of genocide past infiltrated the corridors of power and were invoked to support new political and diplomatic commitments. In 2004, the US Congress told the State Department to report on anti-Jewish prejudice worldwide. When the department objected that other racial and religious groups might demand similar treatment, Congressman Tom Lantos, a survivor of the Nazi occupation of Hungary, retorted that "the current eruption of the age-old disease of antisemitism is more pernicious than anything we have seen since the Holocaust." The State Department was overruled, the Global Anti-Semitism Review Act was passed, and today twenty-plus governments have created posts to combat antisemitism. No other form of racial or religious prejudice enjoys comparable international attention.[11]

The 2004 act changed things in another way too. In a break from earlier decades, it understood antisemitism to include "vilification of Zionism...and incitement against Israel." Opposing antisemitism and supporting Israel had formerly been considered two largely separate matters. "To attribute condemnation of Israel's actions in the Sinai Campaign to anti-Semitism," a commentator wrote in 1967, "is stretching the term beyond recognition." For most American Jews in the 1950s and 1960s, antisemitism was chiefly a domestic problem connected to a larger American struggle against discrimination and prejudice: If it had an international dimension, this lay in the Soviet Union and West Germany, not in the Middle East. For their part, the first

Israeli governments saw antisemitism as a curse of the diaspora unrelated to its own regional problems. Only from the 1970s onward did more and more Israelis begin to read Arab hostility as antisemitic; only then did American Jewish anti-hate campaigners start to include the defense of Israel in their remit. Once seen optimistically as something capable of being dispelled by education, antisemitism came to be regarded in the light of the Holocaust as a hatred unlike any other. Today many people would be astonished to learn of a time when defending Israel from criticism and fighting antisemitism were not connected.[12]

In conflating these things, an important part has been played by some of the well-established Jewish defense organizations like the American Jewish Committee (AJC) and the Anti-Defamation League (ADL). People used to joke that as a think tank the famously discreet American Jewish Committee was more "think" than "tank" because of its commitment to analytic rigor. In the 1940s its watchwords were, according to a recent historian, "dialogue, compromise, rationality, and research" and its wonderfully named Division of Scientific Research enjoyed great prestige. But organizations change and it is hard to fundraise and campaign in our charged times while maintaining a reputation for impartial expertise. Today the think-tank joke has passed its sell-by date. Indeed, it is now at least a decade since its long-serving antisemitism expert quit on the grounds that the AJC had sacrificed "an instinct for serious thought...in favor of ardent pro-Israel advocacy." Beholden to a new class of mega-donors with pronounced ideological agendas, old bastions of Jewish philanthropy struggle to preserve even a semblance of the long-standing fiction that they are inherently apolitical. So partisan have some of them become that the critic Peter Beinart has asked if the fight against antisemitism has lost its way.[13]

Part of the problem is that it is very easy to label an individual or an institution as antisemitic, and this facilitates attention-grabbing tactics like the Simon Wiesenthal Center's "Global Anti-Semitism Top Ten," a made-for-media list that once named the makers of Ben & Jerry's ice cream alongside Hamas and Iran.[14] And because donors often give more when anxiety about antisemitism rises, and hate crime data are notoriously liable to manipulation, campaigning groups are often tempted to paint conditions in the most terrifying colors. ADL OFFICIALS SAY ANTISEMITISM RAMPANT THROUGHOUT THE WORLD announced the headline of a skeptical piece in the Jewish press half a century ago. Twenty years later, the historian and rabbi Arthur Hertzberg remarked that the ADL's own data did not bear out its "sensational conclusion." Not much has changed: Even the ADL's own researchers complain about the reliability of its leadership's warnings. Activism set in permanent panic mode makes it hard to know whose figures or assessments to trust, and this does not really help anyone except perhaps antisemites. In the words of the editor in chief of *The Forward*: "Calling everything a crisis is bad for the Jews."[15]

As if all this were not enough, the enormous attention given in recent times to defining antisemitism has created its own problems. For as scholars in the field know well, the definition of antisemitism has always been a minefield. The concept, which derives its very name from a discredited racial theory, is routinely applied to everything from prejudices and stereotypes to feelings, attitudes, and forms of legislation, not to mention acts of violence ranging from petty abuse to massacre and genocide. That's already a broad spectrum. It also involves attributing motives that are frequently murky even to the perpetrators and interpreting contexts that are ambiguous in meaning. And it often hides dubious generalizations about human psychology, the nature of social interactions, and the identity of the Other.[16] None of this makes defining it straightforward. The Israeli historian of the Holocaust Yehuda Bauer once called antisemitism "the wrong term" that "makes a mess of research projects" and involves "talking nonsense." "The term 'antisemitism' is a snare and a pitfall that traps us in spite of knowing its dangers," wrote the author Ben Halpern. "It shows up the objects it brings to our attention in a dim and distorted focus at best, if not in utter confusion." Halpern tried parsing the term's many tangled connotations; the more he persisted, the less his efforts looked like a definition.[17]

As if to bear out the force of these warnings, a recent effort at definition sponsored by a little-known organization called the International Holocaust Remembrance Alliance (IHRA), demonstrates the kind of trouble a poorly conceived approach can cause.[18] Purporting to clarify the line dividing antisemitism from reasonable criticism of Israel—something that is unquestionably needed—it has served merely to blur it further (for details see chapters 9 and 10). Yet the IHRA definition has been adopted in dozens of countries, and in the United States, a 2019 executive order that extended federal antidiscrimination protections to include antisemitism cited it. A 2023 bill (H.R. 6090) even proposed ruling out the use of other definitions lest they "fail to identify many of the modern manifestations of antisemitism"—meaning criticism of Israel. We have traveled far since 1981, when an outstanding scholar could meticulously discuss how to define antisemitism in the journal *Modern Judaism* without making any mention of Israel at all.[19]

Some recent researchers usefully suggest making a distinction between antisemites and antisemitic beliefs: The former refers to those who are possessed by an ideology and really do have an obsession with Jews because they regard them as holding some power over the life of nations and individuals; the latter are that large repertoire of stereotypes and prejudiced clichés about Jews in general that the past has bequeathed us. The former originated the term *antisemitism*, often proudly called themselves "antisemites," and saw themselves as political actors in a movement that reached its apogee in the middle decades of the twentieth century. The latter form part of a vast cultural reservoir of prejudices and generalizations to be found in many socie-ties about not only Jews but also many races, faiths, and ethnic groups. These days, hardcore antisemites are as yet relatively few compared to before the Second World War, and the policies they once espoused—discriminatory and eventually murderous—are still largely discredited in the West. But society has no more banished every antisemitic belief than it has other kinds of bigotry, and an openly racist Right is in the ascendant on both sides of the Atlantic.[20]

At a time when Jewish communities around the world have had to become accustomed to having to study or pray under armed guard, there can be no question but that Jews continue to be among those groups who are targeted these days for who they are. Anyone who takes antisemitism seriously as an ongoing problem must surely there-fore be dismayed by the confusion that exists around the term, not to mention the overuse that threatens to strip it of meaning. Not only does this do a real disservice to those who are its victims, but by help-ing to dampen down political dissent over Israel's actions in the occu-pied territories, it also provides a cover for continued injustice and systemic violence against Palestinians. And while some anti-Zionism masks anti-Jewish sentiment, much of it does not, and it surely does not benefit Israeli governments to be encouraged to think that any criticism of their policies invariably reflects ethnic prejudice. Nor—need it be said?—will it benefit Jews or anyone else when the ongoing strug-gle against discrimination and prejudice is used opportunistically to try to destroy the autonomy of universities, political freedoms, and liberty of thought itself.

Definitions and theories are available aplenty elsewhere. This book offers another approach, suggesting instead that we view antisemitism in its historical context as a term that has been used to mean different things at different times. To avoid misunderstanding, let us be clear from the outset that antisemitism is much more than a word, and history is about far more than language alone: The issues at stake certainly cannot be tackled simply through semantic analysis. But, as the cultural commentator Raymond Williams once observed, there are occasions when the issues that concern us probably cannot be understood without viewing particular words as integral aspects of a larger problem in their own right. And because words do not exist outside time and place, we need to understand them in their setting. "We must know, if possible, the date and place of their birth," wrote the Victorian philologist Dean Chenevix Trench, "the successive stages of their subsequent history, the company which they have kept, all the road which they have travelled, and what has brought them to the point at which we now find them." What follows then is a kind of historical sketch that looks at the rise and fall of antisemitism as a chiefly European political movement in part 1 before shifting gears in part 2 to analyze the origins and spread of a new conceptual paradigm that originated in the 1970s largely as a way to rationalize growing criticism of Israel. In the early years of the new millennium this led to an international campaign directed against what some termed a *new antisemitism* that partly overlapped with, and partly contradicted, older understandings of the term. The word was the same, but the world had changed. The hope behind this book is that an account of how the concept emerged and spread can help us figure out what sort of work it does today and may remain capable of doing in the future. As George Orwell wrote: "The worst thing one can do with words is to surrender to them."[21]

Part 1

Europe in the Age
of the Antisemites

CHAPTER I

God, Nation, Eternity

After being introduced [Professor Cohen] said, "I have been asked to
speak on the Jewish problem. Gentlemen, there is no Jewish problem"—and thereupon he sat down.

A TRIBUTE TO PROFESSOR MORRIS RAPHAEL COHEN,
TEACHER AND PHILOSOPHER[1]

Idealist conceptions of Zionism are naturally inseparable from the
dogma of eternal anti-Semitism.

ABRAM LEON, THE JEWISH QUESTION: A MARXIST INTERPRETATION[2]

Nineteenth-century nationalists projected the idea of their People
deep into a distant past. Struggling for independence, Greeks dreamed
of the ancients, Italians of Rome. As for Germans, some opted for the
Teutonic tribes, while others preferred the less brutish-sounding Aryans. It was this particular pseudo-racial pedigree that—as an anony-
mous French journalist reported shortly after the Franco-Prussian
War—provided inspiration for a new political movement. "An anti-
Jewish party formed...and was called the *antisemitic* party," he wrote
in 1881. He went on to explain that

> in Germany, everything has an essentially scientific allure....
> Today when the progress of comparative linguistics has made
> the names of the Aryan races more or less popular...people
> know too that the Aryan races are opposed in the name of gram-
> mar and ethnology to the Semitic races which have no close
> kinship with them at all.... To call the Jews *Semites* is to under-
> score their foreign origin, to indulge the Teutonism currently in

vogue, in short to excite the national fiber so sensitive whenever it rubs up against whatever is not German.[3]

A recently unified Germany, the new insights of scientific racism, nationalist sensitivities: The invention of the concept of antisemitism in and around 1880 was part of the birth of the modern. It was in fact a reaction against modernity itself, which portrayed the Jews as single-handedly responsible for pretty much every grievance contemporary life presented and did so using the preeminently modern vehicles of the popular press and party politics. As the movement spread it attracted critical attention. Liberals saw it as an outrage to reason and a spur to educate public opinion; the revolutionary Left saw it as a mistaken diagnosis of a real problem—capitalism—and regarded it as a "socialism of fools." For both, it was a mark of modernity gone astray.

But one group of thinkers was not surprised and saw nothing very new in what was happening. Zionism emerged around the same time as many of its European nationalist counterparts and like them it was a modern political phenomenon that encompassed a vast range of ideological possibilities. It too turned traditional religious faith into a political aspiration: Embracing the Romantic nineteenth-century attachment to territory, with stunning boldness its leaders advocated the Holy Land, where generations of devout Jews had aspired to go to die, as a place for Jews to live. And like other European nationalisms of the time, Zionism thought about the future with and through history. It saw the Jews not merely as those who shared a common faith but as a national unit, a People who had been plunged into exile before they were to be redeemed through restoration—under one political dispensation or another—to their ancestral land. Nothing short of a miraculous combination of a positive and a negative force had kept them together through their many centuries of wandering and misery: The positive force was the promise of Israel's return to Zion; the negative was antisemitism. "Who can tell us," wrote Josef Hayyim Brenner in 1914, "whether, had there been no universal and understandable hatred of such a strange being, the Jew, that strange being would have survived at all? But the hatred was inevitable and hence survival was equally inevitable!"[4]

The first Zionists generally argued that legal and civic equality alone would never truly end anti-Jewish prejudice since freedom for Jews was impossible so long as they lived amid societies that hated them. National independence would finally bring them normalcy and perhaps even allow the genuine international cooperation that they dreamed of like so many nineteenth-century nationalists. "The legal emancipation of the Jews is the crowning achievement of our century," wrote the activist Leo Pinsker in 1882.

> [But] the civil and political emancipation of the Jews is not sufficient to raise them in the estimation of the peoples. The proper and only remedy would be the creation of a Jewish nationality, of a people living upon its own soil, the auto-emancipation of the Jews; their emancipation as a nation among nations by the acquisition of a home of their own.[5]

For most Zionist thinkers, the hatred Jews faced from those around them was to be expected: Jews, they preached, were bound to be seen as alien by non-Jews. It was "a general law," wrote Pinsker, "that no people, generally speaking, has any predilection for foreigners." The historian Lewis Namier stated baldly that it was a fact of life that "nations do not like each other": Antisemitism was in his telling merely another form of national animosity, analogous to the enmity between, say, Germans and Poles. Others said that hatred of Jews was different because it was unique and timeless. Either way most Zionist thinkers agreed that antisemitism was part of the natural order of things with an obvious remedy: a Jewish state. What that state would look like was unclear: Few imagined a politically independent entity of the kind that eventually emerged, and fewer still that the great Jewish heartlands of central-eastern Europe could ever be wiped out. But the benefits of Jewish self-government were largely unquestioned: Bring that into being, preferably in Ottoman Palestine, Jews would surely emigrate there, and antisemitism would vanish. Why it had taken until the late nineteenth century for God to reveal this solution was a problem they did not dwell on.[6]

For Zionism's Jewish critics, this approach betrayed a complacency toward—and even an acceptance of—antisemitism. "Throughout the 40 years of Zionism's existence, the following rule has practically always held: the darker the world, the brighter it gets in the Zionist tent; the worse for Jews, the better for Zionists," wrote Henryk Erlich in an article in the New York Yiddish press in October 1938. Erlich was a leader of the left-wing Jewish Labor Bund, the largest Jewish political party in interwar Poland. The Bund's supporters believed in what they called "hereness"—the need to fight for a future where Jews actually lived—not the "thereness" of Zionism, which in their view was likely to re-create in Palestine the very intolerance Jews wanted to vanquish in Europe. Erlich warned of an inherent contradiction in the Zionist program.

> When Zionists speak to the non-Jewish world, they are outstanding democrats, and they present the conditions in today's and future Palestine as exemplary of liberty and progress. But if a Jewish state is to be founded in Palestine, its spiritual climate will be: an eternal fear of the external enemy (Arabs), unending fighting for every little piece of land, for every scrap of work, against the internal enemy (Arabs)....Is this the kind of climate, in which freedom, democracy, and progress can flourish? Is this not the climate, in which reactionism and chauvinism typically germinate?[7]

The Bund—a onetime rival to Zionism in the Russian lands—was to meet a tragic end as a political force, effectively crushed between the dual enmities of the Nazis and the Communists, and Erlich himself was murdered on Stalin's orders while held in Soviet captivity during the war. Yet there was a striking prescience in what he wrote. After the establishment of Israel, the journalist William Zukerman, a kindred spirit, reflected upon the connection between antisemitism and the new state. "Without anti-Semitism," he wrote, "Israel would be but another small state, like Ireland, Greece, Denmark and Lebanon. With anti-Semitism, it is a state with a special Messianic mission to redeem all Jews." For Zukerman, it was thus not only Zionism but also Israel that somehow needed antisemitism in the world to justify itself—the same Israel whose leadership promised to make Jews safe by allowing them to escape antisemitism's hold over them. Could antisemitism in fact really be brought to an end in this way, through the triumph of Jewish nationalism? Or would it simply be replaced, as Erlich had warned, by a new enmity created by the establishment of a Jewish state in Arab lands?[8]

As if to bear out Zukerman's insight, the idea that antisemitism was a hatred that held the key to understanding the Jewish past shaped professional scholarship in Israel's early years: A group of Zionist historians—the so-called Jerusalem School—framed the centuries of Jewish life in Europe as the story of "a people apart," doomed to persecution so long as they remained "in exile," endlessly beset by what one termed "the longest hatred" of them all, a visceral Gentile loathing that might vanish from view for a time but must always reemerge.[9] In their telling, history turned into an eternal cosmic drama in which "neither Jew nor antisemite changes, only the masks the antisemites wear." It was a kind of Jewish history that highlighted not so much *our* achievements and doings, as it were, but rather a set of unremitting feelings, stereotypes, and ideas that *they* have had about *us*. (This view in the works of a historian of the Spanish Inquisition called Benzion

Netanyahu would influence the outlook of his son, Israel's longest-serving prime minister.)[10]

The first leaders of the new Jewish state were repelled by this depressing view of the past. They frowned upon discussion of the Holocaust lest it perpetuate the idea of Jews as weak; obsessing over antisemitism, they felt, could only accentuate the old story of passivity and powerlessness. In their view, the establishment of Israel was supposed to mark the moment when antisemitism ceased to matter, or more precisely, when it mattered solely as a motivation for the Jews of the diaspora to return from their "exile." The historians of the Jerusalem School, however, disagreed: Antisemitism would never cease to matter. Nor was it only the European past they painted in dark tones; they argued that such a deep-rooted phenomenon as antisemitism could not have ended with the Holocaust, and they discerned it around them in Stalin's Soviet Union and the United Nations, metastasizing into a global force with footholds in the Middle East and the Muslim world. For these scholars, Arab hostility in particular was neither the kind of natural reaction to the fact of Israel's existence that the Bundists had warned about nor the reflection of a sense of ethnic or religious solidarity with the dispossessed Palestinians. It was all much simpler than that: It was the latest incarnation of the hatred that would never die. This interpretation fundamentally turned diplomacy into a holding action or a fool's errand—for what could be done in the face of an eternal antipathy other than to remain permanently vigilant? Any peace would only be temporary. It was, at heart, a view that abolished the room for political thought and left only the figure of the immortal enemy.

If we were to ask how it was that Zionism—whose original dream had been to restore the Jews to political normalcy if not to turn them into a beacon for other nations—came to adopt such a bleak view, we would have to say that in this case, as in others, it was drawing upon ideas it had inherited from the religious tradition. In particular the Hebrew phrase *sinat Yisrael* (hatred of Israel) was a well-established axiom in rabbinic thought that non-Jews invariably hate Jews. Insofar as we can tell, this trope became entrenched somewhere between the end of late antiquity and the early medieval period as part of a larger process that was taking the place of conceptually demarcating the boundary between Jews and non-Jews. Since then, many generations of rabbis have accepted it as a truism. "One of the unique aspects of our history," noted the leading Talmudist and Orthodox Rabbi Joseph B. Soloveitchik, "is surely our capacity to evoke *sinat Yisrael*, the persistent and ever-present hostility which humanity directs at us as a people; it is a strange and inexplicable fact of our history."[11]

Actually the evidence suggests that in ancient times Jews had accepted that nations were of different kinds and that not all of them were necessarily hostile; the starker and simpler view came later. Nonetheless many commentators look to the Bible to confirm their own vision of a Jewish nation surrounded by hostility, citing in particular the Old Testament story of Esau, the brother who was cheated out of his birthright by Jacob, losing the primacy that should have been his. In theological terms, the original antipathy of non-Jews for Jews may thus be located in the Biblical assertion that "Esau hated Jacob." In short, *sinat Yisrael* offers a religious explanation of antisemitism as the price to be paid by the Jews for God's favor.

Such a view has not been confined to the rabbis. The view that the Jews are—in the words of the Bible—a "people that dwells alone" has become a commonplace for many Israeli public figures and a corollary perhaps of the equally axiomatic view that Jews have a special obligation to love and look out for one another. There were, to be sure, more positive alternatives—that the Jews were destined to become a "light unto the nations," for instance, or that there was, in nineteenth-century philo-semitic terms, some special "mission of Israel" to the world that God had stored up. But that *sinat Yisrael* may be balanced by counterviews, also biblical in origin, that testify to ideals of peaceful coexistence does not diminish its significance. Prime Minister Yitzhak Shamir often invoked the phrase; the erudite diplomat Yaakov Herzog advanced a formidable defense of it. At various times Yitzhak Rabin both embraced and rejected it and eventually came to see it as an impediment to peace.

How *sinat Yisrael* might be interpreted historically is not an easy question to answer because the theological idea that it is so closely connected with—the uniqueness of the Jews—poses a special problem when thinking about the past. The historian Yosef Yerushalmi, in a classic work, identified this as a central paradox that faced his profession. "Jewish historiography," he wrote, "must stand in sharp opposition to its own subject matter, not on this or that detail, but concerning the vital core: the belief that divine providence is not only an ultimate but an active causal factor in Jewish history, and the related belief in the uniqueness of Jewish history itself." In other words, to identify the Jewish experience as conditioned by some unique relationship to God is to accept a premise that not only lies outside history itself but in some sense contravenes it.[12]

Yerushalmi had in mind those nationalist historians who saw the Jewish past as the story of a unique people whose centrality to God was taken for granted. Shmuel Ettinger, an animating figure in the Jerusalem School, criticized those who would "turn Jews into a marginal or even a casual element...in the framework of world history." The historian Yitzhak Baer once proposed astonishingly that "there is a power that lifts the Jewish people out of the realm of all causal history." As if to say: The Jews, by virtue of their special relationship with God, are exempt from the laws that apply to all others.[13] History, however, as a secular discipline that seeks to explain events by reference to human action, is fundamentally incompatible with a theological worldview that invokes the divine as a cause. For those unable to follow Baer down his mystical path, the conclusion is clear: History basically cannot be understood in terms of a concept such as *sinat Yisrael*. Nor, by the same token, can it deploy the thinly secularized version of this, which is the classic Zionist idea of antisemitism as "eternal hatred." But if antisemitism is not one continuous story taking us all the way back to the emergence of the Jews—or to put it another way, if it is not God's Covenant with his Chosen People that provides the starting point for its history—then what we are left with is the key question historians always face: Where to begin?

Perhaps with the simple and incontestable fact that for centuries prejudice against Jews was commonplace. If it lacked a label, this was because it existed in societies where prejudice of all kinds was normal, as has been the case throughout most of recorded history. The wars of the past, after all, saw vicious hatreds roused against all sorts of people: The Jews were by no means the sole targets. That did not mean prejudice against Jews lacked specific characteristics or rationales—in the polytheistic ancient world they were singled out for their exclusivity, their worship of a single god, and their disdain for the gods of others—but it can be difficult to argue they faced an especially intense animus compared with other groups.[14]

Where Christianity was established as a state religion, however, things changed abruptly for the worse; indeed, the longevity of anti-Jewish hatred in Europe owes much to the political success of Christianity over two millennia precisely because this offspring monotheism could not forgive Jews for their refusal to recognize Christ as the Messiah. That Christianity emerged out of Judaism and ultimately defined itself against it made their obstinacy the more impossible to accept. And yet Christian antipathy to Jews was complicated by the fact that Christians had ultimately also chosen to incorporate the Hebrew Bible as part of their own Holy Scripture, thereby acknowledging their origins in the Jewish faith: When the second-century AD theologian Marcion proposed excluding the Old

Testament as un-Christian, his ideas were rejected. Christian theology thus existed in a state of deep ambivalence about the Jews, who were a tolerated group, enjoying a variable legal status, and existing—in their own minds—in a kind of secular provisionality in the long wait for their Messiah. Over the years, the precariousness of their position became internalized as a feature of their lot: The scholar Simon Rawidowicz noted in 1948 how one generation of rabbis after another believed that the Jews were about to die out, each oblivious to the fact that those before had feared the very same thing. As he put it: "The world makes many images of Israel, but Israel makes only one image of itself: that of a being constantly on the verge of ceasing to be, of disappearing."[15]

This enduring sense of existential dread was reinforced by traumatic experiences of expulsion and massacre behind which lay the many negative stereotypes that gripped the minds of the Christian peoples of Europe, prejudices that were sustained by centuries of church teaching: their supposed secretiveness and untrustworthiness, their clannishness and reputed sense of superiority over non-Jews, the terrifying tales of their desire for Christian blood. Rather later came their purported affinity for money and wealth, a belief cemented in many places by their being forced by law into specific occupations such as moneylending, banking, and trade. All these stereotypes took deep root in the soil of Christendom, markedly influenced Western thought, and flourished into modern times in conspiracy theories believed around the world.[16]

Yet these medieval and early modern prejudices also expressed the assumptions of times very different from our own. When the scholar Amos Funkenstein asked rhetorically how much of modern antisemitism was "rooted in the Christian tradition," he gave a straightforward answer: "Whatever its driving forces, anti-Semitism seems to be worlds apart from Christian anti-Jewish attitudes."[17]

In history there are no hard-and-fast lines, and the Christian prejudices and animosities of earlier centuries continued to nourish antisemitism deep into the twentieth century and beyond. But a fundamental transformation in more than a millennium of Jewish-Christian relations came about with the Enlightenment. Between the late eighteenth and the mid-nineteenth centuries, the transition to capitalism, the spread of new technologies, and the growth of large cities brought radical changes in conceptions of religion, time, and history. The emergence of mass literacy and the rise of a public sphere allowed ideas to circulate and be discussed more widely and freely than ever before. Politics in the modern sense was born, and the rise of the citizen and the modern political subject raised for the first time the question of legal emancipation and the Jews.[18]

With the coming of activists and agitators, the ideological climate of the mid-nineteenth century was in general one of stormy contestation. Fought out in the press, it manifested itself linguistically in something like a blizzard of new oppositional *anti*-words. *Anti-Darwinian* and *anti-Protestant* appeared in Britain; *anti-républicaine* and *anti-révolutionnaire* in France. From the US there came *anti-abolitionist* (1854), *anti-slaveryist* (1862), *anti-Negro* (1862), *anti-Coolie* (1869), and *anti-Chinese* (1872). The German *Antisemitismus* (1879) was thus literally an expression of the times.

The coining of a new word—*antisemitism*—in Europe in the last quarter of the nineteenth century is suggestive in itself of the importance of these epochal developments. Even more striking is the fact that in the ensuing decades an era opened up whose history cannot be fully recounted without the subject of antisemitism playing a central role. The novelty of this development cannot be emphasized enough. For many centuries before then, the Jews had arguably not mattered very much from the perspective of world history: It was not implausible to view them as a small, venerable sect bypassed by power, not unlike the Parsis or the Jains, remarkable chiefly for their ancestral affinity with the two much more successful monotheisms—Christianity and Islam—that owed so much to them.

Thanks to the Nazis, all this changed: Suddenly, around the world, everyone was talking about the Jews. "The Jews have been made what the Nazis always pretended they were—the focal point of history," wrote the social theorist Max Horkheimer in 1942. "Shattering all previous historical precedents, [antisemitism] transcended the boundaries of any particular country or group of countries," the historian Salo Baron noted the same year. "It has become a pre-eminent factor in international relations." In 1950 Hannah Arendt drew attention—as few had done before or have since—to "the outrageous fact that so small (and, in world politics, so unimportant) a phenomenon as the Jewish question and antisemitism could become the catalytic agent for first, the Nazi movement, then a world war, and finally the establishment of death factories." It was, she wrote, "an outrage to common sense."[19]

A few numbers underscore Arendt's point. At the start of the twentieth century, more than 80 percent of the world's Jewish population lived in Europe. Yet Jews represented barely 2 percent of the Continent's total population of some four hundred million people and less than 1 percent of the population of the world. It was this tiny religious group—or to be more precise, a set of hostile and obsessive attitudes toward it—that played a role of outsize importance in the decades that followed. When the Nazis took power in Germany in 1933, they caused extreme antisemitic policies to be officially adopted in the most powerful country on the Continent and then, through conquest and occupation, throughout most of Europe. What started out for the Jews of Germany as humiliation, assault, systematic discrimination, and then physical expulsion turned by the winter of 1941–42 into an unprecedented and still unique policy that attempted the semi-industrialized biological extermination of the Continent's

entire Jewish population and succeeded in killing off more than half
of it before the effort collapsed with Nazism's defeat.

The global consequences were stark: After the Holocaust, Jews
constituted less than 1 percent of Europe's population and barely 0.1
percent of the total population of the world. For the first time in many
centuries, the center of gravity of Jewish history lay outside Europe,
and by 1950 European Jewry represented just one third of the world's
Jews, down from four fifths in 1900. By 2010 four fifths of the world's
Jewish population lived in the United States and Israel. If antisemitism was chiefly a European issue before 1950, this was no longer
true after.[20]

SHIFTS IN JEWISH POPULATION, 1900–2010 (IN MILLIONS)[21]

	World Total	Europe	North America + Israel (post-1948)	Europe as % of World Total
1900	11.3	9.0	1.6	80
1950	11.5	3.5	6.3	30
2010	13.9	1.4	11.6	10

The sociologist W. E. B. Du Bois had pointed out already in 1942
that antisemitism had global implications. Noting how those thinking about it at that time often seemed wedded to gaining admission
into what he strikingly called "white Europe," he wrote—in a review
of two works on the subject—that

> in both these books the problem is conceived as that of the refusal
> on the part of the aristocratic and dominant culture of the day

to admit Jewish culture as an equal partner. There is apparently
no conception of quite another point of view: of regarding the
Jews as one among many groups, composed of Chinese, Japa-
nese, East Indians, African Negroes, American Negroes, and
American Indians—peoples who form the great majority of the
inhabitants of the earth and are also excluded from fellowship
with the ruling world aristocracy....[22]

The demographic shifts brought about by the war made Du Bois's
challenge simultaneously more farsighted and more unattainable. On
the one hand, antisemitism could no longer be conceived of exclusively as a European problem: The relationship Du Bois was positing
between antisemitism, race, and empire could not be evaded. On the
other, the larger anti-racist coalition that he sought—and in which
Jews participated in the early postwar decades—looks harder than
ever to achieve today when the old Left, to whom such a vision came
naturally, has dwindled, when Israel itself stands accused of colonialism, and when US racial categories pit black against white across an
almost unbridgeable divide. Today it is hard to remember a time when
the leading black civil rights organization, the NAACP, had a Jewish
president (three, in fact, between 1930 and 1975) and when the venerable French International League Against Racism and Anti-Semitism
was a beacon for the future rather than a pointer to an unreachable
past. The struggle against antisemitism, which once unified, now
divides, and that development too is part of our subject.

Many things are responsible for this change, as we shall see. But
the main one is that the setting for the contemporary discussion of
antisemitism has changed radically: The historic question of the powerlessness of Jews in the nation-state system of Europe has been
replaced by the very different question of the power of a Jewish nation-
state in the Middle East. The shift has happened with bewildering
rapidity: It is still possible, within a single lifetime, to have been born

into a world where the center of Jewish life was—as it had been for many centuries—in Europe; to have reached maturity in the Cold War when the Jews of the United States became preeminent among their coreligionists globally; and finally to have seen Israel surpass the United States as the country with the largest Jewish population anywhere. For the Holocaust was not only an unprecedented tragedy, it was also a watershed. In the 1920s, most Jews lived as vulnerable minorities in European states, US Jews faced fast-growing discrimination, and in Palestine a tiny population existed on British imperial sufferance under the aegis of the League of Nations. Today things look very different: Organized antisemitism in Europe contends with the memory of the genocide, American Jews have flourished, and Israel has turned into a populous if beleaguered nuclear state with high per capita income, a large Arab minority, and the benefit of a special relationship with the world's mightiest military power. The context for understanding antisemitism has thus changed faster and further than most people realize. We are a long way from the world that coined the word.

CHAPTER 2

Emancipation and Its Enemies

1880–1914

Therefore, the first political aim of the anti-Semite is to undo the original sin of nineteenth-century Europe: to revoke legal emancipation granted to Jews.... [Anti-Semitic ideologues] presuppose emancipation and are directed against it, which makes them a new phenomenon altogether in Jewish history.

AMOS FUNKENSTEIN, *PERCEPTIONS OF JEWISH HISTORY*[1]

The era of the Emancipation has represented a radical break with the entire past of Jewry.

ARTHUR HERTZBERG, EDITOR, *THE ZIONIST IDEA:*
A HISTORICAL ANALYSIS AND READER[2]

Antisemitism emerged as a political movement at a time when Europe was midway through a protracted, epochal transformation. For more centuries than people could remember, it had been a continent of empires, duchies, city-states, and principalities governed almost entirely on the basis of hereditary rule in accordance with Christian precepts. Yet in a process that began in the late eighteenth century and lasted until the middle of the twentieth, Europe turned into a fractious community of more or less secular nation-states governed through diverse forms of mass politics, ranging from dictatorship to democracy. Old habits of deference and markers of distinction vanished, and monarchy was cut down to size where it was not swept away. The powers of the established church were delimited. Landowning aristocracies were dispossessed or obliged to compromise with social inferiors enjoying their own political representation. An ancien régime that had been built around a primarily agrarian, illiterate society and an age-old system of guilds and corporations gave way to an endlessly changing society of huge cities, open markets, rapid communications, mass literacy, and fast money. Its core was the codification of law and the replacement of subjects by citizens. Political parties appeared for the first time with ideological programs fought out on the battle-ground of public opinion. Today this is all so much a part of our world that it is easy to overlook how recently it appeared, what a dramatic break it represents with the past, and how much conflict the process entailed.

The forging of a modern conception of all-inclusive citizenship began with the American and French revolutions, but the process went on well into the twentieth century and continues in some respects to this day. Waged over many decades, and with numerous reversals and contestations, it encompassed the fight to extend suffrage to women, the poor and propertyless, dissenters, and nonconformists. The fight for the abolition of slavery and serfdom formed part of this movement: The emancipation of both was a milestone on a much longer journey. Universal male suffrage was not won across Europe before the early twentieth century; women's right to vote was not secured until even later. And it is within the framework of this great struggle that we should see the continent-wide campaign to remove the political and civil disabilities faced by Europe's Jews—to win them recognition as full members of the countries in which they lived, eligible to serve in armies, buy land, enter politics, move where they wished, and reside without restriction. In his superb recent account of this process, the historian David Sorkin notes that the Holocaust and the establishment of Israel have, between them, overshadowed the fundamental importance of this transition in modern Jewish history. As he puts it: "[The Holocaust and the creation of Israel] were reactions to, indeed developments from, emancipation. In philosophical parlance, they were epiphenomena. Emancipation was, and remains, the principal event."[3]

The importance of this drive for political freedom was well understood at the time. "What is...the great task of our age?" asked the German Jewish poet Heinrich Heine in 1828. "It is emancipation. Not only of the Irish, the Greeks, the Jews of Frankfurt, the blacks of the West Indies and similarly oppressed peoples but of the entire world." The term *emancipation* itself was new, having spread in Europe chiefly as a result of publicity around the debate in England about Catholic admission to Parliament.[4]

By then the gradual opening up of the previously closed world of Jewish communal life was already well underway. Habsburg rule brought some relaxation of the old restrictions when Emperor Joseph II, influenced by ideals of Enlightened despotism, issued an edict of toleration to the religious dissenters of his Catholic empire in 1781. Personally, he was not sympathetic to the Jews—many Enlightenment thinkers were not—but this mattered less to him than the rationalist principles of abolishing discrimination on the basis of faith and moving toward legal equality among his subjects. In the name of making "the Jewish population useful to the state," he opened some trades to them, granted them a very conditional admission to university, and allowed them to settle in places previously barred to them. These measures illustrated one route to emancipation—via the decrees of an autocratic monarch in the form of privileges that could be granted with one hand but removed with the other.

A very different approach was provided by the revolutions in North America and in France, where political upheaval led to new constitutional orders that proposed a universal model of citizenship and severely curtailed, where they did not outright abolish, religious denomination as a marker of privilege or disadvantage. Napoleonic armies spread these new ideas in the towns and provinces they occupied, and Jews there received freedoms they had never before enjoyed in history. More than forty years after Napoleon's death, his memory as the "immortal hero who had carried the Rights of Man and of the Citizen to the Israelites of Europe on the wings of his victorious eagles" still evoked gratitude in Jewish circles. The triumph of state *indifference* to Judaism represented an astonishing change in the political culture of a Christian Europe, one that was hailed by some with rejoicing but that left others—both Jews and Christians—disoriented and in some cases distressed. It represented a radical departure from a past in which government, military service, and most professions and forms of work had remained the preserve of Christians.[5]

The innovations brought by French conquest did not long survive Napoleon's defeat, but it is worth noting that when the Congress of Vienna met to discuss the post-Napoleonic order in Europe in 1815, it was the conservative Metternich who argued for removing Jewish civic disabilities. In other words, the cause of Jewish emancipation—like its belated and desperate enemy, antisemitism—found support both in the French Revolution and in the world of Restoration Europe that succeeded it. It became an ideal of salons and Enlightenment rationalists, a kind of political movement battling for public opinion in magazines and newspapers, with a capacity to wage campaigns and countercampaigns across borders. Great gains were to be made over the ensuing half century, but these would elicit growing opposition as well.

There were, overall, three fairly distinct geographical zones of emancipation. In the first, comprising the United States, England, France, and Italy, the battle for Jewish equality was won relatively rapidly. Rights were secured quickly in the United States, thanks to the federal constitution's guarantees and its clear separation of church and state, though more slowly in individual states, where minor legal restrictions survived into the nineteenth century. In England, bills to remove all civil disabilities against Jews were stymied more than once, but the strength of liberal sentiment across the country and a series of compromises and piecemeal settlements meant that there were few institutional impediments to integration by the end of Queen Victoria's reign in 1901. In France, where it was a Jewish minister of justice, Adolphe Crémieux, who in 1848 abolished slavery in the colonies and eliminated the death penalty for political offenses, Jews enjoyed equality under the law by mid-century. In independent Italy, there were Jewish generals and government ministers. A Jewish mayor of Rome, Ernesto Nathan, held office between 1907 and 1913, presiding over the new capital's building boom and laying the foundations for its secular schooling system and public transportation network.

If these countries represented the extreme of liberal possibility, it was also true that they contained only a small fraction of the Jews in Europe at the time—somewhere between 5 percent and 10 percent of the total. The Jewish population of Europe had grown very fast, from under one million in 1700 to two million in 1800 and around five million by the mid-nineteenth century. But the fastest growth took place in entirely unemancipated Russia, which, including the Polish provinces it had won by the start of the nineteenth century, contained two thirds or more of European Jewry, the vast majority of whom were regarded as "alien subjects." Confined mostly to an area known as the Pale of Settlement, Jews endured the restrictions and violence of tsarist rule with little obvious means or hope of change. The fiercest struggle over their place in political life was the one that took place between the two zones on either side, in the heartlands of central Europe. It was in Germany and the Austro-Hungarian Empire— where Enlightenment arguments for emancipation collided with growing ethnic nationalism—that tensions were most acute.

"The emancipation of the Jews has become such a volatile issue," remarked the sympathetic German writer Karl Gutzkow, "that one can hardly mention it without immediately finding oneself embroiled in controversy." Vociferous opposition existed in many states. In

Sweden, the 1838 decree abolishing discrimination against the Jews was rescinded because of public protest; in Hungary, the diet ventured an emancipation bill and then gave up. In early nineteenth-century Italy, the kingdom of Sardinia reintroduced its old special dress code, and the papacy reactivated sixteenth-century measures to restrict Roman Jews to the ghetto.[6] Nor were reactionaries the only opponents of Jewish freedom. At the opposite end of the political spectrum from the pope was the French anarchist Pierre-Joseph Proudhon, whose virulent hatred spilled over into private tirades against this "enemy of mankind" who should be "sent back to Asia or exterminated." Proudhon's murderous views were too extreme to be representative of the revolutionary Left but plenty of socialists shared the antisemitic commonplaces of the day. Karl Marx, whose own writings were imbued with anti-Jewish stereotypes, was more typical—not opposing legal emancipation but rather arguing that it did not go far enough: For Marx, "the Jew" epitomized all that was wrong with bourgeois society, an embodiment of alienation who thus stood as much in need of revolution as anyone.[7]

The revolutions of 1848, which swept across France, northern Italy, and the lands of central Europe, showed clearly to what extent the cause of the Jews was closely associated with liberals and radicals: As the German philosopher Bruno Bauer noted, *emancipation* was, together with words like *freedom*, *human rights*, and *justice*, part of the new liberal lexicon of the time. Jews themselves participated as never before as political activists; reform-minded rabbis hailed the dawn of a new era. "Praise be to God—there is no longer any talk of 'Jew' or 'Christian,'" wrote a young scholar called Moritz Steinschneider to his fiancée from Berlin in March 1848.[8] (The polymathic Steinschneider is credited with years later coining the term *antisemitic*—long after the bloom of revolution had faded.) But there were some episodes in those eventful months that showed that not everyone welcomed such an unprecedented prospect. News of revolution in Paris led to anti-Jewish riots in Alsace. In towns across Europe, assaults on Jews became commonplace, often carried out by national guardsmen or police. The ostensible motives for such violence ranged from the old religious prejudices to soaring food prices (always a concern each spring) that were blamed on Jewish speculators, to outraged opposition to Jews moving into previously protected trades or neighborhoods. And yet most had at the core a new element: opposition to the new civic order that their emancipation presaged.[9]

Opposition to liberalism extended deep into Jewish communities as well. The poisoning of a reformist rabbi by his opponents in the city of Lemberg in Habsburg Galicia in the midst of the 1848 revolutions has been described as the first murder of a Jewish leader by another Jew since Roman times. What it demonstrated was that emancipation did not only lead to debate within the larger societies in which Jews lived, but also triggered equally passionate debate among Jews themselves because of the dramatic changes it presupposed to the tenor and organization of their lives.[10] In Lemberg, the clash between Jewish advocates of Enlightenment and their Hasidic opponents had been brewing for years. But among Jews everywhere in Europe, what some saw as opportunity others regarded with deep misgivings. For many of them the price of admission into modern political life seemed unbearably high, threatening the essence of their faith and habits.

The accustomed communal way of life was an isolated one. As late as 1740, being caught in the Berlin Jewish community carrying a book in German could lead to your expulsion. Thus one of Emperor Joseph II's most remarkable demands had been that Jewish children should learn the language of the society they lived in: "What we want is that all our subjects should be able to read, write and sum. For this, learned men are scarcely necessary." Many rabbis and their followers now feared the undermining of Jewish learning, the sudden changes in dress, fashion, and sociability, as well as new perils such as the theater, philosophy, or the mustache (in place of the beard). The Lithuanian rabbi Jacob Halevi Lifschitz lamented the time when

> the Torah alone was still the only nationality we had.... The people at large were disciplined, pious and humble...and did not presume to speak their minds in public, questioning the thoughts of the leaders.... Then it was as yet unheard of to pay heed to the opinion of the crowd in the name of "public opinion" and internal disputes were brought before God, through those who were great in Torah.[11]

The failure of the 1848 revolution meant a setback for the cause of emancipation, and as one uprising after another was crushed, the scale of the forces ranged against it became even clearer. Rumors of emancipation themselves triggered riots and protests. In at least one Baden commune, the Jews actually asked not to be emancipated, fearing the outcome. Polemics in favor of their freedom were answered by pamphlets denouncing it. The first recognizably antisemitic tracts denouncing Jews for their control of the economy circulated: Refuting the premise of the Italian politician Massimo d'Azeglio's *Emancipation of the Jews*, his opponents warned that emancipation would simply grant them license to oppress Christians. What was needed was what the composer Richard Wagner, among others, referred to as "emancipation *from* the Jews."[12]

In the German lands, the scale of Christian opposition prompted supporters of emancipation to adopt a gradualist program, beginning with educational reforms aimed at creating a new kind of Jew whose private faith would not preclude fluency in the national language and patriotic participation in the country's life. The obvious end goal was assimilation; a less foreseeable outcome was the restructuring of Jewish religious institutional life and the emergence of Reform, Conservative, and Orthodox denominations. In this way the movement for "reform of the Jews" emerged as an accompaniment to the expansion of their civic and political rights, and the religion itself was transformed. The assimilationist wager was that by ceasing to differ from their Christian fellow-citizens except in the matter of private faith, Jews would thereby succeed in eradicating the grounds for hostility toward them. The future was to show otherwise.

It was the rapid political changes of the years between 1867 and 1871—at the moment of liberalism's apogee—that were the real turning point in central Europe. With the unification of Germany and the creation of the German Empire under Prussian leadership, legal equality suddenly became a reality there for the first time. Major constitutional reforms in the Habsburg Empire brought about a similar result at almost exactly the same time. Neither realm was yet a recognizable democracy in the modern sense, but in both most of the constitutional impediments to legal equality had been cleared away.

The achievement was celebrated in concrete form as a multiplicity of great synagogues sprang up in the second half in the nineteenth century in central locations in the towns and cities of Europe. Symbols of Jewish middle-class pride and newly won respectability, they testified to the transformation of communal life brought about by the growth and prosperity of a Jewish urban elite participating publicly for the first time in the life of their countries. The trend had started with the vast Leopoldstadt Synagogue in Vienna in 1858, followed by its equally massive counterpart in the Hungarian city of Pest the next year. The Oranienburger Straße central synagogue, with a capacity of three thousand worshippers, opened its doors in Berlin in 1866 in the presence of Bismarck himself. But they were merely the best known of dozens. No fewer than fifty synagogues, some of them enormous, were constructed in the eye-catching neo-Moorish style that evoked a voguish connection to medieval Spain and the Arabs. Found in cities everywhere from Manchester to Kiev, this style had been inaugurated with the Semper Synagogue in Dresden, before inspiring others in Leipzig and Cologne. Zagreb, Prague, Stockholm, Besançon, Florence, Turin, Pilsen, Saint Petersburg, Esztergom, Timişoara, Trieste, Antwerp, Kiev, and Sarajevo all followed, their lavish polychromatic interiors, golden domes, and pillars hinting at the influence of the Alhambra, the Taj Mahal, and the mosques of Constantinople. Others paid homage to Byzantium, the Romanesque revival, or Art Nouveau. In Rome, the ghetto that had confined the city's Jews for three centuries was demolished; in its place arose the vast columned edifice of the Great Synagogue, a mélange of styles remarkable even for that eclectic era that combined Greco-Roman with Babylonian, Pharaonic Egyptian, and Art Nouveau, topped by a square aluminum dome that can still be seen for miles around.[13]

Symbols of a desire to partake of a common historical past and a common future, and expressing above all an unquenchable confidence that the tide was flowing in the direction of liberty and progress, these synagogues stand today—where they survive at all—as forlorn monuments to a time long past. Many in the German lands were burned down during Kristallnacht in 1938 or in the war that followed. Others found postwar uses as stables, warehouses, or offices. The survivors remind us that even as this remarkable continent-wide architectural phenomenon testified to the historical scale of the European Jewish transformation, the countercurrents were growing in strength as well. From the late 1870s, this opposition crystallized in the discourse of a new political movement: antisemitism.

Prejudices against Jews were held in some form by many if not most people in Europe, independent of social class or geography, and they stretched across the political spectrum. They were among the enormous number of negative and unflattering stereotypes Europeans held about one another and others, and they could be found on the Right and the Left, among clerics and *philosophes*, among people obsessed by "the

Jewish question" and those unconcerned with it. They could, for that matter, be found among Jews themselves. The Enlightenment itself had not ended the old myths so much as it had added new ones. And yet despite them emancipation had proceeded and gained ground. Our concern here is not therefore with attitudes, symbols, or stereotypes but with political actions, theories, organizations, and outcomes. What the antisemitism of the 1880s represented that was new was a kind of political movement, one that notched up both successes and failures in the decades ahead. It emerged as a countermovement aiming to check, slow down, and perhaps even, for some, reverse the achievements of the Jewish emancipation campaigns, and its success depended not so much upon persuading people of negative stereotypes about the Jews—these were common currency—but rather in getting them to believe that the Jews were a serious threat to their core social or political concerns.

Aside from the teachings of the Church, the intellectual underpinnings for such arguments had been laid over the preceding two or three generations by intellectuals and academics working across the scholarly disciplines of comparative philology, Bible studies, anthropology, and history. Their publications gave credence to the idea that Jews were a cohesive group fundamentally alien to the societies around them. Some antisemites defined them against Christianity, others against some ideal of Hellenism, and others again said it all boiled down to race. Some criticized them for standing out, others for blending in. Coherence was not the point: There were multiple versions of the basic idea. What this scholarship popularized was a kind of theory about power, increasingly connected to the new language of biological struggle, that enabled the issue of Jewish emancipation (in itself a minor issue for most people) to be linked to other, more deeply established and more widely discussed concerns of the day: the nation's future, respect for monarchy and church, the health of the masses, and the virtues and vices of capitalism.

Sometimes this worked; often it did not: In a Europe where anti-semitic stereotypes were commonplace but not in themselves seen as especially worthy of comment, thoroughgoing antisemites could as eas-ily come across as obsessive as prophets—the importance they attached to an issue others regarded as marginal marking them out. They often struggled for social respectability, for in its dependence upon the press and publicity, its historical consciousness, and above all its call to action, antisemitism was to a large extent a movement of the new mass politics, reaching out to sectors of the population such as peas-ants, students, and artisans who were only now for the first time emerg-ing as actors on the national stage. If emancipation was an achievement gained through the work of intellectuals and elites, antisemitism was a kind of potential uprising from below, a hint perhaps that a demo-cratic future held a darker side.

Many of the mixed feelings elicited by Jewish emancipation reflected the fact that it had coincided with another far more impor-tant and sweeping change in the pattern of European life—the spread of capitalism and a monetized way of life across the Continent. Like emancipation, the coming of capitalism was far from uncontested and produced losers as well as winners. It increased indebtedness in the countryside, while the availability of cheap manufactures and the rise of the first department stores left many guilds, shopkeepers, and arti-sans at a disadvantage and produced a deep reservoir of potential dis-content. Cities grew extraordinarily fast, creating huge slums with a large, poorly housed proletariat. Antisemitism was thus a kind of counterreaction to the accelerated rhythms of modern times that held out the promise of a better life, a return to older and more familiar ways. A salvific vision whose acceptance depended only upon a set of assertions about Jewish culpability, it had the advantage of giving a physical embodiment to the otherwise abstract forces behind social upheaval.

There were of course other ways of explaining and criticizing the emergence of capitalism that did not focus on the Jews. Socialism was the most obvious and influential of these. But whereas socialists identified the chief political cleavage as the one between social classes, the antisemites emphasized race, religion, and ethnicity: In this way their ideas lent themselves to the new spirit of nationalism that was sweeping Europe. A thread of antisemitism could be discerned in some socialist writings too, especially when targeting the international power of financial and banking elites, but there were few socialists for whom this was a major part of their thought, and for many of them antisemitism was intellectual idiocy and anathema.

It was in 1874, amid a sudden economic downturn in Germany, that an anti-liberal journalist called Otto Glagau published a series of articles attacking his enemies for creating an economic free-for-all that had led to swindles, bankruptcies, layoffs, and wholesale moral degeneration. It was, in his view, a social crisis of the first order and the culprits were "the Jews." They were

> everywhere forcing their way to the front, to the top, seizing the leadership and doing the talking.... They actually exercise sovereignty over us; they have a dangerous supremacy and they exert a very ominous influence. After many centuries, it is once again the case that an alien tribe so small in number is dominating the great true nation. The entire history of the world knows no other example of a homeless people, of a race that is decidedly degenerate both physically and psychologically, having dominion over the entire world.[14]

Much of what was to unfold may already be seen in this. A new threat is posed by Jews not only acquiring rights but domination over Germans, and not only over Germans but over "the entire world." Their power is economic, and they have benefited—dishonestly—while honest Germans have lost everything. They have no home and no national feeling. They are not secretive in their quest for power—on the contrary, it is their forwardness that is condemned—but they are unfettered by morality. They are, despite emancipation, irredeemably "alien," and their relationship with German society is not a religious but a racial and biological one: They threaten physical degeneration. In short, the problem here is not just a stereotype or faith: It is an entire theory of world history.

A more extensive, not to say rambling, historical framing of these ideas was offered in a pamphlet that became a bestseller. Running through some twelve editions in less than a decade, *The Victory of Judaism over Germandom* was written by the journalist Wilhelm Marr, who warned that the Jews were close to triumphing in their eighteen-hundred-year struggle for supremacy and were about to succeed in turning Germany into "the new Palestine of Europe." In 1879 he established the League of Antisemites (*Antisemiten-Liga*), a political organization for "non-Jewish Germans of all denominations, all parties and all walks of life" to work toward saving the country from "complete Judaisation." Emphasizing his commitment to "legal means," Marr pledged that the league would fight to "force the Semites back into a position corresponding with their numerical strength." In hindsight, one can see this as proposing a political model of racial unity that regarded all other ideological differences as secondary, a kind of distant forerunner for the Nazi Party and its dream of a "Community of the People" (*Volksgemeinschaft*).[15]

Marr was of course by no means the first. A kind of protopolitical hostility to Jews had been developing in Catholic circles for at least two decades before this: Petition campaigns in Bavaria, for instance, had successfully opposed civic equality legislation immediately after the 1848 revolutions. Many German liberals had their own doubts about emancipation, and antisemitism was a great unifier across the Christian confessional divide.[16] What Marr brought was the political energy and mobilizing power of the radicals of an earlier generation, shocking the political establishment of the time with his racialized politicization of the emancipation aftermath. For the next few years, the "antisemitism movement" was widely discussed in the press, especially with the weight of one of Germany's most prominent scholars, the historian Heinrich von Treitschke, behind it. But as quickly as it arose, the struggle fell apart amid personal rivalries and arguments. Some of the self-professed antisemites wanted emancipation revoked; others did not. Some were devout Christians appalled by the mention of race; others disliked any hint that the movement might be based on religious prejudice. And there was snobbery too: Many conservatives felt that the movement's leaders were rabble-rousers, ex-radicals with suspect pasts and not entirely respectable. By the middle of 1885, one of its younger members had become quite gloomy.

> In its outward appearance, antisemitism (or at least the antisemites) has become more or less bankrupt.... These "entrepreneur-antisemites" who now float on the surface are, as a matter of fact, absolutely unreliable fellows: they burst like soap bubbles under the slightest pressure, and will disperse like "chaff in the wind."[17]

The antisemites can thus be seen as a fringe group of obsessives who failed to enter the mainstream and made a quite marginal impact on German party politics before the outbreak of war in 1914. But political marginalization is not the same thing as failure, and the antisemites introduced ideas that turned out to have a long life ahead of them.

In France, political antisemitism emerged at much the same time as in Germany, and there too journalists and the press were the initiators. There were other similarities as well: stock market crashes, swindles, and scandals that put the new capitalism in the spotlight, bewildering transformations in national life such as railways and fast-growing capital cities that dominated the provinces and attracted immigrants. But the political context was quite different and therefore the character and meaning of antisemitism were as well. Long before the declaration of the Third Republic in 1870, French Jews were already more integrated into national life than their German counterparts. In Germany, with its delicate composite of Protestants and Catholics, anti-Jewish nationalism could not easily assume a confessional form: Race was the unifier. The situation in France was different, in short, and not only because France was overwhelmingly Catholic. It was also a republic, born out of the country's defeat in the Franco-Prussian War, and a contested one at that. After the anticlerical laws of 1880–82 suppressed the Jesuits and established free obligatory state education and civil marriage, many French Catholics regarded the Third Republic with hostility and struggled to explain how the country had fallen into the hands of the enemies of church and monarchy. Antisemitism offered a kind of answer.

When the journalist Édouard Drumont embarked on the series of violently antisemitic screeds that would make him famous, his starting point was thus defense of the faith. An ardent Catholic who saw himself battling Satan, Drumont was influenced by earlier writers like the now-forgotten Roger Gougenot des Mousseaux, whose 1869 *Le Juif: Le judaïsme et la judaïsation des peuples chrétiens* had warned that the chief threat to Christian values in the modern world was the assimilated Jew. The book that made Drumont's name was a two-volume, twelve-hundred-page bestseller, *La France juive*, a vitriolic critique of the Third Republic as a Jewish creation.[18]

The fanatical Catholic was a racist too, and his antisemitic newspaper, *La libre parole*, was a widely read vehicle for ethnically stereotypical caricatures of a kind still relatively unusual for the time. "Semites," according to the writer, "have a brain made differently from ours." He outlined their takeover of France and their sinister conspiracy to gather all power into their hands. To help his readers recognize them, he described their external markings: "The famous curved nose, the blinking eyes, the body too long, the feet flat, the legs bowed, the hair sticking out all over, the hand moist and juicy in the way of the hypocrite and the traitor. They often have one arm shorter than the other." It was on the basis of scientific knowledge such as this that Drumont led his followers into battle in the Dreyfus affair.[19]

The infamous case that helped to define the course of French history for more than half a century began in 1894, when a French Jewish artillery captain called Alfred Dreyfus was wrongly accused of spying for the Germans. Found guilty on the flimsiest of evidence by a military court, he was dismissed from the army and sent to the penitentiary on Devil's Island, a penal colony off the coast of French Guiana. The fight to prove his innocence dragged on for more than a decade before his sentence was annulled in 1906. In that time, the case became a battleground over competing visions of France. Against Dreyfus's supporters ranged an assortment of monarchists, Catholics, and defenders of the honor of the French army, including the artists Edgar Degas and Pierre-Auguste Renoir. The streets of Paris and other French towns became the sites of clashes. One side stood for emancipation, the legacy of the Revolution, and the benefits of assimilation into French civilization; the other identified France with Christianity, the Catholic Church, and a willingness to stand firm against the temptations of modernity. It was not by chance that these very years saw the rise of the shrine at Lourdes as the great inspiration to popular Catholicism and the emergence of a new Catholic politics.

Drumont's followers had an undeniable talent for shock tactics and bloodthirsty rhetoric. Yet as in Germany, the antisemites found immediate success in politics more elusive than literary and journalistic sensation. His comrade in arms, the Marquis de Morès, was an unstable duel-loving aristocratic adventurer whose speculative career had taken him to North Dakota, where he had published *The Bad Lands Cow Boy* and founded the Northern Pacific Refrigerator Car Company before losing a fortune and trying his luck in India and

French Indochina. Running out of money and back in France, Morès discovered Drumont and, sharing his loathing for the Republic, helped him to organize a congress of self-professed antisemites in a suburb of Paris. A few months later they formed an antisemitic league (*Ligue antisémitique française*), a precursor of the far-Right paramilitaries of the interwar years: Their main target was the Jews, but not far behind in their loathing were Freemasons, Protestants, and the British. Morès even formed a squad of out-of-work thugs whom he dressed up as cowboys to attack Dreyfusards and break up their meetings. The high point of the antisemitic leagues came in 1898, when more than fifty riots broke out across France, involving crowds of hundreds or even thousands who targeted and pillaged Jewish homes and businesses. The leagues broke up soon after, but the participation of students, shopkeepers, soldiers, and workers indicated how wide their support went.[20]

Morès's politics were a confused blend of royalism, anarchism, and syndicalism that his biographer describes as an "ideological tossed salad"; Drumont's were not much clearer. Both men were better at hurling insults than policymaking. Morès was dead before he was forty. As for Drumont, his parliamentary career lasted only a few years. After the pope called on French Catholics to accept the Republic, Drumont turned on him too, confusing many of his supporters. A third leader of the Antisemitic League, Jules Guérin, tried to organize a coup d'état and was arrested following a police siege of his holdout: He spent the last decade of his life in prison. "Today antisemitism is in a period of decline," wrote one of Drumont's former followers, the journalist Raphaël Viau, in 1910 in a nostalgic memoir of the years with his idol. Like most people, Viau had left the movement long before.[21]

Only in Habsburg Austria, in the imperial capital, Vienna, did political antisemitism thrive in a parliamentary setting. A formative model for the young Adolf Hitler, the Christian Social Party, under the leadership of the Vienna-born Karl Lueger, dominated municipal politics so emphatically that the emperor was eventually obliged, against

his own inclinations, to recognize him as mayor in 1897. He enjoyed
the backing of Pope Leo XIII and benefited from universal male suffrage, which had been introduced in 1897: Lueger's value was that he
showed how to create a successful Catholic mass political party. An
admirer of Drumont, he was a born politician and a pragmatist who
recognized antisemitism as a route to power though he made little
systematic use of it once in office. Known to his adoring followers as
"the King of Vienna" or "handsome Karl" (*der schöne Karl*), he was an
affable ideological opportunist. His speeches castigated Jews for
oppressing Christians, and he nominally supported efforts to restrict
Jewish immigration into the empire. Yet his famous remark—"I decide
who is a Jew"—summed up his underlying insouciance on the issue.
Despite the understandable alarm expressed in a leading Austrian
newspaper that Vienna was "the only great city in the world whose
administrator is an anti-Semitic agitator," there was no major assault
on Jews' legal rights under his watch.[22]

Nearly thirty years later, in his cell in the Landsberg fortress,
Adolf Hitler, who had been imprisoned in 1923 after the failure of the
Beer Hall Putsch in Munich, recalled Lueger's Vienna. The city had
been a kind of laboratory of antisemitic politicking, and the penniless
student had been a keen observer. Lueger, in Hitler's judgment, had got
the "Jewish question" wrong by his indifference to matters of race. On
that score Hitler preferred the Pan-German Georg von Schönerer,
who had also been active in the Habsburg capital but far less successful politically. Schönerer's importance, wrote Hitler, was to appreciate
the essentially racial rather than religious nature of the struggle. If he
had failed, it was because unlike Lueger, or for that matter the Austrian Social Democrats—Lueger's great rivals—Schönerer had no gift
for mass politics. Hitler would combine the racialism of the one with
the political genius of the other. But it would require the First World
War and its chaotic aftermath to create the conditions that allowed
this to happen.[23]

"Though anti-Semitism has been unmasked and discredited, it is to be feared that its history is not yet at an end." Thus the writer Lucien Wolf concluded the entry on "Anti-Semitism" that appeared in the *Encyclopaedia Britannica* in 1910. Wolf's warning reflected not only the basic failure of the antisemitism movement in the three decades since its appearance, but also the worry that there was more to come. In western and central Europe by 1914 not a single party devoted to the cause survived, and none of the civic rights Jews had won over the previous century had been revoked. But racial antisemitism was on the rise, and in the press, insulting tropes and stereotypical caricatures circulated ever more widely. In France, the Dreyfus affair showed how deeply antisemitism impregnated the entire anti-republican movement, reinforcing a new kind of nationalism that idealized the regions, the Church, and the soil, and saw the Jews as the archetypal intruder. The literary propagandist Maurice Barrès claimed he did not need evidence to confirm Dreyfus's guilt since his race was enough. The Action Française, another anti-Dreyfusard emanation, reshaped the French Right and drove it toward what would later become known as Fascism: Its chief ideologue, the writer Charles Maurras, ended up as a supporter of Marshal Pétain and the collaborationist government of Vichy during the Second World War when finally France's anti-Dreyfusard tradition tasted real power. Neither Barrès nor Maurras, it is worth noting, was a marginal figure: Both enjoyed great literary success and cultural influence.

Right-wing intellectuals (like intellectuals in general) failed to find this kind of adulation in Britain. Yet there too the mass immigration of Russian Jews near the end of the century generated a rumbling of nativist antipathy. "On the continent, the Jewish question erupted," writes a historian of British Jewry; "in Britain, it merely simmered." There was no organized antisemitic politics—after all, the Tories had even been led by a prime minister of Jewish descent—and at the beginning of the twentieth century, Jewish notables gained easy admittance to the court of King Edward VII. Yet there was widespread discussion as to whether Jews could really be assimilated, and concern at mass immigration led to the passing of the 1905 Aliens Act to stanch the flow. Anti-immigrant sentiment extended even to the small, impoverished town of Limerick in the west of Ireland, convulsed briefly by anti-Jewish mob violence in 1904 after a local priest targeted the thirty-five Jewish families who had settled there. The lexicographer James Murray, the founder of the Oxford English Dictionary, admitted around this time that he regretted not including an entry for "Antisemitism" in his dictionary from the start. He had doubted the term would last but realized he had been wrong. "The closing years of the nineteenth century have shown, alas! that much of Christianity is only a temporary whitewash over brutal savagery," he wrote. "It is unbearably saddening to one like myself, who remembers '48 and the high hopes we had in the fifties."[24]

In the German lands, antisemitism's impact upon society went much deeper, especially after the monarchy passed into the hands of the deeply chauvinistic Kaiser Wilhelm II in 1888. His parents had regarded antisemitic demagogues as "lunatics" and on several occasions they even attended synagogue so as to make their views known. They knew their son to be a vulgar and vigorous hater of—in no special order—Jews, Austrians, liberals, Catholics, the English, Slavs, and the Chinese. A believer in antisemitic conspiracy theories, Wilhelm became more open and extreme in his views with time. "The Jews are the parasites of my empire. The Jewish question is one of the great problems I have to deal with," he said. "And yet nothing can be done to cope with it!" In exile after the First World War, the kaiser's antisemitic obsessions reached the point of derangement, and he died in June 1941 hailing the German conquest of Europe as a "succession of miracles" that would sweep the Jews out of Europe.[25]

Elite attitudes in Germany followed the kaiser's lead. Racial science enjoyed enormous prestige and advanced there further than anywhere else. Student fraternities, a useful indicator of the outlook of the country's future leadership, had by the start of the twentieth century more or less purged themselves of Jewish members. Similar prejudices circulated lower down the social scale and erupted in things like the name-change controversies of the era. With the emancipation decree of 1812, Jews in Prussia had been obliged to choose a surname to register for citizenship. But antisemites hated the idea that in changing their names Jews would be harder to distinguish from the rest of the population. In 1893 the "Schmul-Goetze" case made national news after a Jewish merchant called Schmul applied to change his name to the more German-sounding Goetze on the grounds it had been his grandfather's. When his application was approved, another Goetze wrote in to protest and organized a letter signed by twenty-six more who asserted it was a "truly German Christian name" and not one to be utilized by someone for the "express purpose of concealing his Jewish descent." Antisemitic organizations added their support; the lists of signatures multiplied. A petition of 116 bearers of the name that was sent to the kaiser claimed the name change indicated that "[the Jews] are very well aware of their inability ever to become German"; they were, the petition stated, an alien "tribal species."[26] Episodes such as this were both farcical and tragic: They suggest that the political failure of organized antisemitism was not the whole story. In much of central Europe, emancipation had aroused enmities and suspicions that were certainly not dying down and increasingly permeated daily life.

And then there were the lands of Europe's east. In 1898, the very year that anti-Jewish riots took place in France, a much more widespread and serious wave of rioting erupted in the Habsburg Empire's remote eastern province of Galicia. The perpetrators were mostly Polish peasants, workers, and miners, and the targets were Jews living in the small town and villages of the region whose shops and homes were looted and vandalized. Some four hundred attacks were reported before they were suppressed by the gendarmerie and the army. The volatility of the situation took the authorities by surprise, but eventually more than five thousand arrests were made and more than two thousand were sentenced.[27] As for the lands of the Russian Empire, which gave the world a new word, *pogrom*, violence was on an even larger scale and the state's attitude to it was much more ambiguous. The setting there too was an agrarian economy that functioned on the basis of an ethnic differentiation between the Christian peasantry and small-town Jewish intermediaries who ran the estates, owned taverns and shops, and acted as middlemen in the grain trade. The forces of modernity—the railways that facilitated the bringing together of large mobs and the sensation-seeking press (still a novelty in a largely illiterate society)— created a combustible mixture in a world where the old blood libel was still widely believed. Although outright mass violence was relatively rare, it flared following the assassination of Tsar Alexander II in 1881. More spectacularly still—at and around the Bessarabian town of Kishinev in 1903—scores of Jews were killed, a death toll that shocked the world. Just fifteen years later it would seem comparatively trivial.[28]

Like the Habsburgs, the imperial Russian authorities regarded public disorder as a challenge to their own legitimacy. But the difference was that the Romanov court was antisemitic and saw a potential threat in party political activity of almost any kind. Anxious (with good reason) about terrorist conspiracies, it supported the growth of pro-monarchist and pro-church organizations that could be utilized for antisemitic or anti-revolutionary violence. Adding to the volatility was the persistence of popular antisemitism and old-fashioned Jew-hatred whipped up by the local press, which was itself hard to control and in the hands of nationalists. On the eve of Kishinev, for instance, it was the regional daily, *Bessarabets*, that had publicized the ritual murder libel and brought together a group of local ardent antisemites who spread rumors of malign Jewish plots against the peasantry.[29]

The violent nature of Russian antisemitism led to one international cause célèbre after the other, contributing to the country's low standing in the eyes of liberal public opinion abroad. A decade after the Kishinev pogroms came the scandalous trial of Mendel Beilis in Kiev, where local antisemites who had been backed by the tsarist authorities put a Jewish man on trial for supposedly murdering a local boy so that he could use his blood for matzo. The case would have been ridiculous had it not been so serious in its implications. It was an extraordinary and chilling reminder of what many ordinary Russians believed about Jews and the persistence into the twentieth century of the medieval blood libel across swaths of Europe.[30]

One remarkable response to the trial itself is worth noting in particular. Within weeks, half a dozen theaters in New York—home to a huge number of newly arrived Russian Jews—had put on plays about the case in Yiddish, and the name of Mendel Beilis had become a household word on both sides of the Atlantic. The fact is that an era of internationalization left neither antisemitism nor its critics unaffected. This process had started almost as soon as organized antisemitic agitation began in 1880, with the effort of agitators from France, Germany, Romania, and Austria-Hungary to create an antisemitic movement through a series of international conferences in the early 1880s. These had little effect. Far more successful was the counter-internationalism by which Jewish communities and notables in the United States, Britain, and France banded together, mobilizing in defense of coreligionists abroad who were facing persecution, especially in eastern Europe and the Ottoman lands, not so much from these political activists but rather from discriminatory or permissive states. Already at the Congress of Berlin in 1878, German and French Jewish groups had lobbied the Great Powers to withhold recognition from newly independent Romania until its politicians committed the country to Jewish rights. The Kishinev pogrom marked the arrival on the international stage of American Jewish organizations for the first time: The American Jewish Committee was founded in New York City in its wake in order to "prevent infringement of the civil and religious rights of Jews and to alleviate the consequences of persecution."[31] In the Balkan Wars of 1912–13, Jewish groups again lobbied the Great Powers about minority rights, slowly developing an expertise that would stand them in good stead a few years later. In this way, the so-called Jewish question became part of European diplomacy, and it was integrated into the liberal project to "civilize" the Continent and the world through international law.

But Jewish internationalism prompted a counterresponse of its own. To antisemites, the signs of Jewish influence upon European diplomacy confirmed their nightmares: It seemed to them that prominent Jews, operating behind the scenes, really did control the fortunes of the world, using their legendary wealth to bend nations to their will. Radical international conspiracy was of course not a new fear: Catholic monarchists had feared the threat from Freemasonry since the late eighteenth century and fantasized about underground revolutionary networks in the 1820s. Secret policemen feared an anarchist international. By the century's end, the tendency in the increasingly racialized imagination of the times was to see the Jews pulling the strings. The growing internationalization of the fight against antisemitism thus reinforced already well-established fears of a secretive and malign system of Jewish domination. The best-known expression of these fears was a text known as *The Protocols of the Elders of Zion*, published for the first time in a Saint Petersburg newspaper by Pavel Krushevan, a journalist who had been at the center of the agitation behind the Kishinev pogrom: It was very likely he who fabricated and issued what purported to be a translation of the minutes of a secret meeting of a cabal of Jewish elders planning global domination. These days we need no reminding of the damage conspiracy theories can do. After the Great War of 1914–18, the threat outlined in the *Protocols* haunted the minds of men like Adolf Hitler and would lead, with the rise of the Nazis, to a second world war that would make the fate of the Jews a central issue.[32]

CHAPTER 3

Antisemitism on the Rise

1914–33

A crusade of anti-Semitism has been raging from the Rhine to the Vistula, and from the Baltic to the Aegean Sea, during the past six months, with a vindictiveness that almost surpasses all previous manifestations of anti-Jewish hatred since the end of the war.

ISRAEL COHEN, "THE REIGN OF ANTISEMITISM"[1]

Had the First World War never been fought at all, we might today be paying Wilhelm Marr and his ilk as little attention as we do to those obscure fin de siècle French royalists who continued to hope for the return of a king who would never come. By 1914, despite the ubiquity of stereotypes and prejudices against the Jews, the tide of emancipation was flowing in their favor, and antisemitic movements had made little headway against it. Where civil rights had been won, they had not been rolled back. A few episodes around Europe in the war's early days and months were of little consequence compared with the targeting of other minorities. But the length of the conflict, the staggering death toll, and the remarkable upheavals that followed across the Continent changed everything: The triumph of the antisemites was essentially a product of the ideological earthquake that came out of the first total war.

When the war broke out, Jews entered the ranks of European armies, merging their fate with that of their countrymen. For the more politically conscious among them, it was an opportunity to demonstrate their patriotism and to show they would share in the obligations as well as the rights of emancipation. Among the many educated German Jews who joined in the chauvinism of the moment was the poet Ernst Lissauer, composer of the infamous wartime "Hymn of Hate Against England." The ranks of the French army included the young Jewish anthropologist Robert Hertz, who hailed the comradeship he found in the trenches and began an ethnographic study of his fellow soldiers before he was killed in action. One of the best-known of the British war poets from the Western Front was Siegfried Sassoon, scion of a wealthy Anglo-Jewish dynasty and the cricket-playing, Cambridge-educated grandson of a Baghdadi merchant tycoon. A remarkable writer and an almost suicidally brave officer, Sassoon won the Military Cross on the Western Front before going on with equal courage to denounce the war.[2]

However, in the zone stretching from the Baltic to the Black Sea, the military remained a closed and hostile caste to Jews. Indeed, the outbreak of war brought enemy occupation, mass deportation, and destructive violence against civilians on a previously unknown scale and turned the Jews and other minorities into an immediate object of suspicion. From late 1914, imperial armies—the Ottoman, Russian, and Habsburg—targeted suspect populations living close to the front lines or sensitive border zones, where the first massacres and deportations often took place. In western Anatolia, misfortune hit the Greeks; in the eastern Ottoman lands it was the Armenians who were singled out for killing, a preliminary to the genocidal violence of the following year. On the southern border of the Habsburg Empire, it was ethnic Serbs. And in the western borderlands of the Russian Empire, it was above all the Jews.[3]

For hundreds of thousands of Jews confined to the Pale of Settlement in increasingly crowded and impoverished small towns and villages, vulnerable to attacks by the hostile peasantry who surrounded them, the only escape before the war had lain in emigration: Around

1.5 million Jews are reckoned to have migrated to the United States between 1880 and 1914, turning New York City into the largest Jewish city in the world by a wide margin. But once the war broke out in 1914 and imperial armies swept across the region, transatlantic emigration routes were closed off and the Jewish communities of the Pale were subjected to violence initiated not by local troublemakers, as in the past, but by the Russian army itself. In late 1914 Russian units advanced westward beyond the empire into the shtetls of Habsburg Galicia, where they precipitated an orgy of destruction. Towns were burned, and their Jewish inhabitants were killed by soldiers, often in a kind of sadistic blood sport. Not surprisingly, the return of the Habsburg army elicited a "frenzy of joy" among the survivors.[4]

With the success of the German counteroffensive, the tsarist army collapsed. On the retreat, it responded by ordering much of the civilian population under its command to move away from the front: The army saw the Jews of the Pale as a potential pro-German fifth column and turned its violence on them. By the summer of 1915, an estimated six hundred thousand Russian Jews had fled or been deported to central Russia, forced eastward in "indescribable terror" by the army as it fell back in the face of the German advance. In this way, it was war itself that finally destroyed the Pale of Settlement and rendered irrelevant the legal prohibitions on Jewish mobility that had existed until then. By the mid-1920s, the Jewish population of Russia outside the Pale was double what it had been earlier.[5]

In London and New York, the same Jewish groups that had been monitoring official Russian antisemitism vainly expected the tsarist government to acknowledge the contribution of the two hundred thousand Jews who had joined up. When the imperial government issued a proclamation of autonomy for the Poles, they anticipated that one for the Jews would follow. "In view of the great liberal principles for which the Allies have been fighting," wrote Lucien Wolf, one of the key Anglo-Jewish experts, "[we believe] it will be impossible for the

Russian government to maintain the present system." And yet the tsar's ministers showed no signs of bowing to demands to make a stand against antisemitism, to rein in the army, or to ease the legal restrictions Jews still faced.[6]

As the war stretched on, another element entered the equation: war financing. All sides began to look to the US money markets to raise loans, and ironically the antisemitic worldview shared by statesmen and diplomats on both sides made winning over American Jewish financiers seem important. "[Russian] antisemitism makes Jewish financial assistance to the Allies very difficult to obtain," wrote a junior British minister in January 1916. "And this war may well turn on finance."[7] Faced with the stubbornness of the Russian elite, British and French diplomats began to look for another issue that might earn the Entente Powers Jewish goodwill. In the minds of a number of senior Foreign Office officials, there was Zionism. Most of them were not very clear about what this was exactly; still less were they in a position to assess how popular it was among Jews themselves. They got mixed signals on the matter and almost certainly had little conception of the deep ambivalence (not to say dislike) that Jewish elites in both England and the United States felt for the whole idea of a Jewish national state. What they did know was that it was easier to pledge enemy Ottoman lands in a future territorial carve-up than to pressure their ally Russia into making concessions. Thus the British gave up their rather half-hearted effort to use the war to fight for Jewish emancipation in Russia and ended up issuing the Balfour Declaration instead. In November 1917, with British Empire troops beginning to push the Ottoman army out of Palestine, and with Russia in revolutionary turmoil, the British Foreign Secretary Arthur Balfour gave his fateful pledge of British support for the "establishment in Palestine of a national home for the Jewish people."[8]

What this actually meant was deliberately left vague: The notion of a "national home" had no precise sense in international law and it was not at all clear who would even be running the territory concerned when the war ended. Moreover, much of the assimilated Jewish elite of western Europe and the United States was strongly anti-Zionist and did not like the idea at all. The lobbyist Lucien Wolf feared the Balfour Declaration would undermine the position of Jews in England and cast suspicion on their loyalty, and he did what he could to ward it off. In a letter to *The Times*, he and the other Jewish signatories insisted that the Jews of the world were not "one homeless nationality, incapable of complete social and political identification with the nations among whom they dwell." In what would become a familiar liberal refrain, the Anglo-Jewish libertarian economist J. H. Levy protested: "If we proclaim ourselves aliens...I am at a loss to understand on what ground we can cry out that we are being unjustly treated as foreigners.... The one thing which Zionism seems likely to attain is the manufacture of a logical basis for anti-semitism."[9]

So far as eastern European Jewry was concerned, the Balfour Declaration elicited enormous excitement. Yet most Jews even there did not want to leave the lands of their birth either, and the Central Powers still remained a more likely guarantor of their rights than their opponents. The German army occupying Russian territory was greeted as a liberator by Russian Jews, and Berlin presented Germany as an emancipator of the captive nations of the region. In 1916 General Hindenburg announced that Yiddish would be recognized as an official language, and he laid plans to give Jewish communities some local self-government. At the start of 1918, with Russia crippled by revolution, and a German peace seeming likely across eastern Europe, the German foreign ministry endorsed the idea of minority rights. Their Habsburg partner offered proportional representation and even a secretary of state for Jewish affairs. Forgotten in the subsequent course of history, and almost incomprehensible to us today, these reminders of how different the Jewish fate in a monarchical German-led Europe might have been were lost in the German collapse a few months later.

It would be one of the first tragedies of Germany's Eastern Front in the Second World War that many Polish Jewish communities greeted the Wehrmacht warmly, expecting it to play the same role that the kaiser's army had played in the previous conflict.[10]

In late 1918 came an entirely unexpected turn of events when the German and Habsburg Empires followed the tsarist fate and began to disintegrate with unanticipated speed. With Russia already plunged into civil war, a vacuum of power opened up in which Poles, Ukrainians, and others battled for their independence: Amid fighting of bewildering complexity, the region's Jews endured bloodshed on an entirely new scale of horror. Reporting on the news from the town of Proskurov, a shtetl in the former Pale of Settlement, where Ukrainian soldiers massacred more than one thousand Jews in February 1919, *The New York Times* described it as "the first of a new series of events which leave the scope of ordinary pogroms and assume the character of slaughter." Nationalists of all stripes clashed with the newly formed Red Army, anarchist bands, peasant insurgencies, psychopathic adventurers, and warlords. In the eastern provinces of the Habsburg lands, Jewish communities were attacked by Polish nationalists. Right-wing German paramilitary units fighting Bolshevism and Polish and Ukrainian nationalists targeted them in a zone stretching from Estonia in the north to Ukraine in the south. A wave of pogroms erupted that dwarfed anything seen under the tsars. The figures are impossible to determine with precision, but the death toll was staggering: As many as one hundred thousand Jews may have perished in Ukraine alone, with millions more displaced before the civil war came to an end. Nothing like the killing of civilians on this scale had occurred in modern times in Europe—only the death toll of the Armenians in Anatolia exceeded it.[11]

Gathering in Paris for the peace conference in the spring of 1919 with the fighting raging in the East, Jewish delegates tried to bring the suffering and distress of their coreligionists to the attention of the victors. But the latter had many other things on their minds, and there was little interest until the news reached Paris of Polish military units on the rampage, and it dawned on the Big Four that redrawing the map of Europe was going to be more complicated than they had first thought since the new nation-states could as easily become fomenters of war as guarantors of peace. The so-called Committee on New States was asked to construct a legal framework for minority rights, and this was duly written into the treaties that conferred international recognition on the postwar territorial settlement, enshrined in international law, and made a responsibility of a new permanent international organization: the League of Nations. This moment was perhaps the apogee of Jewish internationalism, an epoch when concern for Jewish rights and the extension of the benefits of international law to all seemed to go hand in hand, when the benefits of Jewish emancipation were not only extended but girded by protective international oversight. The ideas behind the new League of Nations protections were at first taken very seriously, and in the 1920s the Jews and the Germans were foremost among the ethnic minorities of eastern Europe who came together in the European Congress of Nationalities to lobby for the defense of the rights the peace settlement had granted them.

The peace settlement marked a shift in thinking about the relationship between minorities and majorities. The old nineteenth-century liberal model of emancipation had been premised on assimilation and the equal treatment of individuals irrespective of faith; at Versailles it gave way to a nationalist model that made the nation-state primary and secured collective minority rights on the basis of ethnicity. For the Jews of eastern Europe this was an advance compared with the regime they had previously lived under, but it also made them hostages to the new configuration of power. For as minorities they were subject to the authority of newly established national states that resented the unwanted oversight of the League of Nations. Moreover, the entire system was the creation of the victorious Great Powers,

German defeat, and Russian collapse. Any combined German-Russian recovery might threaten its survival.

All this lay in the future. In the early 1920s, the forces of Jewish emancipation appeared to have triumphed across Europe and antisemitism as a political movement to have been defeated. The most antisemitic regime on the continent—that of the Russian tsar—had been overthrown with no possibility of recovery; emancipation had finally—and suddenly—come to Russia with the revolutions of 1917, while the liberal Great Powers seemed set to exercise their benign protection over the east European heartlands of Ashkenazi Jewry. In 1925 a Polish-Jewish pact to "end anti-Semitism" was announced, following meetings between communal Jewish groups and the government in Warsaw. "The Polish people," the foreign minister was reported as saying on a transatlantic visit, "have awakened to the realization that their anti-Semitism is a mistake." Two years later, there came perhaps the high point of this reaction against antisemitism when the trial of Sholem Schwarzbard opened in Paris. Schwarzbard was a young Jewish man who had lost his family in the 1919 pogroms in Ukraine; in revenge he had assassinated the Ukrainian nationalist leader, Symon Petlyura, who was living in exile in the French capital. The striking thing about the trial, which ended sensationally in Schwarzbard's acquittal, was that both sides agreed on one thing: Antisemitism was deplorable. One commentator noted: "The assassin had not killed a man; he had struck at Antisemitism....Antisemitism was called...Petlyura." The latter, for his part, had always insisted he was no antisemite. For Jewish groups, the Schwarzbard trial offered a chance to try antisemitism before the bar of world opinion. It led to the formation of an International League Against Antisemitism, an active self-defense organization that pushed for new legislation to allow antisemites to be tried in the French courts.[12] The effectiveness of this strategy, however, was to prove questionable. There were to be several efforts between the two world wars to use the courts in different countries to prosecute antisemitism, but none would produce unambiguous success, and the protection of the law turned out to have serious limitations. A high-profile trial of the publishers of the Swiss edition of *The Protocols of the Elders of Zion* in Bern in 1933–34, which put Nazis in the dock, ended with an unsatisfyingly indeterminate verdict.[13]

In fact, far from antisemitism having been defeated, the final stages of the First World War had seen its intensification across much of central and eastern Europe as well. Indeed, it was the anarchic violence of the war's last phase and its aftermath that did most to bring about the ascendancy of antisemitism as a political movement. The cataclysm of the war had been overwhelming, its conclusion a cascade of unforeseen consequences following the millions of deaths in the fighting itself: the sudden defeat of the Central Powers, and the overthrow of centuries-old monarchies; hyperinflation and acute economic instability; pandemic and massive influxes of impoverished refugees; the emergence of the United States as a major power in determining the future of Europe; and looming above all from the east, the unprecedented triumph of a radical revolutionary movement—Bolshevism—in Russia. All this came as a bewildering and, to many, quite inexplicable turn of events. Anti-Jewish conspiracy theories ramified as a ready explanation for dizzying change and so it was in the early 1920s that *The Protocols of the Elders of Zion*, a text little heard of in 1914, reached a remarkably vast audience on both sides of the Atlantic. High-ranking British and French politicians seriously pondered whether the mysterious book held the key to understanding what was happening in the world. In New York, noted one American Jewish magnate, the *Protocols* were "the topic of conversation in every living room and in every social sphere." Henry Ford gave the work enormous prominence and did more than anyone thereby to create a favorable climate for antisemitism in interwar America.[14]

It may be tempting to see parallels with the speed with which conspiracy theories spread in our own times, but whatever the after-shocks caused by the global financial crisis of 2008–9 or of COVID, they do not come close to the magnitude of the impact of the First World War. What fueled this turn to an antisemitic worldview was above all the fear that the triumph of liberal constitutionalism at the Paris Peace Conference was only the prelude to full-blown revolution-ary socialism across Europe. In the turbulent months following the sudden end of the war, this did not seem impossible: There were strikes, factory occupations, and riots from Clydeside to northern Italy that revealed the new power of organized labor and the Left. Reeling from sudden defeat, food and fuel shortages, and the influenza epidemic, Germany in particular was hit by a wave of short-lived socialist revo-lutions in late 1918 with Jewish radicals prominent among the insur-rectionary leaders. Already anxious about the supposed threat posed by the thousands of eastern European Jews (*Ostjuden*) who were escaping westward from the violence of the Russo-Polish borderlands into Germany and Austria, demobilized servicemen went into action. Many members of the right-wing Freikorps, who were defending Ger-many, as they saw it, against Bolshevism, were staunchly antisemitic; the underground Organization Consul was founded as a death squad to "rid the German government of socialists and Jews." Fleeing White Russians and ethnic Germans uprooted by the Russian Civil War and the Bolshevik advance publicized what they claimed was a sinister new foe—Judeo-Bolshevism. Never mind that most Jews were cer-tainly not Bolsheviks, nor most Bolsheviks Jews; this mythical threat gripped many people's imaginations.[15]

It was in these very months that the Jews came to occupy a central place in Hitler's view of the world. During the war, in the regimental headquarters that had become his home, he had given little if any indication to his fellow soldiers of his future obsessions: Indeed, Lt. Hugo Gutmann, the regimental adjutant who had recommended him for an Iron Cross, was himself Jewish. Days before he arrived in

Munich in November 1918 as a young soldier facing an uncertain future, the Bavarian monarchy had been toppled by a group of revolutionaries led by the socialist Kurt Eisner. For German public opinion not the least shocking aspect of this turn of events was that Eisner, Bavaria's new minister-president, along with some members of his government, was Jewish: What made this the more extraordinary was that unlike elsewhere, Jews in Germany had not held governmental positions of any consequence before the First World War. Awakening to a socialist regime under a Jewish leader, many members of Munich's Jewish community were apprehensive: "We found it worrying at the time how many Jews had become ministers," recollected the feminist Rahel Straus. "It was a great misfortune. It was the beginning of the Jewish catastrophe.... We knew it then, and we said so." Interestingly, Hitler himself opted at this time neither to demobilize nor to join one of the right-wing paramilitary formations: Instead he stayed in the army, serving the new socialist republic. He is even captured on film, marching in the funeral cortege after Eisner was assassinated by a right-wing nationalist in February 1919. But in the fervidly antisemitic atmosphere of the counterrevolutionary repression that followed, the future führer—following along with many of his countrymen—came to attribute Germany's woes to the Jews.[16]

In a Munich beer hall in August 1920, barely eighteen months after Eisner's funeral, Hitler gave a speech entitled "Why We Are Anti-Semites." By this time, he was active in the murky world of Bavarian far-Right politics, and the speech, which was two hours long, was deliberately crafted to try to mark out the new Nazi Party from its rivals. At a time when much of Munich was debating the prominence of Jews in politics, it was not sufficient to be antisemitic; what was important was to explain why. Hitler chose to do this in two ways. The first was by laying a strong emphasis on biological racism. Claiming that his party was in the vanguard of the antisemitic movement in Germany as a whole, Hitler warned that the Jews were a bacillus who threatened the health of the German people: Here were the origins of a set of ideas that would lead to state-sponsored mass murder two decades later. The second, which reflected the new party's hopes for gaining support from nationalistic workers and socialists, meant eschewing the usual conservative and Catholic emphasis on the threat of Bolshevism. The speech shows that the future German dictator recognized, however obliquely, that some in his audience did not yet see the relevance of antisemitism to their concerns and even felt ashamed to be identified with it. "How can you be a socialist antisemite? Are you not ashamed?" he imagines them objecting, before boasting, "A time will come when we demand: 'As a socialist how can you not be an antisemite?'" In the same vein, he imagines another objection that "before the war one heard nothing about the Jews." "You say: before the war one had not heard about them," responds Hitler. "But how pitiful are those who hear about it all now and still lack the guts to join us." His task was to win over those who were not already in the far-Right camp, and his comments—which serve almost as a kind of coded account of his own ideological evolution—are a reminder that German antisemitic politics had confronted significant social obstacles before 1914. But amid the shocking humiliation of defeat, the collapse of the monarchy, and the fear of revolution, such reservations and taboos were smashed. Most of the conservative parties adopted antisemitic views and even began to close their ranks to Jewish members. Hitler was following the trend of the times, using antisemitism to appeal across the class divides of German society.[17]

The first wave of right-wing violence ended with antisemitic riots in Berlin and Hitler's failed Beer Hall Putsch in Munich in 1923: Jailed for his role in the Putsch, Hitler occupied the cell in the Landsberg prison that had formerly housed Eisner's assassin and set to work on the story of his early years, told to foreground his path toward antisemitic political consciousness. *Mein Kampf* (*My Struggle*) described his father as a cosmopolitan, an imperial civil servant who had disapproved of antisemitism and nationalism and found both vulgar. Hitler writes that it was only upon moving to Vienna that he finally understood the occult power of the Jews and their desire for world mastery. In fact he read back into his Vienna years—and into his wartime service—an obsessive antisemitism that those who knew him at the time doubted had actually existed, and he skated quickly over his potentially embarrassing decision to serve the Eisner government in Bavaria at the end of 1918. The book served its purpose: Once he was released from prison in 1924, Hitler saw that radical antisemitism, rather than blocking his path to power politically, could help bring the Nazi Party success within the parliamentary system of the Weimar Republic itself.[18]

And it was not just Germany. In Poland, the country with the largest Jewish population in Europe, a new avowedly antisemitic government made it clear it had no intention of fulfilling its minority rights obligations. In Romania there was fury that the liberal Great Powers continued to humiliate the country by defending Jewish rights; the sizable new Jewish populations of the enlarged Greater Romania that had come into being in 1919 were deliberately kept in political limbo. In Hungary a revolutionary soviet had been toppled by the anti-communist regime of Admiral Horthy, which instituted a White Terror of its own: The rightists saw the failed pro-Bolshevik revolution of Béla Kun, himself Jewish, as yet another "Jewish revolution." With the massive loss of Hungarian territory imposed by the Trianon peace treaty, antisemitism exploded there. "Would Hungary become a Jewish country?" a senior Roman Catholic bishop worried in September 1918. Within two years, this had turned into a full-blown vision of Hungary as the bastion of Christian civilization, saving Europe from "Jewish morality." Views that were extremist in 1918 were mainstream by 1920.[19]

Through the decade, however, the counterrevolution was held in check because the liberal victors of the First World War still underwrote the international system. American capital poured into the Weimar Republic, Bolshevism was halted on the Polish-Soviet border, and the League of Nations continued to supervise the settlement in eastern Europe. So long as this balance of power prevailed, the political effects of antisemitic regimes in central and eastern Europe could be contained. But the end of the Weimar Republic amid the global slump marked the beginning of antisemitism's triumph on a European scale. With the Nazi seizure of power in 1933, Germany fell into the hands of a party distinguished from its rivals only by the importance it assigned to fighting Jews: In the Nazi Party's founding 1920 program, no fewer than eight of its twenty-five points deal in one way or another with the issue. Among their commitments were stripping Jews of German citizenship, dismissing them from public office, and identifying them as a racial threat to the nation. In this way the Nazi Party positioned itself to roll back emancipation. What this meant on paper was clear: the whittling away of the rights that had made Jews part of the German nation and their excision from the body politic. What this meant in reality was as yet quite unclear.

CHAPTER 4

Antisemitism as World Power

1933–45

It is bad to be oppressed by a minority; but it is worse to be oppressed
by a majority. For there is a reserve of latent power in the masses which,
if it is called into play, the minority can seldom resist.

LORD ACTON, *THE HISTORY OF FREEDOM IN ANTIQUITY*[1]

The Jewish question is the key to world history.

THE REICH PRESS OFFICE, FEBRUARY 3, 1944[2]

It is tempting and perhaps to some extent unavoidable in a history of
this kind to present antisemitism as if it exists in isolation, something
to be understood on its own terms without reference to broader attitudes and issues. Yet antisemitism is almost never an autonomous
force or program—one of the reasons for the failure of the pre-1914
antisemitic movements was that they had thought it could be—and it
cannot be properly understood when it is framed as if it stands apart
from its historical context. This is especially true of the era of Fascism,
when organized antisemitism reached its apogee. Historians have
devoted much effort to examining how important antisemitism actually was to the interwar and wartime European Right—and how it
impacted its policies in power. These questions turn out, even when
we arrive at the Holocaust itself, to be more complicated than might
seem likely at first glance.

For the Italian Fascist movement, for example, which gave the
larger phenomenon of Fascism its name, antisemitism was of far less
consequence than struggles with the working class in the industrial

towns of the north or between landowners and the landless labor force tilling the estates of the Po Valley. Antisemitism played no real role in Fascism's rise to power. The anti-Jewish prejudices and stereotypes circulating in Italy were associated with the Catholic Church and somewhat blunted therefore by the staunch anticlericalism hardwired into much of Italian political life: Mussolini was himself not much interested in the issue. Indeed, his mistress Margherita Sarfatti was Jewish, and at least one senior figure in the regime had a Jewish wife. There were Fascist Jews as well as anti-Fascist Jews, and the regime, seeking to oppose the British in the eastern Mediterranean, had even allowed Vladimir Jabotinsky's Revisionist Zionists to set up a naval academy to train members of their youth movement, Betar. (Jabotinsky, a major figure in the Zionist movement, was a believer in Jewish arms and an inspiration behind the formation of the Jewish Legion in the British Army during the First World War.) Only in the late 1930s, as he moved closer to the Nazis, did Mussolini introduce antisemitic laws, for reasons that are still debated, with ultimately catastrophic results for Jewish life in Italy: The impact on the assimilated Jewish bourgeoisie of the country is unforgettably captured in Giorgio Bassani's novel *The Garden of the Finzi-Continis*, but the repercussions were felt across the social spectrum and devastated some of the most ancient communities in Europe.[3]

With German National Socialism it was a very different story. Race held the key to history for Hitler, and antisemitism was at the heart of the party's program. Yet even in the case of the Nazis, there is no real consensus as to how much this element of its program contributed to the party's success, especially since by the late 1920s, the Nazis shared a focus on antisemitism with quite a few of their political competitors. Much of Hitler's electorate was almost certainly as motivated by the desire to revise Germany's Versailles borders, to boost employment, and to regain international pride through rearmament as they were by hatred of the Jews. What is clear is that the

German public was well aware from the time Hitler took power as chancellor in the spring of 1933 that Nazi antisemitism was not going to rest content with the old-fashioned legalism of the past. Nazism was a radical, not conservative, right-wing creed, and it was not going to turn the clock back to the nineteenth century. It was going to venture far beyond where the Wilhelm Marrs of Bismarck's era had ever dreamed of going.

Nevertheless, the scale of the anti-Jewish violence that erupted on German streets in the spring of 1933 was shocking even to conservatives in the governing coalition. It involved not only boycotts of shops and businesses but assaults, beatings, the ransacking and pillaging of private homes, even killings: The violence was worse in smaller towns than in the cities and disproportionately targeted the less-assimilated *Ostjuden*, but no one was spared, not even tourists. Because it was accompanied by an equally savage assault on Communists, Social Democrats, and union leaders, the link was made from the outset that the Jews were themselves a political foe. An acute violation of existing social norms, it was soon accepted as the sign of a new ideological dispensation and there was little protest. "An astonishing number of non-Jewish Germans," writes one historian, "were able not to face the knowledge of what was going on all about them, including what they themselves were doing." If we need any further reminder these days of how fast norms and expectations can be revised in a highly nationalistic society, Germany in the spring months of 1933 provides it.[4]

After the initial terror that accompanied the seizure of power, overt violence was scaled back. The purge of the SA, or Brownshirts, which took place in 1934, bolstered the impression that the street fighting phase of Nazism was over, and with the exception of the destruction during Kristallnacht in November 1938, an episode that brought down much internal criticism on its instigator, Joseph Goebbels, the Nazis avoided shocking the public's sense of decorum and order and instead targeted German Jews through laws and decrees.[5] They proceeded gradually by excluding Jews from the civil service, professions, and cultural life, and from schools and universities. New citizenship and racial laws promulgated in 1935 ended civic equality and imposed a form of legal segregation on most German Jews. These measures were welcomed by some sectors of German society, especially those who profited as jobs were opened up and business competition closed down, but when they were felt to go too far or where they introduced new uncertainty and complications into life, they also generated concern and misgivings about the regime itself.

Racial scientists reshaped medical, public health, and social policy and lent their authority to what amounted to a ferocious anti-assimilationist drive against Germany's Jewish population. At the same time, resistance to these policies remained tangible, if discreetly expressed, across sections of the population, notably in Catholic Bavaria and working-class districts in industrial areas. It was the determination of the Party leadership to generate renewed support for their anti-Jewish measures that eventually led to Kristallnacht itself. Even after it, according to SS intelligence, much of Bavaria remained "without any comprehension of the Jewish question." Antisemitic violence was, in the German context, as much a means for those running the state to radicalize a reluctant population as it was an expression of popular attitudes.

Nazism as a movement against Jewish emancipation is not how we generally think of it, but that is how it was seen at the time. "Nazi Germany set the pattern for other countries," noted the scholar Bernard Weinryb in his wartime study *Jewish Emancipation Under Attack*. "The conquest of Europe by Germany finally brought an end to both democracy and Jewish emancipation in most of the states on that continent."[6] From 1933 one state after another in eastern Europe was emboldened to reimpose discrimination, and restrictions replaced the achievements of the 1920s. In Poland, where many tsarist-era restrictions affecting Jews had remained in place until 1931, the reversal was marked by a government abandonment of its minority rights obligations. Hungary's government passed so-called Jewish laws. As the course of nineteenth-century Jewish emancipation was thus reversed, any embarrassment felt at being labeled an antisemite vanished in much of continental Europe. In the 1920s, wrote the commentator Oscar Janowsky, "whatever their private opinions and practices with respect to the Jews, in public [the new states of Europe] felt constrained to repudiate antisemitism and to denounce its worst excesses. The case of Nazism, however, has removed from antisemitism the stigma which is associated with intolerance and had made Jew-hatred all but respectable."[7]

Romania was perhaps the most pervasively antisemitic country in the region if not the world. Its liberal elites had been notorious in the nineteenth century for refusing to emancipate the Jews at independence, and its intellectuals had concocted a heady mix of Orthodox spirituality and romantic nationalist hatred that left them obsessively fascinated with the figure of the Jew. The term *antisemite*, which had been regarded as vulgar in the 1920s, gained new acceptability. "I know two kinds of anti-Semites," wrote Mihail Sebastian, the Romanian Jewish author of *For Two Thousand Years*, first published in 1934. "Ordinary anti-Semites—and anti-Semites with arguments." Among the latter were friends of his who rarely seemed to glimpse the absurdity of their own words. "Antisemitism resolves neither the national nor the social problems of a people," wrote the ardently antisemitic philosopher Emil Cioran. In this way, antisemitic intellectuals looked down on their vulgar cousins. "Antisemitism? A legend, nonsense or a political sham, or simpler still a gang of vagabonds, hooligans," wrote Cioran's no less antisemitic friend Mircea Eliade. "It is much more difficult, more dramatic and, why not admit it, practically speaking much more inefficient, to try to think for yourself." Such arguments, however much they seemed to allude to a greater truth—that antisemitism was a substitute for thought rather than thought itself—circulated within a milieu that appeared to be incapable of doing without it. As the paramilitary Iron Guard rose to win 16 percent of the vote, new discriminatory measures were introduced under a sequence of increasingly antisemitic governments. By late 1939 more than one third of Romanian Jews had been stripped of their citizenship.[8]

The European continent was gradually dividing into two armed camps: in one the liberal victors of the war, with their faith in democracy, the Geneva system, and international capitalism, and in the other the revisionists led by the Third Reich, who believed they were destined to sweep away this antiquated order and replace it with a new system of racially conscious, nationally pure dictatorships. This new ordering of Europe would, in their eyes, provide a more effective bulwark against the threat of Soviet Bolshevism; be better placed to grapple with the effects of the world depression; combat the materialism sweeping across the Atlantic from America; and remake European society in a more disciplined and hierarchical way. Antisemitism was integral to this program because the Jews were identified with all the ills the Right aimed to eradicate—from socialism to jazz. Indeed, the prefix "Judeo-" was increasingly attached to each and every ideological foe—including Judeo-Bolshevism, Judeo-capitalism, and Judeo-democracy. Eventually, of course, it would come to what Hitler called "the Jewish war." "I have long resisted the assumption that we . . . should really be at the centre of Nazism in this way," wrote Victor Klemperer, a Jewish convert to Protestantism who had been dismissed from his job and forced to wear the yellow star. "But it really was the case."[9]

Closer ties with Germany, which were adopted mostly for economic reasons by one country in the region after another after the gold standard collapsed, were widely understood to imply a new official intolerance toward Jews. "Romania is bound to go Nazi," wrote the cold-blooded Sir Orme Sargent at the British Foreign Office, "and that will automatically settle the Jewish question." A few months later, a "decent-minded" Czech remarked to another British diplomat: "We were never in our history anti-Semitic, but the world is forcing us to become so."[10] On the eve of becoming prime minister in February 1939, the Hungarian Count Pál Teleki analyzed the situation for a British diplomat. It was tempting, he noted, to attribute what was happening to German influence. "It is but natural that a movement and ideology so strong as the German antisemitism must influence the mind of peoples living in the neighborhood." But he went on to emphasize that antisemitism was not new to Hungary. It had grown in 1919 because of the Communist revolution and its Jewish leadership but had then subsided because "Hungary is too small and too weak to start a European movement... in the midst of a different, uninterested Europe... opposed to such ideas." It changed "as soon as the European atmosphere, surrounding us, got favorable to this.... There is nothing astonishing in it; every expansive idea, every successful leader, has enthusiasts. There are still thousands of people who keep a portrait of Napoleon in their room."[11]

As a movement against Jewish emancipation, antisemitism fundamentally involved a critique of the idea that the law should treat all alike: Whether on racial or religious grounds, Jews were regarded as unassailably alien and therefore not to be granted equal citizenship, still less any say in the running of the country. The problem for the antisemites, however, was to spell out exactly how to effect this and how far to take it. It was hard if not impossible to turn the clock back to medieval times, especially for militaristic regimes that needed modern industry and modern methods of control and communications. So what, then, did these regimes actually want? Citizenship could certainly be redefined, exclusions introduced into schools, universities, professions, and public life. Jews could be segregated from the larger society, but what did that mean exactly for daily life or for economic activity? That they should—as in a decree of the Berlin police in December 1938—be banned from certain streets ("the North sidewalk of Unter den Linden from the University up to the Armory")? Or in another piece of Nazi retroactive legislation, be made to stick to "Jewish names"?

Much like emancipation itself, therefore, its reversal was not a one-off event but a tortuous process in which goals were articulated, unforeseen obstacles appeared, and new possibilities opened up. The drive to exclude the Jews from ever greater areas of social and economic life implied that they would eventually cease to be self-sustaining. Then what? That they should somehow disappear was clearly, one way or another, the goal, even if rarely articulated. Looming in people's minds, in the pithy phrase of the historian Alon Confino, was "a world without Jews." But not even the leaders of the Third Reich had figured out ahead of time what their disappearance might mean or how it might be effected.

After Kristallnacht in November 1938, many local councils in Germany put up signs indicating that Jews should keep away. Some Jews were afraid to return to their homes and wandered the streets or tried to shelter in parks. "People [are] about to rot away in starvation," reported an observer.[12] By the end of 1938 the most senior figures in the Reich were being obliged to grapple with an urgent sequence of thorny practical questions, some of them major and some minor, raised by their anti-Jewish policies. At a high-level meeting, one of them mused that Jews should not be allowed to travel with non-Jews, but then what? Did that mean they should have their own compartments, or might that risk them traveling in greater comfort, especially at rush hour? It was not easy to decide. Did keeping them away from other Germans in parks and at beaches mean allocating them special benches and resorts? Even woods and forests came up:

> *Goebbels*: It might...become necessary to forbid the Jews to enter the German forest! In the Grunewald, whole herds of them are running around....

Göring: We shall give the Jews a certain part of the forest [and make sure] various animals that look damned much like Jews—the elk has such a crooked nose—get [put] there also and become acclimated.

Undistracted by Hermann Göring's efforts at humor, the Gestapo director, Reinhard Heydrich, got the discussion back on track by reminding ministers that even with forced emigration at the maximum level imaginable, large numbers of Jews would remain in the Reich for some years, earning less and less. Should they be confined to ghettos, a prospect Heydrich disliked since it might make it easier for them to hide out? What about creating special reserved towns? someone suggested. Heydrich liked this no better. Should they be allowed to work? To buy from Aryan shops? Heydrich: "The German won't serve the Jew anymore." Göring: "One moment. You cannot let him starve." It was here that the first halting and hesitating steps on the path to genocide and total destruction were taken, via the complex bureaucratic minutiae of racial persecution and the dulled imaginations of heartless men, before the war revealed new horizons and the prospect of a Final Solution.[13]

In his highly successful 1922 satire, *The City Without Jews*, the Austrian writer Hugo Bettauer had imagined a sudden mass expulsion of Jews from the Austrian capital, the celebrations that followed, and then—ironically—the city's collapse. Nazis were furious at his mockery of one of their cherished ideas and he was shot dead by a fanatic in 1925. But in fact, forcing Jews not merely out of Vienna but out of Europe entirely had been a widely discussed idea since the nineteenth century if not earlier. The rise of the theory that the Jews formed part of a separate "Semitic" race gave a quasi-scientific rationale for such a program: It suggested that in Europe they were aliens and that their true place was in their own state in their biblical lands. Christian Zionists were one group who embraced the idea of mass eviction. "There is an attitude for which my friends and I were for a long period rebuked and even reviled," wrote the English writer G. K. Chesterton.

> It was always called Anti-Semitism; but it was always much more true to call it Zionism. At any rate it was much nearer to the nature of the thing to call it Zionism, whether or not it can find its geographical concentration in Zion. The substance of this heresy was exceedingly simple. It consisted entirely in saying that Jews are Jews; and as a logical consequence that they are not Russians or Roumanians or Italians or Frenchmen or English-men....My friends and I had...the desire to give Jews the dig-nity and status of a separate nation. We desired that in some fashion, and so far as possible, Jews should be represented by Jews, should live in a society of Jews, should be judged by Jews and ruled by Jews. I am an Anti-Semite if that is Anti-Semitism. It would seem more rational to call it "Semitism."[14]

Christian Zionism should not be confused with the Jewish move-ment of the same name; for one thing, a strand of obsessive anti-semitism, replete with the usual stereotypes, ran through it. But one thing the two shared was a powerful sense that the Jews were aliens in other lands, that emancipation was thus based on a false and dan-gerous premise, and that it would be best for all concerned if they had a home of their own. Many right-wing politicians in central Europe would not have dissented but were much more concerned with forcing Jews to emigrate than with where they went; some regarded the idea of a Jewish state as itself undesirable. Yet the world in the 1930s offered few options; the age of large migration flows and open borders was over. A new League of Nations high commissioner for refugees faced the impossible task of trying to broker international arrangements to find homes for growing numbers of desperate people: He resigned in

1935. The 1938 intergovernmental Evian Conference that had been called to search for a solution to the German Jewish refugee issue created by the Nazis was a failure. As the British clamped down on immigration into Palestine, geographers, antisemites, and increasing numbers of desperate Jews scoured the globe for possible alternatives to little avail.

Ethnic disappearance and ethnic survival had become obsessions not just in Germany but across eastern Europe, and the problem of Jewish communal "viability," which had first appeared in the overcrowded Russian Pale in the late nineteenth century, became an issue discussed in much of the Depression-era region. Economists openly wondered whether not only Jews but all kinds of categories of people—first and foremost the "surplus labor force" on the land—were not somehow surplus to national requirements. In Poland, which had by far the largest Jewish population in interwar Europe, the regime organized anti-Jewish boycotts and restrictions, and observers in 1938 worried that this policy "if carried to its logical conclusion...means starvation and slow death for hundreds of thousands." In an era when economists were starting to think about the problem of long-term national economic development, the antisemitic policies pursued by the Poles and others can be regarded as a kind of eliminationist alternative. That is to say, they proposed a solution to the national economic development problem by identifying a surplus population and then hoping somehow to get rid of it either through economic growth (more or less impossible in the midst of the Depression) or through forced emigration. Given that no one in government, it is safe to say, was thinking in the 1930s of physical extermination, the question was how to push them out.[15]

Confronting the same issue, the Nazis actually managed to force out around 400,000 Jews from the Greater German Reich by the autumn of 1939. This was an enormous figure that represented more than half the original Jewish population of interwar Germany and Austria, effected in the face of international resistance. But then came the German invasion of Poland, which launched the Second World War and made Poland's Jewish problem the Reich's. As one military success led to another, and the Wehrmacht conquered one country after another, the most antisemitic regime in Europe confronted the problem of what to do not only with its own remaining Jewish population, but also with that of occupied Europe as a whole. By late 1940, fewer than 250,000 Jews were left in the Reich (excluding Austria and the Sudetenland), but the Jewish population in countries under direct or indirect German control had soared to more than 5.5 million. More than another million lived in states allied with the Reich, and the invasion of the USSR put at risk around 3 million more. In short, military success posed a racial challenge for the Third Reich's ardent antisemites on a scale that dwarfed any they had faced so far. Astonishingly, there is little or no evidence that the Nazis had thought systematically about any of this ahead of time. Now they would have to, especially as the war that they had launched was one they defined as an existential struggle with the Jews, which gave it an ideological dimension that had been entirely absent from the war of 1914–18.[16]

In a notorious speech made in January 1939, Hitler warned that

> if international finance Jewry inside and outside Europe should succeed in plunging the nations once more into a world war, the result will be not the Bolshevization of the earth and thereby the victory of Jewry, but the annihilation of the Jewish race in Europe.

Some historians have suggested this shows that Hitler was already thinking of a mass killing policy. The truth is that such an extraordinary idea still lay around three years in the future. In fact, the key word in his speech was not *annihilation*—antisemites since Marr had been making dire warnings of this kind—but *Europe*. There were to be several false starts on the twisting road that led to the extermination camps, and the German leadership was to contemplate organizing a policy of general expulsion beyond Europe's borders—first to the island of Madagascar (an idea briefly floated in 1940) and then into erstwhile Soviet territories—before the phrase "evacuation to the East" turned into a bureaucratic euphemism for mass murder. As the historian Christopher Browning has suggested, what Hitler was most probably doing in 1939 was signaling that Nazi policy toward the Jews was now aiming to make not only Germany but Europe as a whole "free of Jews" (*judenfrei*). This required coordination with partners and collaborators on a continent-wide scale. Yet the precedents for an international antisemitic front were not encouraging, and forging it would turn out to be no simple task.[17]

Both liberals and Bolsheviks had manifested a capacity for international cooperation and some Fascists believed the Right should be able to bring together a coalition of ideologically like-minded allies too. Back in 1934, Fascist Italy—still fancying itself as Hitler's senior partner—had convened an international conference of Fascists at Montreux in Switzerland. Even before the war, Fascist propaganda had harped on the need to defend Europe from the twin perils of Soviet Bolshevism and Anglo-American plutocracy. Yet antisemitism had not been high up on the agenda at Montreux. When the Romanian delegate had insisted that "we must discuss the Jews," the conference passed a rather weak resolution demanding action. Delegates had argued among themselves quite fiercely about the importance of the issue, a signal perhaps not only that Fascism was—unlike liberalism—not an ideology well suited to international cooperation, but also that antisemitism was something that potentially divided ideological allies as soon as you moved from propaganda platitudes and rhetoric to policy.[18]

None of this made much impression on Hitler. After 1939 he saw the war itself as a unique opportunity to remake the continent, and because race in general and antisemitism in particular drove his thinking about Europe, he was confident he would obtain widespread support for his anti-Jewish policies from among his allies. If the pioneering historian Lucy Dawidowicz, in her 1975 book *The War Against the Jews*, exaggerated how far back in time Hitler's antisemitic worldview went, she was not wrong in emphasizing his central role as the principal agent of radicalization, especially once the war was underway and older constraints on his power disappeared. Where the führer detected faltering, he endeavored to whip up enthusiasm. Even as the Final Solution was attaining its murderous apogee, in September 1942, he gave a long speech in Berlin at the Sportspalast in which he depicted the war as a battle for existence between "the Aryan peoples" and the Jews that would end with the extermination of the latter. At a time when he knew better than anyone that extermination was a policy and not merely a phrase, Hitler hailed the "wave of antisemitism" that was spreading from one people to another and would, he predicted, cause a kind of alliance of antisemitic states to coalesce.[19] In fact, the more the outlines of Berlin's exterminationist intentions became known among Germany's allies, the more the difficulties of coordinating a European approach to antisemitism emerged.

It is of course true that one of the basic ideas behind the Nazi New Order—that Europe's ills were attributable to the Jews—was widely shared beyond Germany's borders and shaping persecutory legislation in many countries in the late 1930s. Across much of Europe, the Left had been crushed or marginalized, one version or another of the Right was in power, and the antisemites—whether pro-Nazi racists or religious conservatives—were in the ascendant. In speeches by Hitler's allies, the Jews were often identified as the enemy, and antisemitism was portrayed as the continental solution to the cause of Europe's ills. All this reflected more than merely an effort to curry German favor; it expressed the views of a swath of homegrown opinion as well. As soon as the scale of the German triumph became clear, many states targeted their own Jewish populations. And when German units marched in, it took little to encourage antisemitic thugs in towns and cities across eastern Europe to embark on murderous killing sprees. Nonetheless, there were limits to Axis cooperation at a diplomatic and military level, which became more and more evident with time. For although persecuting Jews was understood by pro-German elites as a politically acceptable response to a regrettable demographic reality, that did not mean everyone in power in Hitler's Europe attached the same importance to the issue as the führer did or was willing to go to such extremes. On the contrary, many Axis leaders who were happy to go along with German wishes so long as the costs of doing so seemed low began to hesitate when they rose.

Perhaps the best example is from Romania. In the summer of 1941, the murder of thousands of Jews in the streets of the city of Jassy had shocked even the Nazis by its brutality, and yet the same Romanian government that had sanctioned it temporized a year later when confronted by German demands to accelerate Jewish deportations. This was not because the Romanian leadership had suddenly become less antisemitic but rather because German demands to hand over the country's Jews threatened a vital state interest: sovereignty. Being ordered by an all-powerful Reich to hand over fellow citizens suggested a subservience and inequality that Germany's allies and vassals found humiliating and alarming (for where might it end?) and that induced them to assert themselves. Similar considerations of prestige help explain why other collaborationist regimes were willing to hand over Jewish noncitizens but then became less cooperative. It was one thing to get rid of stateless newcomers to placate an ally, another to abandon Jewish fellow citizens, however disliked, to what they increasingly understood to be a sinister scheme of state-sponsored mass killing: Even many antisemites balked at that. In Hungary the aged anti-Communist dictator Admiral Horthy, whose regime had passed antisemitic laws and allowed some deportations, outright resisted Hitler's angry demands, leading to his ouster and the German occupation of the country.

The Germans might, in the words of the historian Salo Baron, have turned antisemitism into a world power. But the murderous anti-Jewish coalition that they had tried to forge in their New Order was an unstable one. Gradually the Nazis came to appreciate the diplomatic sensitivities that were hindering them and slowing down their efforts, and this made them resolved only to accelerate the genocide, as a specialist on Jewish affairs wrote in March 1942: "The Jewish question must be solved in the course of the war, for only so can it be solved without a worldwide outcry."[20] The regime's growing insistence on secrecy was itself an implicit acknowledgment that the contemplated Final Solution of the Jewish Question was shocking even for a world in which the antisemites had apparently triumphed. Thus at the very beginning of large-scale killing, the mass shootings that started in the occupied Soviet territories in the late summer of 1941 often took place in plain view of nearby army units and local civilians: Orders even had to be issued forbidding unauthorized crowds of spectators from gathering at the killing sites and taking photographs. Such prohibitions were honored in the breach: A much-discussed exhibition featuring hundreds of such snapshots of genocide shocked postwar Germany when it toured the country five decades later. In contrast, the planning, design, and operation of the extermination camps from 1942 onward took place under conditions of extreme secrecy.[21]

By early 1944, facing foot dragging and unmistakable signs of resistance, Berlin was seeking to stiffen the backbone of its ideological allies. The Germans drew up plans for a Pan-European antisemitic congress to discuss "the global Jewish peril"; the organizers planned a busy program for the two hundred or so guests with concerts, plays, and films. But having been left late, the congress never took place, though smaller seminars were convened at a "guest house for enemies of the Jews," where professionals could discuss such topics as "Jewish Power over Europe" or "The Judaization of the English Upper Class." Aware of the dangers of heavy-handed Nazi claims to continental leadership, German diplomats worried about damaging "the delicate little plant of anti-Semitism in many countries."[22]

It is not generally appreciated that to a large extent neither the degree of antisemitism in a given society nor even ideological affinity with Nazism was as important a factor in determining the eventual death toll in the genocide as the juridical status of the countries concerned. Prejudices and attitudes mattered less than the nature of the state and the bureaucratic constraints. (Factors such as geography and timing were also critical.) Where German killers were freest to act, the toll was high, and so in the occupied territories of the former USSR, where the Nazis faced no legal impediments to mass murder, the SS death squads continued their terrible work with little regard for international public opinion: The Nazi economist Otto Ohlendorf, head of just one of the Einsatzgruppen operating in these territories, would be arraigned after the war on charges of having himself overseen the execution of no fewer than ninety thousand people. In the rump Poland of the General Government, the large Jewish population was equally defenseless because the occupation had placed them under the control of an ambitious cluster of Nazis who were keen to kill them off as quickly as possible: As a result, most of the 2.3 million Jews trapped in the General Government perished in the death camps in the space of just over a year. Paradoxically, the tiny number of Jews remaining inside the Reich (usually in mixed marriages) were perhaps marginally better off, because the power of the SS was constrained by the fact that other ministries retained jurisdiction in Germany. In the rest of Europe, the Germans often found the bureaucratic assistance they demanded but sometimes ran into unexpected diplomatic difficulties. In the Italian-occupied zones of the Balkans, army officers and diplomats obstructed them. In Bulgaria, where the authorities had initiated antisemitic measures in 1940, the government deported to the Treblinka death camp the entire Jewish population of the territories the Bulgarian army had occupied in 1941; but in the face of remarkable popular protests, Bulgaria's prewar Jewish subjects were saved from the same fate and sent out instead into forced labor camps in the provinces. Bulgaria itself was an ally, not a defeated power, and there was little the Germans could do.

Yet despite the occasional foot dragging of its allies, there was no real check to the overwhelming power of the German war machine. By the conflict's end, and despite the enormity and complexity of the task they had set themselves and the lack of time at their disposal, the Nazis had succeeded in enacting an extermination without precedent. The magnitude of the crime was an indication of the overriding importance the leadership of the Third Reich had attached to their antisemitic worldview. The Germans had killed almost all the Jews who were living in the Reich in 1939: A mere nineteen thousand survived out of the half million or so in Germany when Hitler came to power. They had also murdered approximately 90 percent of the Jews living in the Polish lands at the start of the war, most of them in the extermination camps constructed specifically for this purpose: The survivors had mostly kept alive by fleeing to the safety of the Soviet Union early on; very few made it through in hiding. Auschwitz-Birkenau, which had started out housing Polish POWs in old prewar barracks, had metastasized into a monstrous killing and labor camp complex. Overall, the Nazis and their helpers killed somewhere close to six million Jews—along with millions of other civilians—which comprised almost half the total population of European Jewry identified by the Reich's senior leadership at the Wannsee Conference at the start of 1942. Europe's centuries-old Jewish past—so important a feature of its historical experience—had been all but wiped out and could thereafter only be glimpsed through the annihilation that had taken place on its soil.[23]

The Final Solution of the Jewish Question was still underway when some of the key German officials involved became aware that they had been named by the Allies as war criminals. Among them was Adolf Eichmann, whose role organizing the deportations across Europe implicated him as deeply as any of them. The man who once dreamed that he would have a monument erected to him in recognition of his achievement and hoped that Hitler would make him "World Commissar of the Jews" began as defeat loomed to flaunt his high standing on the list of the United Nations most-wanted. In hiding in Argentina after the war and talking with friends, he boasted: "I found the war criminals in a list once. I was no. 9, and had a bit of a laugh about it all." His reaction points to a vein of grandiosity and delight in his mission at odds with the self-image he created during his trial in Jerusalem in 1961, but his knowledge that Germany's enemies had identified and targeted the murderers of the Jews as criminals was not surprising. After all, international understanding and condemnation of the genocidal implications of Nazi antisemitism had started as far back as December 1942, when, shocked by reports from Poland, the Allies publicly denounced what they described as "this bestial policy of cold-blooded extermination." In 1944, a book on Nazi occupation policies appeared in which a Polish Jewish lawyer, Raphael Lemkin, coined the term *genocide*. The true implications of what antisemitic politics had led to were becoming clear. As the war neared its end, an American Jewish commentator evaluating the prospects for the postwar world felt that antisemitism had been irredeemably harmed by association with National Socialism: "The Nazi war on the rest of the world has more clearly than ever before... identified the cause of antisemitism with the forces of political reaction, corruption and aggressive war."[24] In the long run, he was to be proved right. Yet we should not leap to conclusions: The Allies' desire to denounce antisemitism explicitly was limited, and the United Nations Declaration of 1942 had been most unusual in speaking out about Jewish suffering. The British and American governments had their own concerns about antisemitism at home and tried to avoid singling out the Jews for mention as victims thereafter. In the October 1943 statement on atrocities that was signed by Churchill, Stalin, and Roosevelt, Jewish victims were not mentioned, and instead there was a general reference to "atrocities, massacres and cold-blooded mass executions."[25]

In the immediate postwar period, the victorious Allies sent a similarly mixed message. Abandoning the idea of minority rights or special protections for vulnerable ethnic groups, they were certainly not inclined to present the war as having been fought for the sake of the Jews. (At the main Nuremberg war crimes trial, the genocide did not form a central aspect of the prosecution case.) But that does not mean they were indifferent to the issue. On the contrary, in their treatment of the defeated Axis powers they did attempt to draw a line under the official racism of the Nazis and in this way to counterpose the cause of victory to the prejudices of their defeated foe, especially because there was a widespread view that race hatred and extreme nationalism more generally had played a key role in the origins of the war itself. Fighting any revival of antisemitism was thus seen to be bound up with larger questions of peace among nations, respect for international law, and the rebuilding of democracies in a continent where they had collapsed.

One immediate if little-remarked-upon consequence of Allied victory was therefore the repeal of anti-Jewish citizenship laws across Europe. In occupied Germany, the Supreme Allied Commander abolished Nazi-era racial legislation with his first decree. In France, Vichy's antisemitic laws were declared null and void. In Italy, the 1938 Law for the Protection of the Italian Race was abrogated. Every armistice agreement signed in eastern Europe committed the new authorities to repeal discriminatory laws and decrees. Austria saw the highly democratic constitution of 1921 restored, and most remarkably perhaps the Soviet-backed Polish government that took over in the summer of 1944 announced the restoration of the old interwar constitution that had outlawed all religious and racial discrimination. The full rollback of racist and antisemitic legislation would take several years, eliciting bureaucratic foot-dragging and opposition; in some ways it was never completed. But it should not be ignored or downplayed: It indicated a genuine desire to distance postwar Europe from Nazi values.[26]

And yet: Was there any reason to believe that the repudiation of antisemitism would last? After the First World War it had surged: Would it be any different this time? At one level, contemporary commentators were surely correct: Nazism had become equated with antisemitism, and its memory would hang like a millstone around the neck of postwar antisemites; the effect of the Third Reich was to discredit antisemitism as a positive program for decades to come. Moreover, Germany was not only defeated but occupied and partitioned: The victorious coalition, discordant on many things, was united in its determination to ensure Nazism never threatened the European peace again. Europe after 1945—whether under Stalin in the East or Anglo-American sway in the West—was under the control of powers that, whatever their internal shortcomings, limitations, and hypocrisies, repudiated antisemitism as a matter of official policy. Yet politics was one thing; how far the defeat of Nazism had changed popular attitudes toward Jews was quite a different question. The antisemites had been defeated. But what of that larger array of antisemitic attitudes that had been inherited from the past? Combating those would of necessity require different weapons and take place on a different battlefield in a war that was certainly far from over. James Parkes, a pioneering British expert on the subject, was not sure of the outcome. "To discover effective means for dealing with this worldwide scourge," he wrote in 1946, "will tax the skill of statesmen and educationalists for many years to come."[27]

CHAPTER 5

Aftermath: Cold War Europe

The Jews, yes; there were difficulties with the Jews. But, my dear sir, Germany no longer has a Jewish problem. In all Germany there are only about 30,000 Jews left. They are mostly old, and keep quiet. The young ones go away when they can; I suppose that is in a way understandable. The Jews no longer preoccupy us.

FAR-RIGHT POLITICIAN ADOLF VON THADDEN[1]

WESTERN EUROPE

In Western Europe, the three decades that followed the end of the Second World War saw democracy rise from the ashes of defeat. "Europe" turned into a peace project, and several decades of unprecedented economic growth transformed society. By the 1960s, observers were talking about the "end of ideology" as voters on the Left and Right abandoned the extremes and fought out their policy differences in the middle ground. Aging dictators in Spain and Portugal were reminders of a polarizing Fascist past the rest of Europe had left behind. The far Right, the spiritual repository of political antisemitism, was relegated to the margins in every country, hampered both by public despair about what Fascism and Nazism had wrought and by constitutional prohibitions against the re-formation of prewar parties. And yet none of this had been foreseeable in 1945.[2]

To the very end of the Third Reich, Nazi propaganda had continued to warn Germans about the "Jewish menace" that lay in wait should the fighters for racial purity not prevail. The "world revolution against the Jewish race," declaimed Goebbels, "[will not end] until its objective has been attained." As Allied armies converged on Berlin, his Propaganda Ministry warned German soldiers that Jews were celebrating the Sabbath in the Reich while ordinary Germans were starving. The poison of his messages would take a long time to dissipate. It is hardly surprising that early reports from occupied Germany stated that the Jewish survivors "mistrust the non-Jewish Germans, many of whom are trying to cover up their previous crimes with a servile, cringing manner." In Berlin, park benches marked with the sign "Not for Jews" were still visible a year after the war's end; popular attitudes changed no more quickly: A US military survey from occupied Germany in 1947 suggested antisemitism remained a serious issue. The Allies' decision to give Austria a status different from Germany's allowed antisemitism to parade there even more openly. Returnees from the camps were asked by civil servants: "Are you Jews or are you 'Aryans'?" as if they were still under Nazi rule. Vienna's Jewish community organization described the city as "the center of the ugliest and most treacherous anti-Semitism." University students hailed the return of Nazi professors, and among the politicians in the elections of November 1945 were well-known antisemites. "I myself have always been an anti-Semite," the new president of the Federal Assembly was said to have remarked. The Austrian chancellor excused this, saying that he was "not an anti-Semite on racial grounds but on economic grounds."[3]

In short, antisemitism was not killed off by the war. How could it have been, when it had achieved extraordinary political predominance across much of Europe only a few years before? A reporter saw the early postwar months and years as a "between-times" in which Jewish survivors gauged the safety of their situation chiefly from the willingness of governments to protect them and to take action through the courts and the law against wartime perpetrators and profiteers. Many of those who had profited from Jewish suffering during the war remained in possession of their wealth, and when Jews sought to reclaim property or to gain compensation, they risked reawakening hostility. In some countries—Austria was a notable example—the beneficiaries of Jewish possessions actually banded together to oppose restitution. They also used political parties or the courts to block such efforts and keep black market gains.[4]

There were, after all, numerous survivors of the Fascist ancien régime still in government and political life. The Italian historian Claudio Pavone has made us aware of the modern state's great powers of administrative continuity even through abrupt ideological change and war, and purges of Fascists and denazification did not by any means bring a total changing of the guard. The West German government formed by Konrad Adenauer in 1954 included four cabinet ministers who had been in the Nazi Party, and two who had actually been in the SS. Such men usually avoided making antisemitic pronouncements, but some, like the Free Democratic Party's Friedrich Middelhauve, were happy to try to exploit the issue; Middelhauve even worked with one of Goebbels's former Jew-baiters in what appears to have been a plot to take over the party with neo-Nazis that was discovered and disrupted by British intelligence.

Fears of a Nazi revival led British intelligence to employ—among other lowly agents—a young Oxford graduate called David Cornwell. His generally unexciting mission is evoked brilliantly, along with the anxious atmosphere of the times, in *A Small Town in Germany*, the novel that appeared under his pen name, John le Carré, launching a distinguished literary career. Much of it describes fictionalized versions of the fledgling neo-Nazi parties that momentarily rose and fell in those years. A Hamburg court ended the activities of two neo-Nazis who had formed a Freikorps Deutschland in 1952. Two years later a Cologne judge sentenced a twenty-three-year-old who called himself *Reichsführer* of a new German Reich Youth Movement whose members wore uniforms styled after the Hitler Youth's and spent their time reading Hitler and Goebbels. There was even an association called "Sufferers of de-Nazification"; hundreds of its members gathered in rallies demanding compensation for their time spent in internment. In the mid-1950s, denazification wound down and the war crimes trials came to an end, reminders of a past that the bulk of the West German and Austrian public had decided to put behind them. Voters who had once meekly supported dictators now adjusted without complaint and often with relief to democratic life. But governmental and cultural power remained mostly in the hands of those who had grown up under Nazism.

Slowly, public expressions of antisemitism waned along with the other reminders of the Third Reich to the point where they signaled an extreme political position rather than merely the currency of the time. As early as 1955, it was reported that "overt expressions of anti-Jewish prejudice were infrequent." Antisemitism was on the way to becoming politically taboo, and far-Right leaders in West Germany in particular came to understand that they needed to avoid the subject of the Jews: They raged instead mostly against the power of the Americans, the threat of Communism, the degeneracy of the new consumer society, and the loss of discipline and moral values in an increasingly egalitarian world.

Yet the issue of the Jews remained beneath the surface and sometimes emerged as if in defense of free speech. NO HARM IN TALKING ABOUT IT: ANTISEMITISM IN OUR TIME was the headline in the right-wing NPD weekly in September 1966; the article starts out with a nod and a wink by admitting that "we must not talk about Jews in the same way as certain Jews do about Germans and in the past certain Germans did about Jews" before going on to warn that Soviet Communism and "the politics of organised Jewry are one and the same."[5] The Six-Day War in the Middle East the following year increased such commentary, though conspiracy theorists could not always decide who was pulling the strings. For the Belgian leader of Jeune Europe, Israel was "a bulwark of American imperialism." For the French antisemite Maurice Bardèche, it was "the citadel of the international Jewish Power." Bardèche, a wartime collaborator and literary scholar, was the brother-in-law of the collaborationist writer Robert Brasillach, who was executed by the resistance in 1945. Brasillach's death turned Bardèche into an obsessive apologist for Fascism and an early Holocaust denier, whose antisemitism was the obverse of his desire to rehabilitate the Right. Such antisemitic language was commonplace among those who had given up on parliamentary politics and preferred forming small intellectual discussion groups or circles of armed militants. A good example was the Italian Centro Studi Ordine Nuovo, which existed from 1955 to 1971 as a vehicle for Italian neofascists impatient with the demands of electoral politics and nostalgic for real Fascism. But its extremism did not suit the strategy pursued by far-Right politicians in Naples or Rome: Most of them preferred to defend the myth of the "good Italian" and to emphasize their hatred of Communism rather than to dwell on their Fascist credentials or get overly worked up about Jews.[6]

There were occasional far-Right successes. In West Germany the National Democratic Party was formed in 1964, scaring everyone before declining again in the 1970s. In Italy, more enduringly, the Movimento Sociale Italiano was formed in 1946 by former Fascists and managed to establish a constant parliamentary presence throughout the Cold War. But the truth is that compared with the persistence of Fascist sympathizers in state bureaucracies, businesses, and judiciaries, the organized far Right mattered so little politically that several major studies of postwar Western European democracy fail to say much about it at all. It is striking that even though the study of Fascism flourished from the 1960s onward, there was next to no scholarly interest among historians in its postwar successors. The war was too close and the Right's historic failure too recent to allow them to make much headway, least of all in an era of unprecedented economic prosperity.

One marker of failure was the far Right's endless fragmenting and factionalism. It did not help that the Fascist leaders of the 1940s—worse off in this respect than the monarchies of the past—had avoided the question of their succession, with the result that there were no anointed leaders to carry on the struggle. To those who remembered the glorious old days, the men who now put themselves forward were second-raters. The gulf between activists and nostalgics gaped wide, between the well-born and the street fighters wider still. The postwar Bayreuth salon of Winifred Wagner, the English-born daughter-in-law of Richard, which gathered various elderly Nazi widows together with aristocratic has-beens such as Oswald Mosley, resembled nothing so much as those clusters of snobbish geriatric royalists who had once peopled the fringes of French life. Reviewing a pioneering study of the "neo-fascist temptation" in France that appeared in 1984, the reviewer commented acerbically that the endless parades of factions and flags, old nostalgic ex-Vichyites and small numbers of youthful obsessives, served only to disprove the author's thesis: "There was no neo-fascist temptation in France because no one was tempted."[7]

Fascism and Nazism had boasted they were the future, founding new civilizations that would last for centuries; their emphatic failure to do this was a mark against them not easily overcome. It did not help that their failure had been accompanied by genocide and mass murder, civilian bombing and destruction. Their successors, unable to boast of these as accomplishments, were forced down the path of "revising" the facts via historical revisionism and Holocaust denial: Things had not been as bad as was claimed, or alternatively, the other side had been just as bad. These were approaches to the subject sufficiently shocking to mark out a political space and garner the occasional headline, but the vast majority of the public, much as they might resent being obliged to confront the crimes of the past, were not willing to go down the revisionist path. In short, history itself was a trap for the postwar far

Right that only the passing of time would help them escape once the veterans, the old Waffen-SS men, and the Pétainists died out.

Another sign of failure was, paradoxically, the Right's internationalism. Unable to work their old magic domestically, Fascists held endless but essentially meaningless "European" meetings in Venice, Munich, Malmö, and other pleasant cities, where they denounced the outcome of the war and bemoaned the Continent's enslavement. "Europeanism" was still a far-Right favorite, but their version of it was undercut by still-vivid memories of what a Nazi New Order had meant the first time around, as well as by the evident success of the rival democratic Europeanism through the Common Market. There was a European Declaration by far-Right leaders in Venice in 1962 and the launch of the National Party of Europe, an idea of the British Fascist Oswald Mosley that went nowhere. Ten years later in Munich, the largest meeting of Fascists since the Second World War, with some twelve hundred participants, again failed to bring about an effective institutionalization of the movement.

A third sign of failure was the drift to violence, whether through street gangs as in the UK or through terrorism or political subversion as in Italy. The thuggery of Britain's National Front skinheads was never sympathetically received by the public and lost its support. The right-wing turn to a "strategy of tension" in Italy was a lot more serious because behind it there was a well-financed network of ideologues and activists, with support from several intelligence services and sympathetic regimes in the dictatorships of Portugal and Greece, which aimed to subvert democracy through bombings and other outrages: Initially attributed to anarchists, the Piazza Fontana bombing in Milan killed more than a dozen people; other attacks followed, culminating in an explosion at the main railway station in Bologna in 1980 that killed dozens. But none of this had the desired effect, and the result was that extremists fled to the last sympathetic holdouts available to them—the fading dictatorships of the Iberian Peninsula, the author-itarian regimes of South America, and the white settler colonies of Africa, where they lent their services to the last-ditch colonial struggle. This was perhaps appropriate: Postwar neofascism was fundamentally a lost cause, drawn to other lost causes. As for the ideology of anti-semitism, it seemed to be increasingly the obsession of those for whom the clock had stopped in the early 1940s.

Which was not to say that either antisemitism or, still less, racism had vanished from Western Europe. Far from it. While politically organized antisemitism faced a dead end, in fringe journalism and publishing the old prejudices and stereotypes still circulated. Holo-caust denial was a key vehicle. Like a similar debate carried on by Turkish nationalists about the Armenian genocide, there was an end-less disputing of the numbers of dead. But unlike Turkish national-ists, Holocaust deniers insisted on appealing to the notion of hoax and conspiracy as if the whole subject had been made up for gain. Israeli-German reparations negotiations were transformed into the allegation that international Jewry was perpetrating a fraud, or using moral black-mail. The publication of the first major study of the Final Solution, Raul Hilberg's 1961 *The Destruction of the European Jews*, sparked off a wave of attempted refutations. Paul Rassinier, a confused, troubled, and contradictory figure who had survived SS torture and Buchen-wald before passing via pacifism into the arms of the German far Right, achieved notoriety by alleging the entire genocide had never happened. The English historian David Irving opted for other lines of argument, pointing out that war crimes had been committed on both sides, and later arguing there was no proof Hitler had authorized the Final Solution. Far-Right circles in West Germany asked why no one touched the question of the expulsion of millions of ethnic Germans, an early exercise in comparative victimology.

Today the Second World War is widely understood as a struggle against racial intolerance with the genocide of the Jews at its center.

But this was not the public perception in the immediate postwar years. A partial exception was Britain, where images of the liberation of Bergen-Belsen and Buchenwald circulated widely and shocked public opinion. In West Germany, the debate over the memory and meaning of the war took the form of a generational struggle, spurred in the early 1960s by the trials of Auschwitz guards and the Jerusalem trial of Adolf Eichmann: By the end of the decade, the country's commitment to research into the Nazi era was already well established, thanks not least to the Institute for Contemporary History in Munich, the city where half a century earlier the movement itself had emerged. From 1972 the Institute there was run by the historian Martin Broszat: An exemplary figure who illustrates the capacity for generational change, this former Hitler Youth member had completed a doctorate on German antisemitism as early as 1952, testified at the Auschwitz trials, and played a key role in helping his countrymen understand how Nazism had rooted itself in German society. In Italy, where historians were studying Fascism as early as the 1950s, the study of its racial policies lagged far behind. In France, where the Gaullists liked to pretend Vichy had never happened, a reckoning with the antisemitic Right took longer still. It might have been true, as a political scientist wrote in 1968, that "antisemitism is not a paying proposition in French politics today," but most of the French did not believe Vichy or Pétain had been fundamentally antisemitic, and so they saw no reason for scrutiny of their record: It took a young American historian, Robert Paxton, alongside filmmakers like Marcel Ophuls, Louis Malle, and Joseph Losey, to blow apart the silence over Vichy and the French record of wartime collaboration in the Final Solution. Meanwhile, the Catholic Church remained a bastion of unreconstructed prejudices, keeping a genteel antisemitism alive in provincial towns and elite circles.[8]

At the same time, the French Right provides an example of how the older antipathy to the Jews was blunted by unexpected new developments, notably the creation of Israel. Generally, Europe's far Right was torn on the question of Zionism, especially as Israel's Labor government was still a popular cause on the Left: For some, it was yet another Machiavellian Jewish ploy, but for many, it was a kind of dream solution. They had little difficulty, after all, with the idea that the rightful place for Jews was not somewhere in Europe, and by supporting Zionist claims they could dispel the accusation of antisemitism while in fact retaining their prejudices. As early as March 1945, one extreme antisemite wrote that "the French...are 100% partisans of Zionism and respectfully demand to these Jewish gentlemen to return to Palestine." "One must have the courage to say with them [the Zionists] that there are cases in which assimilation is impossible," wrote a contributor to the popular far-Right *Écrits de Paris* in July 1948. After the Suez crisis of 1956, right-wing attitudes toward Israel became more positive, and the new country was increasingly seen not merely as a dumping ground for the unwanted, but as a useful ally in the struggle against the enemies of the West. The struggle against Algerian nationalism brought some of the old antisemitic French *pieds-noirs* and Algerian Jews together in a conservative alliance that would flourish over the decades. Resettled in France, many of the latter found a common cause on the Right: "I am a Fascist Jew" (*"Je suis un juif fasciste"*) was how one described himself, no doubt conscious of the historical ironies. By the mid-1960s, expressions of admiration for Israel had become commonplace in the right-wing press. "To be sure, the Jews can be exasperating," wrote a correspondent for the popular *Rivarol* in 1965. "[They are] always invoking the obviously exaggerated figure of six million victims." Yet in the same breath, he insisted that "the most intractable of antisemites" should approve of the idea of settling the Jews in a single territory. Israel was not only an ally; it "remains in 1965, the only country in the world to live in a harmonious synthesis of nationalism, socialism and racism. Perhaps that seems paradoxical... [but] certain abhorred values of national socialism have found a refuge on the banks of the river Jordan."[9]

Such statements should be put in perspective. The French Right had not so much fallen in love with Israel—that would not happen until Israel itself moved sharply to the Right decades later—as it had found a new way of expressing its detestation of de Gaulle, whose betrayal, as they saw it, of French Algeria was compounded by his attempted rapprochement with the Arab world. Support for Israel was perfectly compatible, as the statements above show, with continued antisemitism. It persisted among the old Vichyite conservatives who had never seen the Jews as truly French, among Catholics who opposed the Vatican's 1963 disavowal of antisemitism, and above all in the writings of Fascist nostalgists who dreamed of an authoritarian Europe. But they were aging: Except in the form of Holocaust denial, antisemitism rarely surfaced directly in public; it persisted, but as an electoral liability rather than an asset, a vestige of the past that would soon be overtaken by a new wave of prejudice against France's postwar migrants from Africa and the Caribbean. Antisemitism, in short, became a taboo even as racism against those who came from the former colonies grew into a major electoral force across France and Western Europe.

BEHIND THE IRON CURTAIN

"[The Council of People's Commissars] instructs all Soviet deputies to take uncompromising measures to tear the anti-Semitic movement out by the roots. Pogromists and pogrom-agitators are to be placed outside the law." Thus ran the extraordinary decree signed by Lenin at the end of July 1918 in the midst of his battle for power in Russia. Even before this, the provisional government had abolished the tsarist-era legal restrictions against the Jews and other minorities. "A miracle has happened," wrote the main Russian Zionist newspaper. "Within a few days Russia has become a free country." The revolution thus brought emancipation to Europe's largest and most long-suffering Jewish community. In a continental first, the Bolshevik leadership declared their ideological commitment to opposing and eradicating antisemitism.[10]

Once the civil war was over, the Jews thus in theory existed on a plane of equality with other groups in the USSR. They suffered the same gradual imposition of political restrictions as one party after another was banned or broken up; they too suffered the demands of a state built upon a Marxist-Leninist ideology of materialism, inherently suspicious of both class enemies and organized religion. But what they did not have to endure was the officially tolerated antisemitism of the tsarist past. And because the regime had its hands full in the early years trying to bring socialism to Russian society, the result was an unexpected resumption of many aspects of Jewish daily provincial life. Despite state control exercised through a Jewish section of the Communist Party, many of the old religious institutions and practices survived into the 1920s or were tacitly tolerated. In Minsk, visitors were surprised to find kosher butchers still dominated the local meat-supply business, while hundreds of yeshiva students continued to be taught in semi-clandestinity and to receive funding from American Jewish charities. But for many of the same reasons, popular antisemitism also continued: Indeed, it was if anything renewed and fed by socialism's triumph. For many Jews, after all, the Bolshevik revolution meant unprecedented upward mobility and access to professional opportunity. "Of the many Russian revolutions, the Jewish one was the most successful," writes historian Yuri Slezkine. As a result, there were mutterings of "Jewish domination." A polite antisemitism flourished discreetly among the old Russian cultural elite, surprised at the sudden visibility of Jewish names in the public sphere and the number of Jews who were settling in Moscow and Leningrad now that the old tsarist-era mobility restrictions had been scrapped. Further down the social spectrum, blood-libel accusations surfaced from time to time. The difference was that they were now liable to prosecution as "counterrevolutionary" activity.[11]

"Shame on those who foment hatred towards the Jews," Lenin had insisted in March 1919. For a regime that prided itself on having wiped it out, the persistence of popular antisemitism was a provoking issue. There were discussions and seminars in Moscow party headquarters in the 1920s and anxiety that antisemitism was spreading from the peasantry into the working class. The Soviet premier Mikhail Kalinin warned that it was growing, and the press publicized campaigns against it. Stalin himself led one such campaign in 1927 and denounced it in 1931 as "a survival of the barbarous practices of the cannibalistic period." Once the Nazis came to power, the Soviet press carried articles covering the revival of prejudice in Germany, and Soviet leaders were quoted drawing attention to Marx himself having Jewish origins. (Lenin's Jewish grandfather, on the other hand, remained a closely guarded secret.)[12]

The Second World War, a catastrophe for Soviet Jewry, marked the real break. In the course of invasion, and from its earliest weeks, the Nazi military, together with the SS, waged an ideological war of extermination (*Vernichtungskrieg*) against the Soviet population in general and Soviet Jews in particular. It is worth remembering that likely around 18 million Soviet civilians died in the war compared with 70,000 in the UK and less than half that in the United States. Between 700,000 and 1 million Soviet Jews—a staggering and unprecedented figure—were killed by the Germans in the course of their invasion, mostly shot in massacres by death squads or gassed in mobile death vans across Ukraine and Belorussia. On their return home after the war's end, those who had survived were received with suspicion and hostility. Communal organizations reopened slowly if at all; the region's once flourishing Jewish cultural life had been destroyed.

At the same time, the political calculus around antisemitism changed for the worse. In the ravaged city of Kiev, for example, in the autumn of 1945, vicious competition between returnees and newcomers for shelter and housing led to a pogrom in which sixteen Jews were killed and dozens were injured. Party efforts to clamp down on the rioters and restore order were resisted. Popular antisemitism was flourishing; reports indicated that in some areas it was so strong that it threatened the party's control. A high-ranking official in Ukraine is supposed to have said bluntly that "it is not in our interest that Ukrainians should associate the return of Soviet power with the return of the Jews." The overall outlook for Soviet Jewry after 1945 was thus incomparably bleaker than it had been in the 1920s: Entire communities had been destroyed, and the regime was even more suspicious of anyone who had contacts with the West than it had been two decades earlier. And yet because of the harrowing scale of the losses in Poland, Hungary, Germany, and elsewhere, the Soviet Union's Jewish population was by some margin the largest in Europe.[13]

Jewish survivors now also had to reckon for the first time with the emergence of antisemitism as official Soviet policy under the banner of a struggle against cosmopolitanism and Zionism. The fact that the war in its final stages had involved cultural contact with the West—as the victorious armies interacted with one another and with the populations under their control—had left Stalin deeply worried. He feared political, ideological, and cultural contamination, and he saw the Jews, with their far-flung families and sense of solidarity across borders, as suspect. Despite surrounding himself with several loyalists of Jewish origin, Stalin was notoriously antisemitic. The impact of his personal attitudes on Soviet policy had not been especially evident through most of the interwar era. But the first signs had come with the Soviet rapprochement with Nazi Germany in 1939, which showed that the regime was monitoring the issue among its higher officials. During the war itself the trend became unmistakable: Jews were purged from the foreign ministry and later from elsewhere in the administration. Even the formation of a wartime Jewish Anti-Fascist Committee to garner support for the Soviet war effort in the West was not, as it seemed at the time, a mark of Stalin's favor, but rather another indication that he thought that American Jewry in particular had much more power than it did to sway US policy in a pro-Russian direction: It was thus perfectly compatible with his belief that Jews were well connected internationally and not to be trusted.

In 1946 Milovan Djilas, the chief Communist ideologist among the wartime Yugoslav partisans, visited the Kremlin. He was shocked by Stalin's physical decline and equally astonished by a strange turn in their conversation. Stalin began by asking Djilas why there were so few Jews in the Yugoslav Communist Party and listened as Djilas explained that the country had only a small population and the only prominent Jew on the Central Committee was Moise Pijade, a veteran of the party and the translator of *Das Kapital.* "In our Central Committee there are no Jews!" Stalin burst in, adding provocatively: "You are an anti-Semite, you, too, Djilas, are an anti-Semite!" Djilas, expert in matters of ideology, said nothing, understanding that Stalin was toying with him and in fact signaling his own views on the question.[14]

Stalin's embrace of Russian nationalism had been evident during the war and was made explicit in the famous toast he delivered on May 24, 1945, to the "health of the Russian people." Nonetheless, the anti-Jewish wave that was to sweep both the USSR and its Eastern European satellites after the Second World War took many by surprise. Its origins lay in the Cold War and in Stalin's growing paranoia, which was fueled not only by his anxiety that another world war was imminent and the Soviet Union was unprepared for the struggle, but also by his conviction that the American and British intelligence services were determined to find ways to topple him from power.

Solomon Mikhoels was a prominent Soviet Jewish playwright and director of the Moscow State Jewish Theater. He hoped to turn Yiddish, the vernacular of eastern European Jews, into a recognized dramatic language, and his productions of plays from *King Lear* and *Tevye the Milkman* (the source of *Fiddler on the Roof*) to the 1947 *Uprising in the Ghetto* won him international renown. In the summer of 1941 Mikhoels had organized a rally in Moscow where he warned a huge crowd about the Nazis' plans for the "total annihilation of the Jewish people." By the following year he had been selected by Stalin to head the Jewish Anti-Fascist Committee; other such committees were formed for women, youth, scientists, and Slavs, and all of them reported to a veteran Bolshevik, Solomon Lozovsky, in the Soviet Information Bureau. In 1943 a morale-boosting trip was organized that culminated in a demonstration which gathered in New York that July in support of the Red Army and the Soviet war effort. The writer Sholem Asch noted that the USSR had been the first country to abolish antisemitism, a thinly veiled allusion to the restrictions that Jews continued to face in America. Back in the USSR the following year, the committee under Mikhoels's leadership discussed some sensitive issues: how to document the genocide; how to fight antisemitism; and, most fatefully it would turn out, whether to establish a Jewish republic in Crimea. The committee pointed out the obstacles to displaced Jews returning home and wondered if resettlement in Crimea could help alleviate the signs of growing antisemitism. The USSR had already tried once to create an autonomous Jewish region in remote Birobidzhan; it had not proved attractive. The committee thought Crimea might be a kind of alternative Bolshevik competitor to Palestine.[15]

Zionism's triumph in the Middle East and the establishment of Israel fomented Stalin's anxieties. A series of tentative wartime contacts between Soviet and Zionist representatives had laid the groundwork for the USSR's unexpected recognition of the state of Israel in 1948, but they were riddled with ambiguities that reflected Stalin's own hesitations. The last thing Stalin wanted was to encourage Jewish separatism or Jewish nationalism: Soviet Jewish reintegration and assimilation, not territorial autonomy, were the goals. Internal investigations aroused Stalin's suspicion that the Jewish Anti-Fascist Committee had become a tool of foreign interests and was taking on an "increasingly nationalistic, Zionist character." It had argued strongly, for instance, in favor of a monument to the Jewish victims of the Babi Yar massacre in Kiev, an issue always likely to incur Stalin's displeasure since the official line at the war's end was not to highlight the suffering of any one people in particular, least of all the Jews. Stalin was also well aware of the Zionist leadership's hope that large numbers of Russian Jews would be allowed to emigrate to Palestine, thereby solving their own acute demographic shortfall. Mikhoels's own sympathy for the creation of a Jewish homeland in Palestine was on record; he himself had understood this could cause him trouble. Nonetheless, what happened at the start of 1948 was unprecedented.[16]

As would be revealed a few years after Stalin's death, it was on the dictator's instructions that the Soviet playwright was lured out of Moscow to Minsk and murdered on the night of January 12, 1948, together with his secret police minder: Their corpses were left on a road to be discovered. A traffic accident was officially reported to be the cause, but few were fooled. Mikhoels's death was not the end of the Jewish Anti-Fascist Committee, which came shortly after. In September 1948 Kiev-born Golda Meir arrived in Moscow as the new Israeli minister and was greeted by huge crowds who followed her through the streets, cheering in support. This was more than Stalin could stand, and in November the committee was closed as "a center of anti-Soviet propaganda." In his mind, Jewish nationalism was in full flower and had to be cut down.[17]

The first arrests took place almost immediately and more followed over the next months. But it was not until the summer of 1952, after months of interrogation and torture, that a trial of the purported Jewish conspirators began in the Ministry of State Security. Closed to the public, it was unusual in that only two of the defendants fully admitted their guilt to conspiring against the USSR, and four of them refused to plead guilty to any of the charges at all. In private sessions, defendants were allowed to challenge the prosecutors and to cross-examine one another: What played out was an extraordinary drama, every word of which was recorded by the court stenographers as the innermost discussions of the committee were debated in front of the often-bewildered judges. The chief prosecutor heard enough to seek to stop the proceedings and have the investigation reopened. But there was only one conceivable outcome, and in August 1952 thirteen of the fifteen defendants were executed.

Years later, when the transcript of the proceedings resurfaced in the archives, it was revealed that the star of the trial had been the most senior of the defendants, Lozovsky, to whom Mikhoels and the committee had reported. Lozovsky had told the astonished judge that he had signed confessions only so as to live to be able to tell the truth in the courtroom out of reach of his interrogators. He wrote off the accusations he faced as ridiculous; he mocked the story that they had been planning a Jewish bridgehead for American imperialism in Crimea. He gave the court a lesson in what it had been to grow up as a Jew in prerevolutionary Russia, and he explained in no uncertain terms why he had signed such absurd "confessions."

> Let me explain why I signed. Because over the course of eight nocturnal interrogations Colonel Komarov kept telling me over and over again that Jews are low, dirty people, that all Jews are lousy bastards, that all opposition to the party consisted of Jews, that Jews all over the Soviet Union are conducting an anti-Soviet whisper campaign, and that the Jews want to annihilate all of the Russians. This is what Colonel Komarov told me. I ask you, What sort of language is this? Is this fitting language for a Soviet person, a Soviet functionary?

Accused of being a Jewish nationalist who went out of his way to hire fellow Jews in his office, he responded:

> I did not do that kind of calculation. I never felt drawn to Jews and never denied that I was a Jew. A person who denies his nationality is a bastard.[18]

Lozovsky raised another, highly sensitive issue. He told the court his interrogator had demanded to know which of the senior officials in Moscow had Jewish wives; he had replied he did not collect such information. He was even confronted with the Jewish wife of former Foreign Minister Molotov: She had been arrested, probably because the secret police involved in concocting the plot had likely hoped Lozovsky would implicate her. There was, of course, nothing in which to implicate her. But her arrest—and Stalin's interest in the Jewish wives of other Kremlin higher-ups—points to another reason behind the purge. Stalin had become convinced that American intelligence was hoping to use his inner circle to find out more about his second wife, who had killed herself in 1932, and whose death he had covered up ever since. Increasingly paranoid, he would have heard about Molotova's warm greeting of Golda Meir when she came to Moscow, and in general feared the international contacts of the Jewish figures in the Kremlin.

While the trial was still going on, a number of highly placed doctors were also arrested. One was a pediatrician at a Kremlin clinic; another had been the chief medical officer in the Red Army. From November, the number of arrests accelerated. A surprising number of those arrested bore recognizably Jewish names, as became known when the press—on the Kremlin's instructions—published a list of "saboteur doctors" in January 1953, thus indicating to an astonished Soviet public for the first time since the Great Terror of the mid-1930s that another public show trial was imminent.

The news precipitated an antisemitic panic, and the Kremlin was inundated with warnings and rumors. As arrests were reported around the country, accusations too poured in. In Vilnius a party member warned that a Jewish doctor was killing children by infecting them with cancer. There were multiple stories about Jewish medics routinely murdering patients in hospitals. Poisoning under the pretense of vaccination was a common fear, notably with tuberculosis. Other doctors were said to be giving children pills with stones inside. It was as though the old religious blood libel had found a new lease on life in a thinly secularized form. The Soviet New Man did not seem to have changed very much from the pre-1917 version: Behind the white coat, the doctor was still a Jew, harboring murderous intentions toward Christians unfortunate enough to fall into the wrong hands. The press whipped up hysteria and talked of a "gang of killer doctors."[19]

It remained ideologically important for the regime to deny the charge of antisemitism, and when one of the few remaining Jews close to Stalin died in February, he was given a Red Square funeral. But internationally there were protests, and at the United Nations the Soviet delegate was challenged to justify what was happening. There is evidence that Stalin had indeed determined to play out the drama of the doctors' alleged plot in full view of the public with a trial that would have been followed by executions in Red Square. Preparations were said to have been set in motion for mass deportations, and there were rumors that the entire Jewish population of Moscow was to be sent away to Siberia. A letter was prepared, to be signed by most of the prominent Jewish figures in the Soviet regime, condemning the doctors. Many did sign but there were others who refused: The writer Ilya Ehrenburg, who had served Stalin faithfully for years, appears to have written his own letter to warn Stalin of the repercussions abroad. It was only Stalin's sudden death at the start of March 1953 that ended the threat. Ironically, many of the doctors who could have helped him were in prison. Within days Foreign Minister Molotov's wife had been allowed to return to Moscow, and the following month it was agreed to drop the doctors' plot and release those who had been arrested.

Yet so far as Soviet Jewry was concerned, even that was not the end of the matter. *Pravda* announced that the plot had been concocted to "fan national animosity": It did not say by or against whom but clearly pointed the finger at the Jews themselves. News of the doctors' release was met across the country with consternation, and letters flooded into the press. Some were expressions of support for the authorities and some called for the rehabilitation of the doctors. To judge from digests prepared for senior party figures, the majority fell into two other categories: Many people refused to believe the doctors were innocent and many others simply expressed bafflement. Some accused the press of fomenting antisemitism: "The paper waged a pogrom-like anti-Semitic campaign...and tried to prove, in the manner of fascist leaflets, that they [the Jews] must get what is coming to them....You are prostitutes and beasts...Fascists." Others were outraged that the Jews "*have managed to get off scot-free again!*" Public confusion reigned for months. The one thing that was clear was that antisemitism was alive and well in the country whose government had proclaimed its historic defeat.[20]

In Eastern Europe too, popular antisemitism, which had been endemic before the Second World War, had certainly not been ended either by the defeat of Nazism or by the arrival of the Red Army. Once a major center of Jewish life, Poland itself had been wrecked; its capital, Warsaw, was largely in ruins. Of its large prewar Jewish population of roughly 3.4 million, fewer than one in ten had survived: The vast majority had been killed in the death camps. But the troubles of the survivors were far from over. In the months of near–civil war, before the Polish Communists prevailed with Soviet assistance, hundreds of returning Jews lost their lives. The popular linkage between Jews and wealth continued, and peasants were to be found digging and demolishing

houses, convinced the dead Jews had left behind their hidden valu-
ables. There were other echoes from the past as well: Disturbances
in Kraków in August 1945 were caused by rumors that the bodies of
Christian children had been stashed in a synagogue; in Kielce the
following year a pogrom triggered by claims of ritual murder left forty-
six dead.

The Polish authorities in the immediate postwar period placed no
obstacles in the way of Jews wishing to leave the country. As a result,
more than one hundred thousand Jews left almost at once for the
Allied-run displaced persons camps of Germany, many of them hoping to reach either the United States or Palestine. Together with other
survivors from Romania, Yugoslavia, and Hungary, there were at least
a quarter of a million Jewish DPs in the camps by early 1947. This was
a small proportion of the many millions of people displaced and on the
move across Eastern Europe in these years, but it was a significant proportion of the surviving Jewish population in the region. Between the
end of the war and the mid-1950s, the Jewish population in Czechoslovakia declined from 45,000 to 15,000, in Hungary from 140,000 to
80,000, in Bulgaria from 43,000 to around 5,000. In Romania the population halved to roughly 200,000.[21]

There were many factors behind this exodus, but high among them
were the anti-Jewish campaigns in Eastern Europe, which were extend-
ing into the region Moscow's political strategy of seeking to win
popular support for Communism by scapegoating Jews. As Cold War
tensions between the USSR and the United States intensified in
1947–48, Stalin had become increasingly concerned about his ability
to retain control in territories he regarded as critical to Soviet security.
With Soviet troops demobilizing, the key lay in local Communist parties' capacity to rule what had once been staunchly anti-Communist
societies. When the Yugoslav leader Josip Broz Tito broke with Stalin
in the summer of 1948, prompting the first open resistance to the Kremlin, it raised the specter of a larger nationalist resurgence directed

against Moscow. Tito's defiance came at the same time as Mikhoels's murder in the USSR and Stalin's turn to antisemitism. The merging of these twin obsessions—preserving Soviet domination in Eastern Europe and the bugbear of Jewish influence—now underpinned a sequence of show trials across the region that quickly developed an unmistakable antisemitic tinge.

It began in Hungary, where the fight to unmask "Titoists" eventually toppled the interior minister, László Rajk. When the purge spread to Czechoslovakia in the spring of 1949, the secret police and their Soviet advisers quickly employed the kind of antisemitic reasoning being pursued in Moscow at that time to crush any temptations the Czech party leadership might entertain in pursuing their own route to socialism. The chief defendant in the key 1952 trial of the "Anti-State Conspiratorial Center" was Rudolf Slánský, the Jewish general secretary of the Communist Party; accused of "Trotskyite-Titoist-Zionist activities in the service of American imperialism," he confessed in a show trial and was hanged. Tried along with Slánský were thirteen other defendants, mostly Jewish. There followed a number of minor trials and a purge that eventually targeted more than one hundred thousand people.

As the Rajk and Slánský trials indicated, Soviet Communism might pride itself on having opposed and purportedly eradicated antisemitism, but what it had actually done was more modest and misleading: to make overtly antisemitic rhetoric more or less impossible. Using the term *Zionist* as a euphemism for Jewish had started in the 1920s, but on a small scale and at a time when Zionism was not yet a fact of international life. By the late 1940s, by which time antisemitism was a criminal offense in much of the Communist bloc, *anti-Zionism* had turned into a code word that signaled Jewish ethnic origins. It was certainly not neutral in the Communist context because it alluded—via the associated charge of "cosmopolitanism"—to the idea that Jews could not truly be patriots and, worse, that any Zionist sympathy turned them into a potential agent not only of Israel but of the real enemy that stood behind it: American imperialism.

Ana Pauker, known to some as the "Empress," had been hailed by *Time* magazine at the end of 1947 as the first-ever female foreign minister in the world. She was indeed the Jewish foreign minister of not only one of the most antisemitic countries in the region, but also the one with the largest surviving Jewish community at the war's end. Though she was the chief architect of the party's consolidation of power and rapid growth after the war, she was intensely conscious of the pervasive antisemitism around her: According to British diplomats in 1946, the Romanians regarded the Jews "as traitors *who should be exterminated at the first opportunity*."[22]

A stalwart Communist, faithful Stalinist, and confidante of the Kremlin for many years, Pauker had survived Romanian prison and even her husband's disappearance in the Great Terror of the 1930s. She had been indelibly marked too by the cataclysm of the war. "After all that has happened, how many of us are left?" she wrote sadly to her brother, after she helped him to emigrate to Palestine in 1944 on one of the few boats able to leave in wartime through the Black Sea; she helped her father, an Orthodox Jew, follow three years later. Defying Moscow's wishes on the questions of emigration, collectivization, and other issues—she was surprisingly independent-minded—it was only a matter of time before she was caught in the Stalinist dragnet. New men were rising in the party, as they were elsewhere in Eastern Europe. But her ambitious party boss, Gheorghe Gheorghiu-Dej, did not move fast enough for the Kremlin's liking. In April 1952, he was flown to Moscow to be upbraided by a furious Stalin: "Dej, how many times did I tell you to get rid of Ana Pauker, and you didn't understand me? . . . If I were in your place, I would have shot her in the head a long time ago. . . . I was convinced that only proletarian blood flowed through your veins, but [now I see] it's petit-bourgeois blood."[23]

An anti-cosmopolitan campaign was already underway when Pauker herself was arrested in February 1953: Gheorghiu-Dej had finally understood what was wanted of him and summoned up the courage for a show trial with her as the main attraction scheduled for around the time of the doctors' trial in Moscow. Stalin's death meant Pauker's trial never began, and in late March she was suddenly released—thanks to the intercession of Soviet Foreign Minister Molotov—and put under house arrest. Despite everything, she burst into tears on hearing Stalin had died. "Don't cry," said a colleague. "If Stalin were still alive, you'd be dead." She outlived him by seven years, earning a living as a translator from French and German.[24]

Romania was in some ways an outlier among Eastern European states. It never broke off diplomatic relations with Israel, even after the Six-Day War; it permitted the only Hebrew-language journal to be published in the Communist bloc; and it encouraged limited contacts with the West. To be chief rabbi in such an environment was no easy task, but the position was filled by two remarkable figures. Serving from 1940 to 1948, Alexandru Safran had used his high-level contacts at the Romanian court to persuade the wartime Fascist government to block the Germans' demand for deportations. After he was expelled by the Communists, he was succeeded by Moses Rosen, known to his detractors as "the red rabbi," whose extraordinarily long tenure in the position outlasted Communism itself, only ending with his death in 1994. As both men understood well, antisemitism was but one factor in shaping state policy—in Romania as elsewhere. It was a serious cultural and political force but it was not necessarily determinative.

Milovan Djilas—one of the most acute and least sentimental political analysts of the century—noted that antisemitism had become routine in the region under Communism and incorporated as a feature of postwar Soviet rule: "Great Russian bureaucratic state capitalism has had to become not only nationalist, but racial too.... And it must inevitably become—and already is—anti-Semitic also."[25] But Stalin's death and the ensuing thaw meant that the worst was over.

His successors had seen the potential for popular violence to escape its control and never again played with fire in the same way. Nikita Khrushchev was no Stalin and lacked the Georgian's intensely paranoiac view of the world; his own antisemitism was more likely to express itself in crude jokes and gaffes than in sustained political campaigns. But the Soviet fear of "Zionism" had become entrenched, and suspicion and prejudice against Jews in party circles remained.[26]

In post-Stalinist Eastern Europe, Jews lived in a somewhat freer and less stifling atmosphere. Party policy was generally more liberal than in the USSR, Jewish communal organizations had somewhat greater autonomy, and travel abroad was occasionally possible. But they were living in the shadow of the past and many of the same factors hit Jewish life hard. State officials targeted Jews because of their class origins (as bourgeois), or because they were accused of contacts with Israel (and hence American imperialism), or because they were observant. Popular antisemitism surfaced in the letter pages of the press in complaints at the numbers of Jews in senior party positions or about their supposed access to privileges. In Poland, after a series of internal party purges produced a new wave of emigration, the situation grew serious enough by 1957 for the party newspaper, *Trybuna Ludu*, to comment with surprising frankness that "during the twelve years since the establishment of the People's Republic of Poland, objective conditions were created to wipe out antisemitism. But the results have not been satisfactory." The paper warned that the continued flight of the few Polish Jews remaining would discredit the country abroad and lead people to question to what extent a society of equal rights had really been built under socialism.[27]

A decade later, the last of the major Cold War antisemitic campaigns erupted. Events in the Middle East provided the pretext: In the wake of Israel's victory in the Six-Day War, a nationalist faction in Poland's ruling party saw the opportunity to denounce its internal enemies as "Zionists" and the press launched an open campaign in the name of "anti-Zionism." Because some Polish Jews had openly cele-brated the Israeli victory, the authorities were convinced of their treachery. There was a purge of journalists and officials running Jew-ish communal organizations, and by the spring of 1968 the authorities were organizing demonstrations with banners that read: DOWN WITH THE AGENTS OF IMPERIALISM—REACTIONARY ZIONISM! Speaking to a meeting of party activists, their leader Władysław Gomułka insisted they would nonetheless fight "with complete firmness every manifes-tation of antisemitism." Gomułka's wife was Jewish, and he had once taken the problem of prejudice seriously. But as he navigated the del-icate politics of the 1967 anti-Zionist campaign that had been insti-gated by his own ambitious minister of the interior, he acquiesced in what had become an outright antisemitic drive that removed Jews from public employment: The victims included many members of the security services and judiciary, army officers, leading journalists, pro-fessors, and other representatives of the intelligentsia. Between 1968 and 1970, around twenty-five thousand Jews left Poland, just under half of them for Israel; after that no more than ten thousand remained. Gomułka brought the campaign itself to an end but the reverberations continued and eventually led to his own downfall. Meanwhile, in Czechoslovakia, with the Soviet tanks that rolled into the country to end the "Prague Spring" came not only a return to hard-line rule but also a return to the Stalinist techniques of an antisemitic purge to smear the opposition. There could be little doubt after this that post-war Communism had not only failed to vanquish antisemitism, it had evolved its own form of antisemitism. Across the Soviet bloc, as the last Jewish communities dwindled further, what remained was what one analyst called "anti-Semitism without Jews."[28]

Part 2

On the Battlefield of Ideas

WORLD JEWISH POPULATION C. 1920[1]

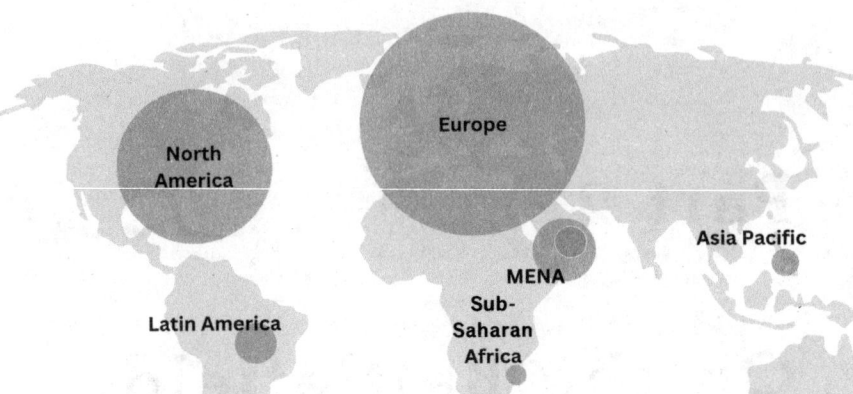

WORLD JEWISH POPULATION C. 2020[2]

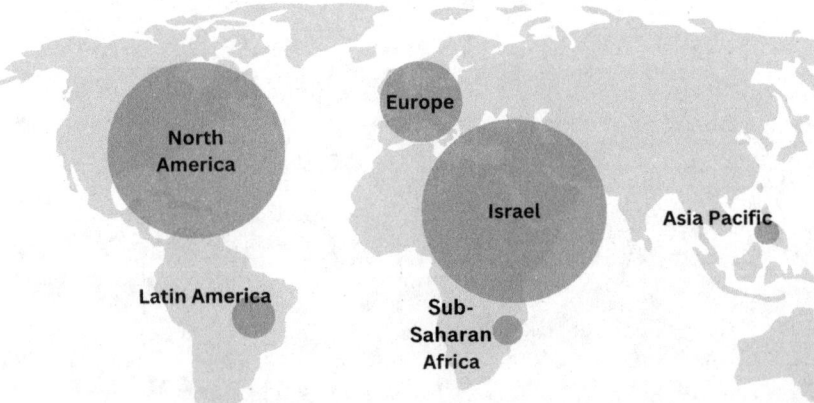

CHAPTER 6

Prelude: The United States, Israel, and the Middle East

1940s–1960s

In the postwar Jewish world, [there are] two major Jewish entities—ourselves and the Israelis.

BEN HALPERN, "THE IMPACT OF ISRAEL ON AMERICAN JEWISH IDEOLOGIES," 1959[1]

Europe had been the historic epicenter of Jewish life for centuries: When it became the main arena for the struggle for Jewish emancipation and the emergence of antisemitic politics, it was home to more than four fifths of the world's Jews. This struggle over Jewish rights culminated in the Nazis' genocidal war that all but wiped out the Jewish heartlands of central-eastern Europe and left not only Germany but the European continent itself devastated, partitioned, and weakened. Anti-Jewish prejudices survived (as we have seen), but antisemitism itself as a political movement was largely discredited in the region that had given birth to it.

Yet the story of antisemitism does not end at this point. Lingering on in the USSR and Soviet-dominated eastern Europe, it was transformed and extended thanks to two fundamental geopolitical changes. The first of these was the emergence of the United States as a Cold War superpower, a factor that over time was to give the concerns, influence, and organized actions of American Jewry a weight they had not previously possessed in international affairs. By 1950, North America was home to more Jews than anywhere else, eventually catapulting the American Jewish community into a new world role, with the result that American understandings of antisemitism would come to possess more and more global heft. The second development was the collapse of European imperial power in the Middle East, the creation of Israel, and the emergence of the Palestinian question. Initially the junior partner, by the end of the century Israel rivaled American Jewry in numbers and clout. Jewish life around the world would henceforth be shaped politically by the dynamics within and increasingly between these two poles. Displaced from its place of origin, the concept of antisemitism acquired new political associations in new settings.

A LAND WITHOUT ANTISEMITISM?

Surveying the depressing panorama of world Jewry in 1934, the year after the Nazis came to power, the great Anglo-Jewish historian Lewis Namier came round eventually to the subject of the Jews in the United States. Their outlook was, he wrote, a "closed book" to someone like him, born into the Polish Jewish gentry in the Russian-Habsburg borderlands and trained at L'viv, Lausanne, and pre-1914 Oxford—a man steeped in the culture of Old Europe. Namier was worried that as they settled in the United States, Jewish immigrants were shedding the cultural vestiges of their eastern European past, leaving behind "a fading, anaemic Judaism." Would they disappear altogether through assimilation? Or would the pressure of antisemitism keep them together even after their own "inner values" had disappeared? He was neither the first nor the last to fear Jews might be threatened in the United States as much by acceptance as by enmity, and to fret over what would happen if antisemitism vanished. As Namier sensed, Jews were relative newcomers in a country with political and social traditions very different from Europe's, and their experience would turn out to be unlike that of any other Jewish community in the world.[2]

The American context differed in two crucial ways. One was that, with only very minor caveats, Jews arriving in the American republic found themselves from the start in a state of civic emancipation. That the political setting was more favorable to them than anywhere in continental Europe—as it was to religious minorities of all kinds—reflected the fact that the US itself had been conceived of as a republican and democratic riposte to the closed and deeply hierarchical societies of the Old World. A riposte with one critical limitation, however: race. The other key difference with Europe was that American citizenship and the American political imagination was structured by a racial dichotomy: Even if the US constitution itself preserved a discreet silence on the matter, no one who lived in the country could doubt its importance, and the 1790 Nationality Act, which limited the possibility of naturalization to aliens who were "free white persons," rendered this colorized dichotomy and its inequities explicit. The fundamental divide was between those who were slaves or their descendants, and everyone else. The first Jewish immigrants from Europe found themselves the beneficiaries of a political dispensation that denied emancipation to American slaves. Those arriving at the century's end found sanctuary in a country engaged in rolling back emancipation for former slaves and their families, introducing Jim Crow laws, and turning a blind eye to the spread of lynching. "They have people who are more Jewish than the Jews, that is to say the Negroes," the writer Joseph Roth marveled in 1927. "Of course the Jews are still Jews. But here, significantly, they are white. For the first time, a Jew's race is actually to his advantage."[3]

We shall explore, in chapter 7, the consequences of this invidious situation for black-Jewish relations, which were unsurprisingly complex, intense, and entangled. Here our concern is with the phenomenon of antisemitism, which became a far more prominent factor in American life than it had been before. Thanks to Jewish immigration from eastern Europe, part of an even larger wave of European immigration, the US Jewish population soared from under 300,000 in 1880 to over 3 million before entry was restricted after the First World War; it was against this background that nativism revived, and antisemitism emerged for the first time on a national scale.

Jews soon came face-to-face with the brutal realities of American race prejudice. In 1913 a factory manager called Leo Frank was convicted in Atlanta, Georgia, of the murder of a young girl worker. Occurring in the same year as the Beilis affair in Russia, the case was a highly controversial one; even more astonishing was the denouement two years later when the unfortunate Frank was lynched. Frank had been president of the local chapter of a Jewish fraternal organization, the B'nai B'rith; following his trial, it created the Anti-Defamation League, which was to become perhaps the best-known American Jewish organization specifically combating antisemitism. The ADL and the other national Jewish organizations soon had plenty on their plate: After the First World War, as curbing immigration became a political issue, conservative politicians warned of disturbing changes to the American way of life, Henry Ford helped turn *The Protocols of the Elders of Zion* into an American bestseller, and antisemitic discrimination intensified sharply across the country. With a raft of apathetic or indeed antisemitic university presidents following more sympathetic ones, the rapid growth in Jewish admissions to American universities and colleges was thrown abruptly into reverse and (as in Europe) quotas were introduced. Social clubs, hotels, and resorts declared themselves off-limits to Jews. Restricted covenants kept housing segregated and excluded "Hebrews" (Jews) along with those of "Ethiopian, Malay or Asiatic [black, Filipino, or Asian American] race." The Ku Klux Klan regrouped in what struck observers as "the first serious attempt in the United States to exploit antisemitism—and racial and religious hatred generally—for reactionary political ends." Racial science spread the idea that Jews were a threat to the Anglo-Saxon race; the Red Scare portrayed them as a revolutionary threat too. Organized political antisemitism on the European model never truly took hold, but the Catholic Right in the persona of Father Coughlin, a notorious radio personality of the late 1930s, propagated anti-Jewish poison, and the impact of European Fascism was felt as Nazi funds poured in to bankroll supportive American groups: There had been only one of these in 1932, but a decade later there were more than one hundred.[4]

The ferment continued during and after the Second World War: In July 1945 a reporter noted that "one of the most extensive anti-Semitic campaigns this country has ever experienced has developed in the United States since the beginning of the war." Jewish commentators looked ahead nervously. "Even in the United States there is grave danger of antisemitic reaction if things do not go well in the post-war period," noted Koppel Pinson. "All the factors identifying Nazi antisemitism with the enemy of our own national security are potentially capable of serious back-fire if our hopes and expectations for the post-war world are not appreciably realized." Between 1944 and 1946 polls showed a rise in the number of Americans who thought Jews had too much power in the country.[5]

In the intensely anti-Communist atmosphere of the Cold War, the formerly buoyant Jewish socialist movement shrank. "In a period no longer than the lifetime of one human being," writes a scholar of American Jews and the Left, "the relationship between socialism and the Jewish community in America changed dramatically." Although only a tiny number of Jews had been on the far Left, they represented a high proportion of the militants of the Communist Party of the United States between the wars. The left-wing Yiddish press began its long postwar decline. The largest Jewish newspaper in the country was the leftist *Forward*, but whereas its circulation in the early 1930s had been around 275,000, by 1962 it was under 60,000 and falling. Any perceived association with Communism prompted anxiety, never more so than after the arrest of a Jewish couple, Julius and Ethel Rosenberg, on charges of spying for the Soviet Union. Their 1951 trial—with

Jewish prosecutors and a Jewish trial judge, as if to allay the inevitable suspicions—fanned an international cause célèbre. But most of the major American Jewish communal organizations did not join in the campaign for the Rosenbergs' release, and they did not share the widespread suspicion on the international Left that the case was a product of antisemitic Cold War hysteria. Sartre might describe the case as a "legal lynching"; other French commentators likened it to the Dreyfus affair. In fact, unlike Dreyfus, Julius Rosenberg had indeed been spying and was guilty, though his wife was very likely innocent.

Anxieties lest the old interwar association of Jews with Bolshevism should persist in the US did not fade away quickly; as late as 1961, the AJC had set a committee to work to "disassociate Jews from Communism in the public mind." This engaged a number of prominent Jewish intellectuals who would, over time, move on from worrying about American Communism to pressuring the USSR on behalf of Soviet Jewry. Such a trajectory helps explain the passage so noticeable among some high-profile New York Jewish writers from the non-Communist Left to the anti-Communist Right, a path that eventually led many to neo-conservatism and its culture of fears about Marxism on college campuses.[6]

Historians of antisemitism tend to be catastrophists by inclination and they rarely dwell on the times when the phenomenon subsides: Still less do today's campaigners against antisemitism stop to ask themselves what they can learn from such periods. It is as though they cannot believe these moments mean what they seem but are instead aberrations that must inevitably end in tears. So it is perhaps worth dwelling on what took place in the US from the 1950s onward when, in what the chief authority on the subject has described as a "remarkable metamorphosis," levels of anti-Jewish bigotry fell and overt prejudice became less socially or politically respectable. For as it turned out, the anxieties American Jews felt at the prospect of continued anti-Jewish discrimination were to be unexpectedly relieved, and

American antisemitism as a system of institutionalized discrimination was dismantled with the same surprising rapidity with which it had been constructed. The ADL was already commenting on the decline in formerly pro-Nazi groups by 1948, and by 1956 one observer was noting that "organized antisemitism is already confined mostly to the lunatic fringe." Polls confirmed the trend: Antisemitic attitudes certainly did not disappear and episodes of small-scale violence indicated its persistence, but major discriminatory barriers to housing, employment, and college entry came down. Schools and colleges that had introduced quotas in the 1920s abolished them and Jewish admissions soared; many jobs opened up that had formerly been closed, though the inner sanctums of law and business remained tightly guarded for longer until they too succumbed in the face of a targeted campaign by the AJC. As if to banish memories of life's miseries confined in the shtetls of the Old Country, now relegated to sentimental and sometimes heartbreaking memory, Jewish builders, real estate developers, and architects went into what one observer called "space manufacturing," transforming much of New York and helping create modern Manhattan as a place to live as well as to work, a city of residential cooperatives and elevator-equipped apartment blocks. *Fortune* magazine in 1960 hailed what it called "the Jewish *élan*" that gave New York City its "dramatic character, its excitement, its originality, its stridency, its unexpectedness."[7]

As anti-Jewish segregation in housing became a thing of the past, so too was it abandoned in vacationing. The Borscht Belt, otherwise known as the Yiddish Alps, was a zone of hundreds of Jewish hotels, bungalow resorts, and summer camps in the Catskill Mountains, an easy drive from New York City: It included Grossinger's, a hotel whose dining room could reputedly seat thirteen hundred guests, and the Nevele high-rise, with the Waikiki pool and the country club's renowned Stardust Room. The 1950s were the heyday of such places. But as discrimination waned and cheaper airfares made other destinations more attractive, decline set in. Tastes were changing too: When a Jewish Catskills dairy farmer called Max Yasgur agreed to host a festival of "Three Days of Peace and Music" in the summer of 1969, half a million people descended on his fields to hear Santana, The Who, and Ten Years After (among others), and the name of Woodstock resounded around the world. Today most of the great hotels of the Borscht Belt have burned down, become derelict, or found new uses serving the growing Orthodox Jewish population of the Eastern Seaboard. Those who once vacationed there as children are now likely to be found enjoying retirement on the Florida shoreline or other Sunbelt communities in the southern United States.[8]

The occasional antisemitic episode notwithstanding, observers agreed that American Jewry—like much of the country generally—was entering an era of moderation and opportunity after the politically polarized tensions of the previous half century. Instead of returning to depression, the US economy—already representing 50 percent of world GDP in 1945—boomed, and full employment and mass consumption banished memories of the Dust Bowl and the unemployment lines. American Jews benefited from postwar prosperity and joined in the consumerist boom and the joys of suburban life. A sense of optimism about the future was captured in a 1960 survey of American Reform rabbis and other leaders. Asked to predict what the year 2000 would look like, the consensus was that although none of the three main religious branches of American Judaism would have merged (in this at least they were realists), in the outside world peace would have been reached between Israel and the Arab states, there would have been a Jewish candidate for vice president, and antisemitism in the United States would have declined further. Even though they still faced discrimination—social clubs and school boards remained hangouts of exclusion—on the whole Jews had accelerated faster into middle-class comfort than any other of the ethnic groups that had passed with them through Ellis Island on the journey from Europe. Hailing "the

virtual end of overt antisemitism" in the United States, a director of
the ADL observed in 1972 that the postwar decades were a "golden
age" in which American Jews enjoyed security and social acceptance
to a degree unprecedented in history.[9]

How and why exactly this happened would seem important to
understand and yet defies simple explanation, as cultural shifts generally do. The experience of the war itself surely played a part, although
no more in the United States than elsewhere did victory against Fascism and Nazism discredit antisemitism, let alone racial prejudice in
general. It was unquestionably in part an organizational achievement
by American Jewry, which mobilized to fight discriminatory barriers
with greater success than possibly any other ethnic group. An important part of that mobilization was intellectual: It is worth noting that
antisemitism was not widely seen in this time as something that could
or should be treated separately from other kinds of bigotry or discrimination. On the contrary, Jewish organizations, reflecting the belief
that antisemitism was an instance of a larger social and psychological
maladjustment that could be cured through public education and secure
work, commissioned social scientific research into the causes of racial
prejudice to help bring it to an end: Under the leadership of Columbia
University–trained social psychologist John Slawson, founder of its
Division of Scientific Research, the American Jewish Committee
in particular sponsored major works of scholarly investigation, and
through the Studies in Prejudice series they disseminated this research
in bestselling paperbacks. Although dated today, the 1950 volume
The Authoritarian Personality was perhaps the best-known and most
influential of these works, written by German refugees whose studies
of antisemitism and prejudice dated back to the Third Reich.

But more indefinable cultural shifts were at work too, such as the
passing of generations and shifting horizons of experience. For as a
cohort that had grown up amid the shock of mass immigration and
Bolshevism gave way to one whose chief memory was of fighting

Nazism, attitudes changed. Fighting antisemitism was associated with the larger struggle to improve the quality of American democracy. Within college fraternities it was noticeably the younger students who wanted to open up to Jews and others in the face of resistance from older alumni.

And then there was the impact of the creation of Israel. In 1942 a commentator on antisemitism had daringly but perceptively suggested that establishing a Jewish homeland in Palestine could "normalize" the place of Jews in American life by giving them, like other immigrants from Europe, a country of "origin." It was the opposite of what many in the American Jewish elite feared, which was that a Jewish state might actually raise suspicions of where Jewish loyalties lay (as it was to do in the USSR and Eastern Europe). It was also the opposite of what many Zionists hoped and expected, namely mass emigration from the United States to Israel. The emergence of an independent Israel was to put these propositions to the test and change the place of Jews in America forever.[10]

Even before it existed, Israel was on American minds. Colonial preachers called their new land Canaan; Melville saw Americans as "the peculiar, chosen people, the Israel of our time." In the Second Great Awakening, American Protestants became obsessed with the Holy Land, and it was perhaps in response that one Jewish preacher had called as early as 1818 for Jews to establish themselves in Ottoman Syria.[11] Christian Zionism flourished, remaining a powerful force in American politics to this day. But Zionism in the modern sense was largely a product of the mass migration from the Russian Empire, and even in the interwar years pro-Zionist movements in America were still outranked socially by the officially "non-Zionist" AJC, which represented the leadership of the most assimilated section of the Jewish population, whose arrival predated the "Russians." *Their* attitudes were reflected in the 1898 resolution of the American Reform Movement, which declared itself "unalterably opposed to political Zionism" on the grounds that "the Jews are not a nation, but a religious community." Into the 1930s, the AJC opposed the setting up of an international quasi-parliamentary Jewish organization lest it imply that Jews owed an allegiance to one another that ranked above their allegiance to the political institutions of their own homeland; when the creation of the World Jewish Congress was mooted, the AJC objected to the view that "the Jewish people" were, or could ever be regarded as, "a united national organism." The wartime AJC president, Judge Joseph Proskauer, regarded Zionist propaganda for a homeland in Palestine as "a Jewish catastrophe" and insisted that "from every point of view of safety for Jews in America there has got to be an open, vocal Jewish dissent from nationalism and political Zionism."[12]

The abandonment of this position and the wholesale American Jewish shift in the direction of Zionism only really took place during and after the Second World War. In 1942, against the opposition of both the wartime American Council for Judaism, an anti-Zionist voice, and the American Jewish Committee, several groups convened to demand the postwar establishment of a "Jewish commonwealth" in Palestine. The threat posed by antisemitism was taken very seriously by all sides, but they came down in different places as to how a Jewish state would affect it. The Zionists believed a Jewish national home would end the problem by providing a sanctuary to which all Jews would naturally gravitate. For anti-Zionists, antisemitism was a problem of racial prejudice and incomplete democratization that was best fought in solidarity with other minorities in labor movements and unions and could not be solved by turning another people—the Palestinian Arabs—into a homeless minority in turn. The chief worry of the American Jewish Committee was that American antisemitism would undermine Jews' acceptance in the United States, and so it remained committed to the long-term ideal of political emancipation worldwide. "We refuse to accept the thesis that Jewish emancipation is a failure because it has been repealed in many countries under Nazi pressure" ran an internal wartime analysis.[13]

But with the establishment of Israel, hailed across the board by American Jews as an epochal event, anti-Zionism as a political position was weakened, and the anti-Zionist American Council for Judaism shrank to virtual irrelevance. Of the few figures who stood out against the tide, perhaps the most notable was William Zukerman, a journalist who had been reporting on international Jewish affairs for decades. Arguing that since 1948 the terms *anti-Zionist* and *Zionist* had lost their meanings, Zukerman described himself as "pro-Israel" but "anti-nationalist." He criticized what he called "the wave of Messianic nationalism which the Hitler Holocaust has released" among American Jews: In embracing the ethnic chauvinism that had swept over the world since the late 1930s, he argued, the Jews risked breeding a cruelty that was already changing "the entire character of the people." Israel had turned Jews into "conquerors" whose indifference to the plight of the Arab refugees betrayed Judaism's tradition of sympathy for the oppressed. For Zukerman the Israeli leadership's deliberate efforts to identify the country with Jews abroad served merely to increase the danger of antisemitism faced by the latter since it introduced "new diplomatic and political reasons in addition to the old social, economic and psychological ones."[14]

Zukerman's articles were much discussed by American Jews at the time and are attracting new readers today. Nor was he alone: Other Jewish leaders expressed similar concerns. But such a stance carried costs and he was inevitably denounced as a "self-hating Jew" and an antisemite. What he termed a "perverted chauvinistic reasoning" meant that his opinions were treated "as almost the equivalent of treason": "To criticise any policy of Israel, whether it is the rendering homeless of a million native Arabs, the treatment of the Arab minority as second-class citizens or the transformation of the new state into a racial theocracy, is denounced not only as anti-Israel but as anti-Semitic."

One senses the shock he felt at the term being applied in this way to someone like him, who had done as much as anyone to chart the rise of antisemitism in interwar Europe. We are here at the very beginning of what one might call a kind of Zionist usage of the term that was only conceivable once Israel itself had come into existence. Recent research has revealed that Israeli diplomats were concerned enough about Zukerman's influence to mount a behind-the-scenes campaign against him, enlisting American Zionist organizations and eventually pressuring the proprietors of Jewish newspapers to drop him. As a result, his articles ceased to be widely available, and when he died in 1961 his *Jewish Newsletter*—which he had kept going for fourteen years—folded.[15]

More consequential—because of its powerful position in American Jewish public life—was the transformation of the avowedly "non-Zionist" AJC, whose political sympathies by the late 1940s were adjusting to the establishment of Israel. Alongside the work it was doing to reconstruct Jewish life in Europe, the AJC was also supportive of Jewish refugees making their way to Palestine. But it disliked the Zionists' braggadocio, and its anxieties about American Jewish vulnerability to the dual loyalty accusation were acute, above all in a time of Cold War tensions, spy scares, and mistrust of foreigners. The AJC was constantly worried about the Israelis as well; in fact, it was far from assuming the cheerleading role of recent times. It is worth bearing in mind that in 1950 there were four times as many Jews in the United States as in Israel—and almost twice as many in New York City alone—which meant that an extraordinary tussle for power between the community notables of American Jewry, on the one hand, and the Jewish state and its leaders, on the other, was all but preordained.

Israeli Prime Minister David Ben-Gurion was the new political factor. He had very little time after 1948 for the organized American Zionist movement, which he believed lacked any further raison d'être once Israel had come into being, and he engineered the downfall of its leader, Abba Hillel Silver, whom he feared as a potential check on his freedom of maneuver. "Zionism is not undergoing a crisis," Ben-Gurion remarked with satisfaction in the wake of Silver's ouster. "It is going bankrupt." That is, after all, what he hoped for. He assumed American Zionists worthy of the name would want to move to Israel, and he questioned their fiber—on occasions in public—when to his dismay this did not happen. For Ben-Gurion, as for Zukerman, who agreed at least on this, the underlying issue was a simple one: If the creation of Israel spelled the end of anti-Zionism, understood as a movement opposed to a Jewish state coming into existence, did it not also by the same logic spell the end of Zionism as well?[16]

Although not especially attuned to American sensitivities, Ben-Gurion understood that American Zionists were by and large already his. Winning over American Jewry really meant wooing the "non-Zionists" of the AJC, whose leader, Jacob Blaustein, enjoyed influence in Truman's White House. But this was complicated by Ben-Gurion's repeated calls for American Jews to come and settle in Israel, something that infuriated Blaustein. Driven by his fear that Israel lacked a large enough population, Ben-Gurion saw the United States as a badly needed reservoir of superior "human material" (preferable in many ways to the tattered and traumatized survivors coming in from wartime Europe). BEN GURION URGES US PARENTS TO SEND THEIR CHILDREN TO ISRAEL FOR PERMANENT SETTLEMENT was the headline reporting a speech he gave in Israel in 1949. "We appeal to the parents to help us bring their children here," he had said before pouring fuel on the flames by adding: "Even if they decline to help, we will bring the youth to Israel." The AJC leadership were so angry that they warned Ben-Gurion they would protest publicly if he did not refrain. He needed, they insisted, to revise his assumptions: American Jews were *not* in exile; America, not Israel, was their home, and their families, not Israeli politicians, were responsible for Jewish children. They wanted this message spelled out lest it make them liable to the accusation that their American patriotism was lacking.[17]

Things got so bad that in the summer of 1950, Blaustein visited Israel at the prime minister's invitation to sort out their disagreements. It was an extraordinary meeting. Ben-Gurion's remarks afterward were conciliatory; Blaustein's were longer, tougher, and emphatic. Speaking almost as the senior partner in the relationship, he emphasized "American Jewry" as an equal to Israel itself, willing to support it but nonetheless with its own interests. He stressed the need for liberal democracy to take root in the new country and offered the assistance of American Jews "within the framework of their American citizenship." But he warned that goodwill was "a two-way street."[18]

Both men got what they wanted but perhaps one got more. Blaustein clarified that American Jewry were not in exile but Ben-Gurion did not actually disavow the ideal of aliyah; on the contrary, even though American emigration to Israel in the 1950s averaged under four hundred people per year, Ben-Gurion kept up his calls for Jews to come and settle. It was a constant theme in the campus visits he made to the United States in 1960, when it became clear, especially when he was speaking with students themselves, that he was determined to encourage young, educated American Jews to come to Israel by any means in the hope they would stay. His message was above all an activist one. "Please don't perceive this as blasphemy," Ben-Gurion told his audience at Yeshiva University in New York, "[but we, the government of Israel,] have taken upon ourselves to fix or finish that which the Holy One Blessed Be He chose for some reason not to complete." Blaustein might have seen aliyah as an inherently political issue; for Ben-Gurion, it was a godly one.[19]

For similar reasons, the Israeli premier also insisted that Zionist organizations abroad had an absolute obligation "under all circumstances and conditions" to "aid the Jewish State." This statement was made during the ongoing show trials in Eastern Europe, and was hardly helpful for the Jewish communities in those countries; the AJC was once again furious. Nor was it happy that Israeli officials had begun the practice—not regarded in those days as quite as normal as it is today—of discussing antisemitic incidents abroad directly with governments over the heads of local Jewish communities, as though it were in fact their primary protector. Blaustein especially objected to remarks made by Moshe Dayan in Canada that "his government should not only represent the people of Israel but the interests of all Jews." Eventually he accused Ben-Gurion of contradicting the assurances he had given him at their meeting in 1950. To demand the allegiance of every Zionist to help Israel whether or not their own government wished it was "an unheard-of request for allegiance to a foreign power."[20]

Yet the Ben-Gurion government continued to assert that it had the right and the authority "to speak and act for Jews everywhere." Its 1952 legislation that settled the fate of the old international Zionist organizations begins with the statement: "The State of Israel regards itself as the creation of the entire Jewish people." The AJC had bargained for the inclusion of a crucial clause: "The State of Israel, *representing only its own inhabitants*, regards itself as the creation of the entire Jewish people." But to Blaustein's fury, this clause did not appear in the version passed by the Knesset. Ben-Gurion was not especially apologetic: He told the angry Americans that Israel was like any other state and therefore had no need to define whom it represented. Both men understood what was really at stake and knew who had come out on top. Ben-Gurion caused uproar once again when he told the twenty-fifth Zionist Congress that Jews living in the comfort of the West were violating the faith itself and that Judaism "faces the kiss of death, a slow and imperceptible decline into the abyss of assimilation." Once more the AJC complained; once more to little avail.[21]

In the early years of Israel's existence, as this to-ing and fro-ing suggests, the new state was far from generating the kind of wide-spread support in the US that we associate with it today. The scholar Ben Halpern had shown in 1959 that a general sentiment of sympathy for, and identification with, Israel did not mean that most American Jews necessarily saw their own fates as bound up with its welfare in the way they would come to do later. In 1966 Rabbi Arthur Hertz-berg, among the most acute commentators on the American Jewish scene, even chided American rabbis for their coolness toward Israel. "No one can today make a major career within American Jewry through Zionist political activity," he wrote. The dual allegiance inhibition remained strong; the assimilationist ideal remained powerful and dis-couraged public assertions of American Jewish connection to Israel.[22]

It was the Six-Day War that was perhaps the real turning point, immeasurably boosting Israel's image in the United States and thereby transforming the relationship between Israel and American Jewry. After it, the last of the sharp ideological conflicts and disagreements that had been evident through the Second World War gave way to a mutual embrace, emotional as much as political. Zionism—in a new and attenuated sense of being generally supportive of Israel and feel-ing some special kinship with it—increasingly unified the American Jewish mainstream. In the words of the Israeli historian Evyatar Fri-esel, "not only was Zionism 'Americanized,' American Jewry became 'Zionized.'" It is hard now to recapture the radical nature of this shift not least because it was something of a paradox. As the commentator Henry Feingold noted, "The American Jewish identity, which Zion-ists predicted was destined to fade...was actually strengthened by the establishment of the Jewish state."[23]

How passionately the Six-Day War made ordinary American Jews feel about Israel—and by extension about their own lives—emerges in interviews given by the Jewish residents of a Midwestern suburb to the brilliant sociologist Marshall Sklare. Working for the American Jewish Committee's Division of Scientific Research, Sklare had first visited the place he called "Lakeville" in the 1950s; after the Six-Day War he returned. (Lakeville was likely the Chicago suburb of Highland Park on Lake Michigan.) The people he spoke with said they had been swept up in the intensity of the moment more than with any other event they could remember. All had felt unambiguously pro-Israel and sure which side was right. They had also felt no strain between their loyalties to America and what they felt for Israel, or more precisely, in Sklare's words: "They strove not to perceive any such strain." They had all given money as a way of helping, and Sklare was struck by the fact that "strange as it may seem," and despite the lack of any evidence for the belief, "even today [they] connect their own actions with the Israeli victory." Most said they had been pleasantly relieved that non-Jews too had supported the Israeli side, and they believed American Jews had won a new respect in American eyes because of the Israeli victory. To Sklare's surprise, none of them had visited Israel over the previous decade, even though flights had become cheaper, and more surprisingly still, only one of them had any plans to. As for the idea of making aliyah and settling there, that was a nonstarter: Life was good in "Lakeville."

At bottom, their sense of intense commitment to Israel, Sklare concluded, was less about Israel itself (which most of them knew little about) than it was about the history of the 1930s, and it could only be understood in psychological terms.

For Sklare, the memory of the Holocaust and the significance American Jews attached to it was central. In his view, the Six-Day War had reawakened the thought that the Holocaust could be repeated; and accompanying that, the reflection that if it happened again, American Jews would once more escape unscathed just as they had done during the Second World War, through no special virtue of their own but by mere chance. If their good fortune the first time around seemed hardly justified, they could at least act now in such a fashion as to suggest that their exemption had led to "some good purpose. . . . Thus our support for Israel is intimately connected with our desire to preserve a feeling of our worth as human beings."[24]

Sklare argued that Israel's creation and existence had restored what he called "a sense of meaning" for American Jews after the Second World War: At least for the inhabitants of Lakeville, it could seem that "something new, clean and good was born" out of the genocide. Thus, were Israel to be annihilated, the final victory would—in some metaphysical sense—belong to Hitler, and American Jewry would be faced with a "complete loss of meaning" and "total anomie." Sklare's analysis suggested that it was because the destruction of Israel would threaten the psychic existence of American Jewry itself that people felt so strongly that the country had to be supported. At the same time, he suggests, its victory ensured the even tenor of American Jewish life could continue largely undisturbed.

It is perhaps in this largely forgotten pamphlet that we encounter the most searching and thoughtful exploration of the roots of American Jewry's impassioned engagement with Israel in the moment of its emergence—before "standing with Israel" was taken for granted and before it became regarded as a normal and self-evident dimension of communal life, an aspect so essential to being Jewish that any deviation would itself seem remarkable.

American public backing for Israel in the 1967 Six-Day War revealed the existence of an essentially supportive national political environment that has only begun to fracture in recent years; American Jewry itself, never a monolith, came together in support as never before. "Israel became the focus of American Jewry," writes one scholar. Giving to the United Jewish Appeal rose from $65 million in 1966 to $240 million the next year and to $511 million by 1974. This was the real beginning of Israel political advocacy in the United States, though it was as yet on a small scale compared with today. As American Jewish rallies revealed how popular the cause had become, the AJC abandoned what was left of its residual "non-Zionism." There were still cautionary voices: One board member warned that the AJC had to "proceed with extreme caution.... The world is calling Israel a 'conqueror'... and the fate of five million Jews in the United States is being relegated to the fate of two million Jews in Israel." But this was the old guard speaking. When AJC leaders flew to Israel to urge peace on the prime minister, he asked them not to get involved in the question of territorial concessions: Unstinting backing was now expected, and with only sporadic exceptions it has been given ever since. In the AJC's annual report for 1966–67, "Israel" had come far down the list, below the struggle for civil rights and against discrimination and antisemitism; in 1967–68 it had moved to the top. And there it stayed.[25]

Yet in one critical respect the times remained very different from ours. There were already voices, many of them Jewish, warning that the country's military triumphs and territorial conquests might yet yield only a Pyrrhic victory. But condemnation of Israel was not yet automatically connected to the issue of antisemitism. In the 1950s, this was still associated in the minds of most American Jews with Nazism and ideas of white supremacy and racial prejudice—what was left of a world "that had seemingly been destroyed with Hitler's armies," in the words of the ADL, but that had not been completely eradicated. A conference to discuss antisemitism that the ADL held in New York in 1962 offers an intriguing snapshot of how the subject was understood at that time. Participants focused chiefly on right-wing extremism (which they saw as on the wane), Christian fundamentalism, and surviving patterns of social and professional discrimination. A sociology professor talked about stereotypes and the difficulty of really understanding the phenomenon theoretically. There was discussion of continued exclusion from resorts and private clubs, of the malleability of youth, and of fostering the ability to "agree to disagree." There was surprisingly little discussion of the civil rights movement or the fight to end segregation, however, and two matters, which would today be inseparable from any treatment of the subject, simply never came up. One was the Holocaust; the other was Israel. In only a few years, things were to change radically.[26]

IN THE MIDDLE EAST

On the eve of the 1956 Suez crisis, the Israeli government had become increasingly anxious about Egypt's charismatic ruler, Colonel Nasser. Secret talks with Egypt over their differences had led nowhere, and Ben-Gurion became convinced that "this Nasser Schmasser," as he privately referred to him, needed to be taught a lesson. A series of tit-for-tat raids and killings across the border ensued. Then came the news of an arms deal Nasser had brokered with the Czech government that threatened to alter the balance of power and give the USSR a foothold in the Middle East. Alarmed, Ben-Gurion gave a speech in the Knesset filled with foreboding historical allusions.

> The rulers of Egypt are buying these arms with one goal only: to uproot the State of Israel and its people.... The head of the ruling military faction in Cairo has announced that its war is aimed not only against Israel but against world Jewry and against Jewish finance which rules the United States. This kind of talk is known to us from Hitler's day and it is highly mystifying that the Czechoslovakian government in particular is ignoring the Nazi dogma that is being sounded anew on the banks of the Nile.[27]

Nasser as the new Hitler! The Arabs as Nazis! The challenge facing Israel was thus presented as a continuation of the old antisemitic persecutions of the Jews of Europe. Time and again, fearing encirclement by the Arabs and waiting for that charismatic leader who would lead them to victory, Ben-Gurion repeated the Nazi analogy. And yet that was for the public. In private, to his close confidants, he told a different story, no less pessimistic about Israel's chances of survival, but much less rooted in the invocation of antisemitism.

Nahum Goldmann was head of the World Jewish Congress and one of the chief negotiators of reparations with the West German government in the early 1950s. An ardent and prominent Zionist, he had worked and clashed with Ben-Gurion for years. In his memoirs he paints a vivid portrait of the Israeli leader: dominating and mercurial, a brilliant and utterly unscrupulous politician with an unrivaled sense of history. Their main disagreement was over the question of negotiations with the Arab states. Although Ben-Gurion wanted Goldmann to handle the issue for him, Goldmann believed Ben-Gurion was too suspicious and vengeful ever to allow for peace. A conversation convinced Goldmann he was right. It was a summer evening in 1956 and the two men were alone on Ben-Gurion's balcony. As was his way, Ben-Gurion began talking, and what he said left Goldmann, an experienced diplomat, stunned. "I don't understand your optimism," Ben-Gurion began.

> Why should the Arabs make peace? If I was an Arab leader I would never make terms with Israel. That is natural: we have taken their country. Sure God promised it to us, but what does that matter to them? Our God is not theirs. We come from Israel, but two thousand years ago, and what is that to them? There has been antisemitism, the Nazis, Hitler, Auschwitz, but was that their fault? They only see one thing: we have come here and stolen their country.... It's simple: we have to stay strong and maintain a powerful army. Our whole policy is there. Otherwise, the Arabs will wipe us out.[28]

Arab hostility, in short, even when expressed in eliminationist rhetoric that evoked the past, stemmed from a struggle over land: Ben-Gurion understood that in Arab eyes Zionism was just robbery.

It was hard to square the public rhetoric with the bleaker and surely more dispassionate assessment Ben-Gurion gave Goldmann in private.

Ben-Gurion was not alone in distinguishing European antisemitism from the sources of Arab hostility. In fact, the distinction was commonplace for a generation of Zionists who firmly believed that once the Jews had left Europe behind and possessed a country of their own, antisemitism would disappear. The Dutch Zionist Peretz Bernstein, author of a pioneering 1926 essay on antisemitism, was categorical on the point: Once Jews were no longer minorities, antisemitism would be "finally liquidated." This did not mean, he went on, that Jews would not face enemies. On the contrary: "A Jewish people that lives in closed settlements in its own land will doubtless be exposed to the normal enmities of its neighboring peoples and war will alternate with peace, as has been the way of the world." But this would be nothing more, he stressed, than a *"normal* enmity." For the leading Revisionist Zionist theorist, Vladimir Jabotinsky, whose influential essay on "The Iron Wall" also appeared in those years, Arab hostility to Jewish settlement was likewise to be expected: It was in his view a familiar case of native resistance to colonization, and in his essay the word *antisemitism* never appears. Writing in 1934, Arthur Ruppin, the veteran German Zionist, noted: "The conflict between Jews and Arabs in Palestine resembles...not so much the anti-Semitism of a strong non-Jewish majority against a weak Jewish minority but much rather a rivalry between two equal nations. Such rivalry may be marked, but it lacks the tang of contempt and helplessness which renders anti-Semitism in Europe so hard to bear for the Jews." Ruppin, familiar with the historical struggle of Germans and Poles in the eastern borderlands of Europe, had no difficulty transposing this schema to the Middle East. For him, antisemitism had nothing to do with it. He knew the real thing too well.[29]

It was not just that Zionist thinkers did not believe the Arabs were antisemitic. To the outside observer, what is striking about much early Zionist thought—Theodor Herzl is only a partial exception—is that it seemed to devote relatively little attention to the Arabs as a political factor at all, and if and when it did, the thinking was chiefly wishful. Jabotinsky's acceptance of the likelihood of violence marked him out as unusual. Most of the time, competing Jewish schemes for Palestine were discussed as though the actual inhabitants of the land were less real than the Jews of the past and future, and a less concrete impediment to Zionist plans than the Ottoman authorities or later the British. The "Holy Land," Amnon Raz-Krakotzkin has suggested, was an "empty land" in the Zionist imagination, a terra nullius whose only real natives—those with a claim to it—could be Jews. This is something of an exaggeration: There was a long-standing Jewish interest in Arab culture and even in their supposedly common racial ancestry as "Semites." But such intellectual concerns, often refracted through the lens of European Orientalism or racial science, had few concrete political effects.[30]

Perhaps the earliest exploration of Arab attitudes toward Zionism, which appeared in 1899 in the work of the Jerusalem-born Eliyahu Sapir, implicitly warned of the consequences. He differentiated between Christian antisemitism, which he portrayed as irrational and never-ending, and Arab Muslim attitudes, which allowed for the possibility of Jewish integration, provided the Jews made sure "to feel entirely at home and not as guests in these countries, in their language and in their culture." But most settlers from Europe had next to no interest in the Arabs and never acquired Arabic: Many would likely have shared Max Nordau's view that their mission was to "expand the moral boundaries of Europe to the Euphrates." From his perspective, the idea that "in Palestine we will become Asiatics" was laughable: Were not the Jews, as Europeans, superior to the local population?[31]

It is true that there were dissenters. Ruppin, who had hoped at one stage for peaceful coexistence, was fairly unusual in trying to think through the question of the Arabs' attitude to the newcomers. In the 1920s, a former comrade of Ruppin's on the dovish wing of the Zionist camp, Hans Kohn, fell into despair after two Arabs were shot outside his house in apparent retaliation for some assaults on Jewish girls. Familiar with the problems of minorities from his boyhood in Prague, Kohn was shocked at the reaction of his fellow Jews. When a neighbor told him to say the murderers were Arabs, he wrote to a friend: "We have degenerated in a horrible way due to our nationalism.... One can say today that 95 percent of the Yishuv supports such murders.... Here innocent people were murdered, passersby. Even the Germans did nothing like this. The French intelligentsia was in turmoil about the Dreyfus Affair. Here the murder interests no one. Who can afford to be a part of this?... Where does it lead?... An indescribable racial hatred takes place here." In short, for Kohn, the real problem in the relationship with the Arabs was not their antisemitism but Jewish chauvinism. Kohn eventually left Palestine for good and settled in the United States, where he became a world authority on nationalism.[32]

Ben-Gurion was far more typical in that he never learned Arabic nor betrayed much interest in Arab history and society. An enormous recent biography of him in the crucial war years, which weighs in at more than one thousand pages, has almost nothing to say on his thinking about the Arabs at all. It is as though their hostility is simply assumed. He shared the view of the peace camp that Arab enmity was a threat, but as there was, in his view, nothing to be done about it, there was no point spending time talking about it either. "The Arabs do not seem to deserve political attention," a reviewer of the book has noted. Over time, there was a parting of the ways: Those Zionists who believed that the Jews "are the classic minority people" and should avoid inflicting the sins once inflicted on them mostly either left Palestine, retreated into a kind of internal exile, or ended up, much later, backing the country's fledgling human rights movement, while the rest, as Kohn had noted, mostly avoided the issue or assumed that the deterrent of overwhelming force would remain the best and perhaps the only means to manage the Jewish-Arab relationship. Chaim Weizmann warned, as did others, as early as 1930, that a nationalist movement was spreading among the Palestinians, creating a generation who "from their point of view are as 'Zionist' as we are." Antisemitism was in short an irrelevance; rather than attributing Arab anger at Zionism to it, Jewish nationalists like Weizmann acknowledged the force of nationalism as a political movement among the Arabs too.[33]

What we therefore need to explain is why, if the question of Arab antisemitism was hardly discussed in the 1930s, it was being regularly trotted out half a century later to explain the hostility Israel faced from its neighbors and generating in the process a mountain of mostly polemical literature on the topic. (In contrast, the study of Israeli racist stereotyping of Arabs has lagged noticeably.) Of course, to assert that the fundamental impediment to peace in the Middle East is Arab antisemitism is to say that it is not issues that we need to take into account but an irrational and despicable attitude. A revisionist school of historians has countered this by extolling the relatively secure place of Jews in Muslim societies over the centuries and even highlighting the contrast between this and the fraught predicament of Jews within Christendom. Both schools of thought offer a partial view. If the one exaggerates antisemitism's scale and significance, especially in the pre-1950 Middle East, the other risks skating over the more problematic and troublesome aspects of a complex set of social relationships that extended over centuries. But if we leave the polemics to one side, the basic contours of the story are not hard to discern, thanks to new scholarship that sheds fresh light on it.[34]

Ancient Jewish communities under the sway of Islamic rulers were to be found across the lands that stretched from Morocco to Iran.

Like Christians, they enjoyed a status inferior to Muslims yet were simultaneously respected and protected as people of the Book. They enjoyed a substantial degree of communal autonomy and suffered nothing comparable to the historical scale of Christian anti-Jewish persecution. Islam also lacked the powerful theological animus against Jews that Christians held against them from the start. Thus, although food riots and other explosions of discontent were common in the cities of the region, outbursts on the grounds of faith were relatively rare. Probably the best-known blood-libel episode in the Middle East, the so-called Damascus affair of 1840, when Jews were arrested and tortured to death after an elderly Italian priest and his servant disappeared, turns out on closer investigation to have had little or nothing to do with Muslim views of the Jews—even though the blood libel was widely believed by Arab *Christians*—and more to do with the meddling of European consuls and Great Power politics in the eastern Mediterranean. In the second half of the nineteenth century, when European political conceptions of nationality, statehood, and imperialism came to the Middle East, antisemitism was another of these imports, part of a larger phenomenon of the emergence of interconfessional violence. The very fact that it needed to be imported indicates perhaps the very different kind of society that it was entering.[35]

The first signs of an Arab interest in European antisemitism seem to have come through Catholic channels via translations by Arab Christians of nineteenth-century French antisemitic texts. Reporting on the rise of antisemitic politics in Europe, the popular Arab periodical *al-Manar* described and denounced the Dreyfus affair in 1898, its first year of publication, noting that French antisemites were motivated by racial hatred, not religious difference. Through such examples, the irrationality of European racism could serve to underscore the superior reasonableness of Muslim attitudes—a key concern for Arab modernizers at the time. Before the First World War there was already discussion of these issues in the Arab press of North

Africa, and in the interwar period, as antisemitism grew in Europe, commentary intensified. By this time the connection between antisemitism and the Zionist program was hard to mistake. One newspaper ran a forty-five-part series on Hitler and the Jews; another, *Filastin*, attacked Nazi antisemitism directly: "The Jews are oppressed only because they are Jews, no more, and there is no justification for that." Arab public opinion, emerging around a new middle class in these years, was well aware of the extreme imperialism of the Nazis and Fascists. *Filastin* tried to get a basic point across:

> The Arab Palestinians don't need Fascists or Nazis to be motivated against the Zionists. The hatred against the Zionist plan in Palestine grew long before Nazism and Fascism....But always, when Arabs protest the pro-Zionist policies of England, we heard: Arab Palestinians learned it from the Nazis. And the English believe this? Reality is different. The Arabs don't expel the Jews from their home, but those foreigners want to push the Arabs out of the country.[36]

Well aware that Fascism threatened to put wind in Zionist sails, Arabs in Palestine worried that the Nazi policy of driving Germany's Jewish population abroad was likely to bring more settlers into Palestine. At the same time, growing anti-British sentiment brought some in the Palestinian leadership into alliance with the Third Reich: The Mufti of Jerusalem is by far the best-known case. Having fled to Berlin to escape arrest by the British and thrown his hand in with the Nazis, the increasingly antisemitic Mufti gambled on Berlin's victory in the war. But as his Palestinian rivals foresaw, his policy yielded nothing but failure not only for the Germans—his efforts in Palestine fell on stony ground—but also for the Palestinians themselves. Like anticolonial movements elsewhere around the globe, Arab nationalists sought to hedge their bets during the Second World War. But unlike, say, the Indian nationalist movement—which faced the same predicament of how to resist the British without falling into the arms of the Germans—the Palestinians lacked both organizational capacity and far-sighted political leadership in depth. In fact, despite the Mufti, there is plenty of evidence both in Palestine and elsewhere for a broader Arab stance of either neutrality or pro-Allied sympathy proffered in the hope that the Allies would support Arab independence after the war. In October 1944, by which time the tide of the fighting was flowing unmistakably in the Allies' direction, the Alexandria Protocol that preceded the formation of the Arab League noted with regret "the woes which had been inflicted upon the Jews in Europe, but insisted that their question should not be confused with that of Zionism, because it would be unjust to solve the problem of the Jews by inflicting injustice on the Palestinian Arabs."[37]

It was not so much the European war as the colonial system that preceded it and threatened to outlast it that made the position of the indigenous Jewish minorities in the Arab lands precarious. The rise of pan-Islamism as an anti-colonial movement fueled a discourse ill-prepared to draw a distinction between Zionists and Jews—a distinction that in any case it was improbable the illiterate strata of the population would be likely to make. The Muslim Brotherhood often conflated Zionists with Jews, veering frequently into outright anti-semitism. As for secular Arab nationalists, they too increasingly identified the Jews as proxies for a European colonialism that was seeking to remain in control amid the stresses of its own internecine war. In Iraq the bloody wartime attack on the Jews of Baghdad known as the Farhud took place in precisely such a context—as the Germans and the British tussled for control of the city, the country, and the Middle East: The targeting of women and children on that occasion was unprecedented, as was the scale of the death toll.

On top of all this, growing anxiety about Zionist intentions was also gradually jeopardizing the position of the Jewish communities of the Arab world. Even Arabic-speaking Jews with deep historical ties to the countries they lived in were increasingly associated with Zionism in the minds of many fellow Arabs. In November 1945, riots in Cairo on the anniversary of the Balfour Declaration resulted in six deaths, hundreds of injuries, and a synagogue being burned down. More serious rioting left more than one hundred dead a few days later in Libya: It had been triggered not only by news of events in Egypt but also by rumors that the Great Powers might hand the country back to the Italians. The Jews of North Africa and the Middle East were coming to be seen both as stand-ins for European imperialism and as closet Zionists. It would not take much to undermine their position entirely.

The event that did so more than any other was the Arab-Jewish War of 1948. Months earlier, the UN, faced with an imminent British withdrawal from Palestine, had proposed partition of the territory. Although it was voted through the UN General Assembly, both Jews and Arabs had major reservations. While the plan was hailed publicly by most Zionist organizations—it allocated them around 56 percent of the territory compared with the less than 10 percent they then owned— many Jews nonetheless doubted that the anticipated Jewish state, with its extensive tracts of desert and an envisaged Arab minority of 45 percent of the total population, would be the end of the matter, and they believed they could win more territory with fewer Arabs under their control in the future. Confronted with the loss of most of the mandate's territory, despite their much larger population, the Arabs declared their opposition from the outset.

As in India the previous year, therefore, the British withdrawal created a lethal vacuum of authority. Fighting between the two camps erupted almost as soon as the partition plan was announced, but it escalated in the spring of 1948. Massacres were committed on both sides, but the Jewish Haganah was far better organized and had more to lose than the invading Arab armies: A significant number of Haganah fighters were survivors from the war in Europe and they were under the command of a unitary political leadership determined to come out of the conflict on the most favorable possible terms, both territorially and demographically. Jewish forces soon asserted their military superiority, and huge numbers of people were displaced. Probably around 175,000 Palestinians had already fled their homes by May 1, many of them ejected or expelled by Jewish troops. By the time Ben-Gurion announced the creation of the state of Israel in mid-May, the number of Arab refugees was around 400,000, and by early 1949 it had perhaps doubled again. The numbers and circumstances are, needless to say, disputed, as is the degree to which the outcome reflected a deliberate strategy of what we would now call ethnic cleansing. But an internal Haganah intelligence assessment reckoned that some 75 percent of the exodus was the direct result of Israeli operations.[38]

What came to be known as the *nakba* (catastrophe)—involving the destruction and depopulation of hundreds of historic Palestinian Arab settlements—marked the last and politically the most enduring of the violent demographic upheavals that were driven by nationalism and war and that ran through the 1940s in a zone stretching from the Baltic to the eastern Mediterranean.

The sudden establishment by force of arms of a Jewish sovereign state in historically Muslim lands and this massive displacement of their Arab population was a huge and to this day unresolved shock to Arab expectations, and it was really then that European-style antisemitic conspiracy theories began to circulate widely around the Middle East. We should bear in mind that whereas a taboo against overt antisemitism had just emerged out of bitter historical experience in the postwar West, in the Arab lands, where there had been relatively little antisemitism and no Holocaust, the taboo did not exist. Much as in Europe and North America at the time of the Russian revolution, *The Protocols of the Elders of Zion* were embraced as a way of explaining sudden and dramatic shifts in world power, a means of understanding the otherwise almost inexplicable triumph of a Jewish state and—a little later—the swift rise of American power across the postwar Middle East.[39] For Arab elites, it was also convenient to blame their political, organizational, and military shortcomings on satanic forces rather than ineptitude. Islamicist intellectuals did their bit. References to global Jewish power crop up in the texts of postwar Islamicist movements such as Hamas and Islamic Jihad; Ayatollah Khomeini's 1970 *Governance of the Jurist* is not unusual in warning that the Jews have been the enemies of Muslims from the start and portraying this "cunning and resourceful group of people" as aiming at world domination. Along with the *Protocols*, Holocaust denial spread too, although in the Middle East this did not reflect the right-wing European penchant for quasi-scientific demonstrations minimizing the numbers of Jews killed (as though if they were shrunk sufficiently this would lighten or justify the crimes of Fascism). Rather, the spur was rooted in the post-1948 conflict itself: It expressed chiefly perhaps a desire to refuse the status of victimhood to a people who were perpetrating violence against the Palestinians, alluding to the Holocaust to justify expulsions and engaging in their own form of denialism (about the Palestinian *nakba*) at the same time.[40]

Some Western-oriented Arab critics quickly understood that the spread of conspiratorial antisemitism was a kind of political trap that hindered a realistic appraisal of the balance of forces in the Middle East and undermined those making the case for Palestine in the West. One of them was Fayez Sayegh. The son of a Syrian Presbyterian minister, he had studied in the United States before becoming the acting director of the Arab Information Center and the face of the

Arab League's public diplomacy in America in the 1950s. Over time Sayegh became the most effective spokesman for the Palestinian cause the United States had seen. But cleansing Arab propaganda of any hint of antisemitism turned out to be a challenge. Even if most Americans who met him realized Sayegh himself was beyond reproach, other Arab diplomats were less cautious or careful in their language than he was. Moreover, so far as many American Jews were concerned, the sight of an Arab criticizing Israel was enough to trigger allegations of "anti-Semitism by detour."[41]

In one of his last articles, William Zukerman wrote that Arab opposition to Israel was political and had "little if anything to do with traditional anti-Semitism." But American Jews, in his view, had lost the capacity to appreciate this because they had developed a tendency to "denounce as anti-Semitism any ordinary criticism of Israel's policies which [they] would be the first to make if similar policies were pursued by another state." As if to bear out his words, more or less as soon as the Arab Information Center began operating in the United States, it was condemned by the ADL and accused of working with antisemites. The next year, the ADL followed this up with a book in which these allegations were repeated and extended. It claimed implausibly both that Arab propagandists aimed at "the utter destruction of Jewish prestige in America" and that they were whipping up antisemitism to weaken Jewish voices in support of Israel. These were fairly novel arguments at the time. But as in the Middle East itself, the Arab cause was indeed attracting marginal figures from the far Right who came to offer their support, and while Sayegh understood such contacts were toxic and undesirable and warded them off, some of his colleagues, whether through ignorance, malevolence, or stupidity, were not as careful. Sayegh increasingly felt himself to be undermined by the ignorance and corruption of the Middle Eastern regimes behind him. He openly castigated senior Arab diplomats for circulating antisemitic materials and took to the airwaves to defend the work of the center and to clarify his own position. "I am anti-Israel. I am anti-Zionist also," he said, "but I am NOT anti-Jewish."[42]

In 1965 Sayegh helped establish the Palestine Research Center in Beirut as the Palestinian nationalist movement crystallized around the Palestine Liberation Organization (PLO). There he published a key text, *Zionist Colonialism in Palestine*, a work that was to shape global perceptions of the conflict indelibly. But it was another work (written this time in Arabic), also emerging out of the Palestine Research Center milieu in Beirut, that best illuminates a fascinating debate within the Palestinian camp at this time about antisemitism itself. In his extensive 1970 study of the Talmud and its relationship to Zionism, Ass'ad Razzouk, a PLO researcher with a doctorate in philosophy from Tübingen, argued that the Arabs needed to abandon their credulous acceptance of European conspiracy theories. The Arabs knew little about Judaism, he wrote, and in particular they knew nothing about the actual Talmud even though they feared the very mention of it. Antisemitism was political idiocy and a burden that would alienate Western sympathy and do nothing for the Palestinian cause.

Razzouk's remarkable study briskly disposes of the existing Arabic literature on the subject, a mix of medieval anti-Jewish theological polemic and rehashed antisemitic nonsense, before going on to introduce the text itself and then, in perhaps his most interesting intervention, to explore the connections between Jewish religious thought and Zionist political philosophy. He concludes, after an exploration of various Zionist thinkers, that the Talmud had had a rather small direct influence upon them, even though the influence of religion in some more general sense was undeniable. The findings were squarely in line with debates going on at the same time—and since—among Jewish thinkers. Razzouk's point was a simple one, that the Palestinian struggle stood on its own terms and should not undermine itself:

"Until when will we remain our own worst enemy, continuing to prejudice the justice of our cause?"[43]

One of the rare Israeli commentators who was able and willing to sympathize with the predicament of Arab intellectuals like Sayegh and Razzouk was the writer Nissim Rejwan. Born in Iraq in 1924 and active in the literary life of Baghdad in the 1940s before being forced to leave for Israel in 1951, Rejwan was among the relatively few Jews of his generation to have an insider's understanding of the region. Perhaps for this reason he was an unsparing critic of those polemicists among his countrymen who kept banging on about Arab antisemitism. His particular target was fellow Arabist Yehoshafat Harkabi, the chief of Israeli military intelligence during the Suez crisis and a prominent commentator. Rejwan was unimpressed with Harkabi's work on antisemitism in the Middle East, which he regarded as merely providing people with an excuse to ignore what Arab critics of Israel were actually saying. In 1968 Rejwan wrote to a Canadian colleague that antisemitism was "a totally foreign importation" into the Arab world. Laying bare ambiguities that continue to haunt us today, he went on:

> Harkabi gives me the feeling that he wants to eat the cake and have it. He himself, as a Zionist, would not really make any distinction between Zionism and Judaism, Israeli and Jew—but he asks the Arabs to do so, and the trouble is that even if they do so, he would not agree; he would still call them anti-Semites since, as is often said here, you cannot draw the line between Zionism and Judaism as the former is the "national liberation movement" of the Jews.[44]

Was it fair, Rejwan asked, to impute antisemitism to "people who one knows are anti-Zionists and anti-Israeli rather than anti-Semitic"?

It was, he confessed, a "tricky problem." Some years later, he was still mulling it over. In a long letter to the American critic Irving Howe, Rejwan wrote about the growing prevalence of the term *Arab anti-Semitism*. He agreed that antisemitic literature in Arabic was worryingly popular and he had no doubt about its pernicious character, but he still had misgivings.

> All this granted, for me it remains almost the ultimate in irony that what Arab anti-Semites have been doing is nothing more horrible than accepting Zionism's own definition of itself!...After 1948, Israel—the consummation, however partial, of Zionism—defined itself in such a way and promulgated laws and regulations of such a nature that it virtually turned all the 90 percent of Jews living outside its borders into Israeli "nationals." Who are we, then, to accuse Arabs of anti-Semitism when all they have done is fallen right into the ideological trap which the Zionists set for them?[45]

Rejwan helps us to see how the Arab-Israel conflict was beginning to shift perceptions of antisemitism. In the minds of ardent Zionists, he was saying, the creation of Israel was tantamount to the political fulfillment of Judaism, and so it was tempting to charge antisemitism against critics of Zionism even if they were not antisemites in the old racial sense. Put another way: If one really believes that Zionism and the Jewish state speak for all Jews, then it may in fact become impossible to see criticism of Zionism or Israel as anything but antisemitism. And yet others—Jews and non-Jews alike—may see things very differently and may moreover find it important to preserve a distinction between the two. As we shall see later, it is precisely this divergence that creates confusion and discord today. But in the 1950s, few American or European Jews seriously believed Israel spoke for all Jews: AJC President Jacob Blaustein's argument with Ben-Gurion made clear what *he* thought. The new Jewish state was tiny, made up very largely of immigrants, and in need of help; other Jewish communities around the world were much older or much larger, or both. In the coming decades all this would change. Rejwan was thus in his way anticipating the emergence of what would become for many of today's anti-antisemitism campaigners a self-evident truth, and for their critics and opponents a self-serving elision. The era in which antisemitism could be discussed without reference to Israel was about to end.

CHAPTER 7

A New Antisemitism?
The International Arena

Zionism has become a dirty word. How far this attack on Zionism is
a disguise for old or new anti-semitism and how far it arises from a
genuine disagreement with and a critique of the present character and
policies of the state is a question Jews must urgently seek to answer. It
is far too easy to raise the spectre of anti-semitism, call for unity and
thereby ignore the changes in the Jewish position in the world that
these developments represent.

ANTONY LERMAN, "CONTINUITY AND CHANGE," 1984[1]

In what became known at the time as the "international swastika outbreak," the winter of 1959–60 saw a rash of vandalism against Jewish
sites on at least four continents. It started in West Germany, where
the slogan "Germans demand that Jews get out" was found scrawled
on the synagogue in Cologne, accompanied by swastikas. Within days
similar graffiti had defaced stores, tombstones, and places of worship
in cities across Western Europe, in New York, and as far afield as Australia, New Zealand, and South America. In West Germany alone more
than eight hundred incidents were recorded by the authorities by mid-
February 1960. Hundreds more acts, mostly involving swastikas and
offensive graffiti, were registered in the United States over the same
period. International outrage against the revival of Nazism in West
Germany reached a crescendo, and doubts were publicly expressed
about the country's suitability to be a member of NATO, which it had
joined only a few years earlier.[2]

The German police made numerous arrests but had difficulty tracing the culprits. Two men detained for the Cologne incident turned out to be members of a far-Right party and delivered antisemitic diatribes at their trial. Yet of the suspects picked up in the coming weeks only a third or so appeared to be driven by political convictions; many were very young and a lot were copycats out for some fun. Then it turned out that both defendants had often visited East Germany, and another neo-Nazi confirmed they had been under instructions from an East German agent to intensify antisemitic activities. Police suspicions were eventually confirmed: The whole operation had started as a KGB disinformation plot to strain Western attitudes toward their West German ally. Inspired by news of earlier antisemitic incidents in the country that had prompted press speculation about a Nazi revival, the KGB had launched an undercover operation to weaken the Western alliance and called it Operation Zarathustra (according to a defector) to indicate that German antisemitism was as immortal as Nietzsche's classic text *Thus Spake Zarathustra*.[3]

What was not widely known at the time was that the KGB had first carried out a dummy run inside Russia itself by sending a group of agents to desecrate Jewish gravestones and paint graffiti in a village a little outside Moscow. Other agents then reported on the locals' reaction. Some were appalled; many were frightened and mystified. But quite a few revealed their own prejudices and began to carry out similar actions of their own. Only two months before the start of the "swastika epidemic" in the West, a synagogue was burned down in the suburb of Malakhovka, and the wife of its caretaker murdered. Flyers had been pasted on walls with antisemitic slogans from the tsarist era.[4]

Thus European society revealed itself to be split, on both sides of the Iron Curtain, almost twenty years after the war, between those for whom the swastika brought back fearful memories and those for whom it represented a license to rebel. Of course, there was a significant difference. On the Soviet side, a government agency was responsible for instigating the whole affair, and its creator, Ivan Agayants, head of the KGB's Western European Department, became a legend within the agency as the inventor of what its official history terms "active measures." The Kremlin tried to hush up reports of antisemitism's resurgence at home and never admitted to its role in originating the "epidemic" itself. On the Western side, in contrast, the condemnation was immediate and sweeping; indeed, in several European countries it reinforced voices calling for legislation against hate speech. But the episode also had another consequence that no doubt had not been in the minds of the KGB when it planned the operation: It resulted in the question of antisemitism landing on the agenda of the UN. This turned out to be the beginning of the internationalization of campaigning against antisemitism, a process full of twists and turns that is still underway today and that forms the subject of the chapters that follow.

With decolonization in Africa and Asia, the UN was becoming a genuinely global organization where the tensions and debates around the epic struggle over the fate of peoples under European colonial rule were played out before the world's media. Thanks mostly to incoming African, Caribbean, and Asian states, the General Assembly grew from some 60 members in the early 1950s to 110 by 1962: This transformed the UN's entire relationship to Europe. To the newcomers, European concerns and its recent history mattered less than they did to the UN's original members, and empire, colonialism, and race mattered more. Nonetheless, news of the "swastika epidemic" prompted the drafting of a General Assembly resolution condemning "manifestations of antisemitism and other religious and so-called racial prejudices." Both the Israelis and the US government supported the resolution; raising the issue of antisemitism was, for them, a means to put pressure on the Soviet Union and spotlight the treatment of Soviet Jews. The Soviet delegation countered by pointing the finger at rising neo-Nazism and accusing the West of support for "Fascist" West Germany. When others suggested connecting anti-Jewish prejudice to racism in general, a compromise formula emerged that cited antisemitism alongside other "religious and racial prejudices" that were said to be reminiscent of the Nazis.

But this version, which had originated in committee, was changed once again when Arab League members insisted that any mention of antisemitism required a countervailing reference to the plight of "the Arab minority in Palestine." More significant, news had just arrived from South Africa of the Sharpeville massacre, where dozens of African protesters were shot dead by police; it was this tragedy that turned apartheid into the overwhelming issue of the day and marked the internationalization of the anti-apartheid movement. Compared with the scale of the ongoing struggle against racial discrimination and segregation, antisemitism—though it loomed large in European and American minds—seemed to many of the newer UN members like yesterday's issue. The final resolution that passed condemning "racial, religious and national hatred" made no reference to antisemitism at all.[5]

The fight against antisemitism had clearly become just another piece on the Cold War chessboard, and any attempt by the United States or Israel to advance it met with opposition: The Soviet delegation wanted to "get the Americans off their antisemitism kick" and warned—in vain—that their efforts to raise the matter would be countered by reference to Zionism. But the issue of antisemitism had become overshadowed by decolonization too: A large voting bloc of new states simply did not consider what they saw a European problem to be a priority, and some of them were increasingly sympathetic to charges—which the 1956 Suez crisis made far more plausible—that Israel itself was a beneficiary and an agent of European empire. The colonial connection that Zionists like Jabotinsky had underscored before the Second World War was now a liability.[6]

The old mid-century linkage between antisemitism and racism

was also itself coming under strain. Other forms of racial discrimination seemed more urgent to many UN members and, almost imperceptibly, the meaning of *racism* was shifting. The term had been popularized in the late 1930s by the German Jewish sexologist Magnus Hirschfeld, who had argued for a view of Nazism that placed antisemitism in the context of long-standing theories of racial differentiation. In the 1940s and 1950s, a shared commitment to anti-racism had brought Jewish rights groups into the heart of the civil rights movement in the United States and elsewhere. By the 1960s—under the dual impact of the American anti-segregation struggle and the fight against apartheid—the term was coming to connote first and foremost a problem of black suffering at white hands, whether that meant American slavery or African colonial exploitation by Europeans.

Arab nationalists had traced a connection between Nazi racism and Zionism more or less from the start, and they had consistently argued that Palestine should not be asked to pay the price for Nazi anti-Jewish persecution. In late 1947, during the UN debate over the partition of Palestine, the Syrian delegate Farid Zeineddine, a Sorbonne-trained international lawyer and scholar of nationalism, went further and insisted that Zionism itself was based upon racial discrimination. The UN, he argued, "which had been formed through the common endeavour to destroy Nazism, should not support its parallel, Zionism." Connected to larger theories of empire and capitalism, the concept of racism itself could be extended in support of the Arab cause. Once the PLO found a voice of its own in the mid-1960s, its leaders immediately adopted the idiom of anti-racism and anti-colonialism. "Zionism is a colonialist movement in its inception, aggressive and expansionist in its goals, racist and segregationist in its configurations, and fascist in its means and aims" declared an article in its founding charter. Fayez Sayegh framed the challenge of Palestine in the same liberationist terms. "As a colonial venture," he wrote, "which anomalously came to bloom precisely when colonialism was beginning to fade away, [Zionism] is in fact a challenge to all anti-colonial peoples in Asia and Africa." It was, he concluded, "a racist system animated by doctrines of racial segregation, racial exclusiveness, and racial supremacy."[7]

After Israel's victory in the 1967 Six-Day War and its military occupation of the West Bank and Gaza Strip, a Third World bloc took up the Palestinian cause as part of the larger struggle against colonialism and found in the UN—as the Algerian National Liberation Front had before them—a forum that they could hope to dominate and that offered them global attention. The Arab states' influence was enhanced by the rise of the petroleum producers' cartel, OPEC, in 1973, and was demonstrated when several UN states severed diplomatic relations with Israel. The following year, Yasser Arafat, head of the PLO, was invited to address the General Assembly, and the PLO was granted observer status. But it was the General Assembly's controversial 1975 resolution equating Zionism with racism that showed how far the language of Sayegh's analysis a decade earlier had become common wisdom. The text opens by denouncing not only doctrines of "racial differentiation or superiority" but also "the unholy alliance between South African racism and zionism." It recalls an earlier declaration affirming that "international co-operation and peace require the achievement of national liberation and independence, the elimination of colonialism and neo-colonialism, foreign occupation, zionism, *apartheid* and racial discrimination in all its forms." And it adds a statement from the Organization of African Unity "that the racist regime in occupied Palestine and the racist regimes in Zimbabwe and South Africa have a common imperialist origin, forming a whole and having the same racist structure." After all that, its finding—that Zionism was a form of racism—was something of a foregone conclusion.[8]

The resolution came as a shock to Israel and its defenders. Having failed to produce a declaration against antisemitism, the UN was now apparently allowing Israel to be treated not as if it were heir to the victims of the Third Reich—as it saw itself and as much of the West saw it—but rather its successor. Daniel Patrick Moynihan, the combative US ambassador to the UN, had already understood that the United States would need to "go into opposition" at the UN (as he put it) as the General Assembly became unfriendly territory, and he viewed the resolution correctly as another disguised anti-American vote, a product of post-Vietnam antipathy across the Third World. Washington now not only saw its interests increasingly aligned with Israel's, but also moved to sideline the UN—which it had once dominated—by operating over the next two decades on the assumption that it was basically a lost cause. For their part, Israeli diplomats saw the UN as an institution hopelessly weighted against their nation.

The two countries—the United States and Israel—struggled to make sense of the dramatic shift in global opinion since that time barely a couple of decades earlier when the United States had been widely seen abroad as an anti-imperial power, and Israel had been hailed in Europe and South America as an example of national emancipation. By the mid-1970s, the Vietnam War stamped the United States as the neo-imperialist superpower par excellence, and Israel was now widely seen as an occupying power on the wrong side of the struggle against colonialism. Some commentators believed that this growing criticism reflected a general sense of anti-American Third Worldism or else they saw Moscow's hand at work. But others discerned what they called a "new antisemitism" with Israel as its target.

"What is wrong with current speech and writing," a scholar of the English language once noted, "is not that they use new words but that they misuse the old." (Thus George Sampson in his introduction to Richard Chenevix Trench's classic of Victorian philology, *On the Study of Words*.) Whether or not the concept of antisemitism was being misused exactly by being yoked to Israel is debatable, but we can certainly see it being used in a quite different global setting. As a way of explaining hostility to Israel in terms that connected it to the Jewish past rather than its geopolitical role in the present, the invocation of antisemitism in this context marked a new stage in the history of the concept. Antisemitism did not by any means lose its historical associations with the old animosities shown to a historic minority people; on the contrary, its power as critique derived from those memories and echoes of the past. But these associations were now increasingly overlaid with other political connotations. A reaction to the hostility encountered at the UN and elsewhere, this new reading of antisemitism reflected and emerged out of deeper shifts in cultural and intellectual thought in both the United States and Israel, and it is to explore these more closely that we should now turn.

THE DISCOVERY OF
AMERICAN JEWISH IDENTITY

By the 1970s, American Jewry was by any metric enjoying a period of extraordinary achievement. Its population had increased remarkably fast to some 5.7 million, and rising living standards propelled a move to the suburbs, where a completely unforeseen boom in synagogue construction presaged a vibrant new kind of community. Jewish life was changing: As the immigrant generation died out, their children and grandchildren threw out their old Yiddish books—the tongue from the Old Country that fewer and fewer spoke—and turned to the latest Saul Bellow or Philip Roth. Barriers in the workplace were coming down; the march into the boardroom, government, and academia was underway. As discrimination was curtailed, social scientific research into anti-Jewish prejudice, a flourishing and important field in the 1940s and 1950s, started to seem less and less urgent. A series of surveys starting in the early 1960s showed "a steady decline in the level of conventional antisemitic attitudes held by Americans." Other works drew similar conclusions: A former Anti-Defamation League director described the United States in 1982 as "more hospitable to us than to antisemitism." Polls carried out between the 1960s and the early 1980s overwhelmingly confirmed the trend.[9]

If people remained fearful, nonetheless, of what historian Henry Feingold called "the threat to Jewish survival in America," their perceptions of that threat differed widely. "Some may think American Jewry is threatened by a raging antisemitism," wrote Feingold in 1985, "while others see it drowning in a sea of perfume exuded by a society anxious to absorb it." As this suggests, statistical trends failed to allay the concern that more and more American Jews seemed gripped by antisemitism becoming serious again in the near future. There was, as Jerome Chanes wrote in his survey of the literature, a "perception gap": Increasing numbers of American Jews would tell pollsters they were "comfortable" in America and simultaneously say they regarded antisemitism as a "serious" and worsening problem.[10] Some experts saw this as "cognitive dissonance" or suggested American Jews had become "paranoid"; another talked about the anxiety being "wrongly-directed or excessive." The historian Edward Shapiro looked in another direction: Fears about antisemitism, he wrote, were "stoked by organizations whose very survival is at stake should American Jews come to believe that American anti-Semitism has become a marginal phenomenon. Without the existence of domestic anti-Semitism, much of the raison d'être of organizations such as the Anti-Defamation League...would be called into question."[11]

Feingold, who was among the most acute commentators on American Jewish life, had made the same point more generally. "When the threat to American Jewish survival stems more from acceptance than from raging anti-Semitism, agencies whose agendas rest solely on a defense function are threatened with a loss of function. Success, no less than failure...can be a cause of obsolescence." Feingold was writing about the American Jewish Committee, but the problem was much more acute for the hate fighters at the ADL. So perhaps it was not surprising that it was in fact two ADL leaders, Arnold Forster and Benjamin Epstein, whose 1974 book *The New Anti-Semitism* had sounded the alarm. Forster, a longtime ADL investigator who had spent the war years tussling with pro-Nazi groups, recounts in his memoirs with perhaps a tinge of regret how by the early 1970s "organized anti-Semitism as we had known it for more than thirty years" had fallen; it was at "a low ebb," a pale shadow of its prewar threat. Working for an anti-hate organization in a society where hate seemed to be harder to find, Forster and Epstein asked what at the time must have seemed an odd question: "Is the post–World War II honeymoon with the Jews over?" Their answer was predictable. Featuring hard-hitting ADL types hot on the trail of assorted nefarious bigots, their book inveighed against aging nativist preachers and moralized about the stereotyping of Jews in the media, decrying the film version of *Portnoy's Complaint* as "a cheap, vulgar, smutty, anti-Jewish diatribe." But as if sensing that none of this was truly rousing stuff, they exhorted readers to accept "some redefining of traditional notions of anti-Semitism." The threat from the Right was admittedly declining but—they claimed—a "new anti-Semitism" was on the rise that was manifesting itself in hostility to Israel; the authors castigated what they termed American society's widespread "unwillingness to comprehend the necessity of the existence of Israel to Jewish safety and survival in the world." The source of the problem? The radical Left.[12]

A new orthodoxy—that antisemitism was the same as opposition to Israel, and that it was therefore chiefly a problem of the Left rather than the Right—was being laid down. Thirty years later it would come to seem unassailable common sense to a lot of people, but at this time it was a novel argument. Presaging the neoconservative drift to the Right of some prominent American Jewish figures and organizations in the 1980s and 1990s, *The New Anti-Semitism* cited the radical Left's sins: its criticism of American support for Israel, its cheerleading for Moscow and the Communist movement, its exploitation of post-

Vietnam American war-weariness. The authors were especially worried by what they called "Trotskyist communists" and the impact of
far-Left groups on political attitudes and campus life. Then as now
there was plenty of anxiety about universities as breeding grounds for
radicalism. But from today's perspective, it is fascinating to see just
how unfamiliar such arguments seemed to be. Forster acknowledged
that the book aroused "not a little protest and resentment"; its authors
were even attacked for being overly ready to label people "virtual anti-
Semites."[13] But while admitting that the groups it criticized were
themselves highly vocal about not being antisemitic and saw their
views as purely political, the book nonetheless insisted that their actions
were "clearly anti-Jewish." The proof: They were working with "overt
anti-Semites." Not the American neo-Nazis of the past, these shad-
owy figures turned out, in the telling, to be Black nationalists. Perhaps
inevitably, given the American context, the authors of *The New Anti-
Semitism* thus raised the question of race.[14]

In 1907 the lawyer Louis Marshall, who had helped found the American Jewish Committee the year before, learned to his astonishment
that a Lower East Side Jewish debating club in New York was going
to support the motion that "the South would be justified in disenfran-
chising the Negro." "It seems incredible to me," wrote Marshall, "that
a body of Jews who have just emerged from virtual slavery, and who
are seeking in this country the privilege of voting, which was with-
held from them in the land where their ancestors have lived, should
for a moment consider the propriety of arguing in favor of the disenfranchisement of any citizens of this country."[15] Marshall had identified the key issue shaping black-Jewish relations in the United States.
In the era of Jim Crow, the denial of equal rights to blacks had been
pursued both through the law and through violence, most notably in
lynchings. In those very same decades, hundreds of thousands of eastern European Jews arrived in the United States, fleeing pogroms and

governmental persecution to find liberty: In this fashion, Jewish enfranchisement coincided with black disenfranchisement—their communal fates in America could not have been more starkly contrasting. As James Baldwin once noted, European Jews had found opportunity in America, while African Americans, who had been there for much longer, still had "no place to go."[16]

In the United States, political good fortune presupposed the benefits of whiteness, and Jews were certainly favored over the descendants of slaves, though because racialism was both widely believed and scientifically baseless there was inevitably disagreement about just how white they were. Some said there was no purer race while others viewed them as akin to blacks. "The Jews, the descendants of Shem, in every country... belong to the white race," argued a Nashville clergyman in 1867. "We know on Biblical authority, with mathematical certainty, that they are not Negroes, either before, at nor since the flood, but white." Yet some decades later, another author, Arthur Abernethy, wrote his polemical *The Jew a Negro*, where he insisted to the contrary that "the Jew of today, as well as his ancestors in other times, is the kinsman and descendant of the Negro." Deep into the twentieth century, Jews existed in an ambivalent zone, their racial status indeterminate.[17]

Although black American authors had long felt aggrieved at the way European immigrants were able to win acceptance in a country that denied it to them, they had initially tended to exempt Jews from such criticism on the grounds that they too were a people who knew suffering: "There is a similarity between the Jew and the Negro," wrote the *New York Age* in 1889. "One is despised almost as much as the other." During the Dreyfus affair many writers in the black press condemned the French for their antisemitism. Yet as violence against blacks in the South escalated, people wondered how it was that American Jewish organizations could lobby the US government to protest pogroms in Russia yet say nothing about the domestic persecution of fellow

American citizens. Black disappointment with Jewish silence grew. It scarcely helped that the same Mississippi senators who signed petitions to the tsar had publicly defended lynching in the name of "law and order." For the black press the parallels with Russia were self-evident. In July 1903, after a riot forced hundreds of black residents of Evansville, Indiana, to flee into nearby woods for safety, a local black paper wrote that "Negroes are fleeing from the American Kishineff."[18]

In working-class and leftist immigrant Jewish circles, America was readily viewed through a Russian lens and Jewish journalists frequently spoke out against racism and antiblack violence, especially when writing in Yiddish. *The Forward*, for instance, reported on Evansville under the headline NEGRO POGROMS. Yet not only did the major American Jewish organizations generally stay silent; some Jewish leaders even protested the parallel, claiming that pogroms targeted the innocent whereas lynchings allegedly punished the guilty. "Of all the morally wretched defenders of this American crime of lynching," wrote a black Chicago paper, "the American Jew who defends Negro lynchers while denouncing Russian massacres—and some do—is most contemptible." Shortly after this there was an effort in Maryland to disenfranchise black voters: Two of the main proponents of the measure were well-known figures in Baltimore's Jewish community, outright apologists for restricting the vote on racial lines. "The white race must prevail over barbarism," said Isidor Rayner. "And this can best be achieved by reducing the Negro vote to the utmost minimum in Maryland."[19]

In the interwar years, with the intensification of antisemitic politics both in Europe and also in the United States itself, American Jews did become more outspoken against racism. While many Southern Jews remained cautious and unwilling (even where they privately dissented) to challenge the prevailing bigotry of the white society around them, the far larger Jewish communities of the northern states, and their increasingly organized national leadership, propagated a message of interracial solidarity. Indeed, these years saw the start of efforts by communal leaders on both sides to forge connections.[20] The so-called black-Jewish alliance was in reality always uneven since there was an evident power asymmetry between the two sides: The black population needed much more help because the discrimination and violence they faced were far greater. The question of double standards still remained a sore point. "Why shed crocodile tears over the fate of Jews in Berlin," asked Oklahoma City's *Black Dispatch*, "when here in America we treat black folk the same every day?" Yet despite all this, in the face of Fascism an antiracist coalition took shape. "The race problem," stated W. E. B. Du Bois, "cuts across lines of class and physique and belief." The National Association for the Advancement of Colored People (NAACP) denounced Nazi antisemitism in the belief that this would help in the fight against American racism too. "We Negroes know what this means since it happened to us," said the NAACP's Walter White at the time of Kristallnacht. "What happened to one minority can happen to others—a lesson which Jews, Negroes and all minorities must learn." In 1947, after the NAACP formally requested support for an anti-lynching bill, the once aloof American Jewish Committee declared its intention to "join with other groups in the protection of the civil rights of the members of all groups irrespective of race, religion, color or national origin." For the next two decades, the AJC would stick firmly to the line that Jewish interests were best served by ensuring the rights of all.[21]

This new policy of fighting for civil rights across the board caused strains between Jewish communities in the South and Jews elsewhere. It was not that Southern Jews were supportive of Jim Crow; mostly they were on the liberal end of the white spectrum. But they were worried about their own vulnerability if they became identified with the black civil rights movement and they had some cause for concern: Jewish activists were indeed targeted and several Jewish civil rights workers were murdered. Pamphlets warned that "the Jews have destroyed racial segregation" and a rash of bombings across the South culminated in a 1958 attempt in Atlanta, Georgia, to blow up the main synagogue whose rabbi had supported the civil rights movement. The minuscule American Nazi Party, founded in 1959, made headlines out of all proportion to its size for almost a decade before the assassination of its leader led to infighting and fragmentation, but the real problem was the hate-filled racism endemic in white Southern society.[22] The well-known images of Martin Luther King Jr. and Rabbi Abraham Joshua Heschel arm in arm at the head of a march in Alabama in 1965 marked perhaps the high point of national black-Jewish solidarity. Less noticed at the time were the anxieties and unease of Southern Jewish rabbis, many of whom were conscious of the vulnerability of their constituents.

With the passing of major civil rights legislation in 1964 and 1965, the black-Jewish coalition started to fracture. Black nationalists resented what they saw as the paternalism of well-meaning white allies. The latter felt their support was not appreciated. Intellectuals such as Harold Cruse and James Baldwin penned unsentimental essays exploring black-Jewish relations while the young sociologist Gary Marx carried out the first systemic analysis of black prejudice. Finger-pointing polemics appeared with depressing regularity over the next two or three decades, and by the late 1980s the conflict had worsened on the page and off to the point that even the most farsighted analysts on either side found it hard to see how to move beyond it. "Black anti-Semitism and Jewish antiblack racism are real," wrote Cornel West in *Race Matters* in 1993, "and both are as profoundly American as cherry pie."[23]

Before looking into the range of sentiments and stereotypes often lumped together under the heading of black antisemitism, it is worth spending a moment on the other half of the pie. It goes against the grain for many of those concerned about antisemitism to pay attention to the forms of Jewish racism or to reflect on the larger social and cultural forces at play in race talk of all kinds. (Even, in some cases, to hear talk of racism at all: Lucy Dawidowicz for one was willing as early as 1958 to acknowledge the existence of "anti-Negro feeling among Jews" but balked at calling it racism.) The existence of a specific word for anti-Jewish prejudice—a legacy, as we have seen, of European politics—can itself obscure the fact that Jews have been no more immune to racialized discourse than anyone else. Jewish antiblack racism tended (and tends) to get a lot less discussion than anti-Jewish racism, but it had—as we have seen—offered a means for Jewish immigrants to demonstrate their American credentials and to help win social acceptance, especially perhaps in the South during Reconstruction. Politically, American Jews tended toward liberalism, the Democratic Party, and support for civil rights, but none of this precluded sharing in the antiblack stereotypes and behaviors to be found in white society at large. The subject was widely if inconclusively discussed over the years by analysts of "inter-group relations" at the AJC. In an unusual intervention at an AJC conference in May 1968, the writer Charles Silberman, one of the most interesting commentators on the postwar American Jewish community, insisted that "it's time—no long past time—to face up to the raw, rank anti-Negro prejudice that is within our own midst. We talk—endlessly—about Negro antisemitism; we rarely talk about, let alone try to deal with, the Jewish anti-Negroism that is in our midst and that is growing very rapidly."[24]

Black antisemitism, the half of the pie that the ADL's Forster and Epstein worried about, was a composite and not very precise term that gestured toward at least three distinct elements: suspicion of white folk generally as exploiters of black folk, often identifying the familiar figure of the Jewish shopkeeper or landlord as the embodiment of this; a sense that Jews, of all people, who should have been able to understand their situation, were not doing more to help; and not least, resentment against another group claiming to be victims of history in a setting where they had suffered little in comparison with those still suffering the aftereffects of slavery. But so far as Forster and Epstein were concerned, there was, in addition, a fourth element: the growth of Black nationalist support for freedom struggles in Africa that translated readily into sympathy for the Palestinians. Du Bois had certainly not been the only black leader to see a Jewish nation-state as a positive step for mankind; Martin Luther King Jr. had described it as "one of the great outposts of democracy in the world." Yet their benign view of Israel was repudiated by the generation after them, whose suspicion of American military power abroad and denunciation of the Six-Day War as an "imperialistic, Zionist" war put them into opposition with the American Jewish mainstream.[25]

Prejudice proper thus constituted only one reason for the breakdown of the anti-racist coalition, and although there was plenty of it on all sides, it was probably not the most important. As Harold Cruse suggested in a brilliant treatment of the issue in 1967, black-Jewish relations were fundamentally affected by the changing place of Jews in American society. Citing Arthur Hertzberg, Cruse noted that as the Jews moved, in his words, from the "have-nots" to the "haves," this was leading to disagreement over how to build upon the achievements of the civil rights legislation of the mid-1960s. An old story and not an especially American one, it was in essence a clash between liberals, who believed that the establishment of formal equality in the eyes of the law was a sufficient goal, and radicals and revolutionaries, who regarded it as meaningless without continuing the struggle for equality in the economic and social realms. The specifically American inflection came from the fact that in this case the ideological disagreement was also to a large degree a racial one, with much of mainstream Jewish opinion taking the liberal position, leaving it to black organizations to deal with the many sources of discrimination against them that persisted. The growing black-Jewish estrangement thus extended beyond the question of prejudice and went to the heart of late twentieth-century America's way of dealing with its deep-rooted historic patterns of racial discrimination.[26]

One of the most commonly cited grievances raised by American Jewish groups in the past few years is that antisemitism is not taken as seriously as other racisms. The roots of such a perception lie in these debates of half a century ago and in particular in their resolution in the shape of a new antidiscrimination bureaucracy. For from the mid-1960s onward, the US regulatory authorities, through antidiscrimination provisions and affirmative action, started to use the power of the federal state to dismantle barriers in housing, employment, and education that had been established against black and other minority groups. In the decades that followed, few if any countries intervened as extensively as the United States to improve equality of opportunity for minorities and to enshrine diversity as a principle of public life. Behind this approach lay the activist critique of *institutional racism*—a term coined by Stokely Carmichael and Charles Hamilton in 1967 in their book *Black Power*. Others concurred: The Kerner Report on the urban riots of 1965–68, which sold more than two million copies, identified "white racism" as a chief source of social unrest. From the Nixon era onward, federal agencies interpreted provisions of the Civil Rights Act of 1964 proactively to enforce anti-racist compliance in many areas of social and economic life. This involved a profound shift in the very understanding of racial prejudice: Less and less seen as a psychological or emotional propensity that was manifested in individual actions, it became a societal problem expressed through statistical under-representation. The social psychologists gave way to the rise of a monitoring bureaucracy and the search for ethnic and racial categories that would allow progress in the fight against discrimination to be quantified and measured.[27]

And therein lay the paradox: The civil rights movement of the 1950s had aspired to remove racial categories as a classifying principle of daily life; the new approach required their reinscription. A commentator noted: "The success achieved by the movement to remove race from forms in order to reduce discrimination is now a major stumbling block in the enforcement of powerful policies aimed at removing discrimination." For the sake of reducing racial discrimination, racial categorization became an essential bureaucratic tool.[28]

"To Know or Not to Know"—a 1973 report of the Commission on Civil Rights on the collection and use of racial and ethnic data by federal assistance programs—argued strongly for standardizing racial designators. The six major federal agencies the commission had investigated turned out to use several different systems of classification, and at least one was still using a prohibited racial category (non-white). In fact there was controversy over more or less every potential category mentioned—including white (other names were suggested)—and widespread confusion between "race" and "nationality"; as for "ethnicity," few could figure out what it really was or whether groups like the Poles and Portuguese should figure in some catchall "other minorities" category. Five years later, after much discussion, the Office of Federal Statistical Policy and Standards in the Department of Commerce weighed in. When this obscure but influential agency published its Statistical Policy Directive No. 15 in May 1978, it proclaimed the existence of five classes—American Indian or Alaskan Native, Asian or Pacific Islander, black, Hispanic, and white. Only four of these were said to be racial since Hispanic was deemed an ethnic category but not a racial designation. Despite the confusion, one thing was clear from the start: For bureaucratic purposes and therefore from the viewpoint of monitoring federal antidiscrimination policies, the Jews (along with other European ethnicities) were statistically invisible.[29]

Blackness was being reclaimed with pride by student and protest groups. "A recent accomplishment, mainly attributable to Negro college youth, is the unprecedented semantic reversal of the negative racial connotations formerly associated with the words 'Negro' and especially 'black,'" noted a report from 1968 into student protests at Columbia University. Whiteness not only became an umbrella category that lacked some advantages enjoyed by the others; it was also coming to sound increasingly negative. "How did Jews become white all of a sudden?" questioned one Jewish newspaper. "Which pigeon hole do I prefer?" a journalist reflected. "White? Black? I often check 'Other.'" Many Jews refused to see themselves as white or accept the premise it implied—that they were to be counted with the oppressors, not the oppressed.[30]

In fact, the proposed reinscription of racial categories had initially found both Jewish and black groups opposed to it. The AJC for one had long argued that Jews did not exist as a race; American Jews had ceased to be identified as a separate racial category in US immigration statistics in 1943, and they had long preferred not to be marked out as a religion in censuses and other official documents. The fact that anti-semitism was *not* among the forms of discrimination covered thus not only testified to the general sense that anti-Jewish prejudice was in decline, but also reflected the wishes of Jewish organizations at the time. Yet it turned out that the new regulatory system incentivized being mentioned.[31] When a Maryland congregation sued to have van-dals who had daubed swastikas on a synagogue charged with civil rights violations, the courts found that the American legal system did not recognize Jews as a protected racial group. Only an intervention by the Supreme Court extended them civil rights protections; Jewish demands to be included in the antidiscrimination machinery of the state would accelerate in the early twenty-first century.[32]

Some Jewish commentators argued that the original omission was deeply unfair since Jews were just as much potential victims as any "protected group." Advocating for a new language of ethnicity, not race, the sociologist Nathan Glazer wrote that the United States had simply created "affirmative discrimination" and insisted ethnic disadvantage affected white groups too. Norman Podhoretz insisted Jews too were persecuted in America.[33] And then there were the persecutions of the past. With the rise of victimhood as a form of late twentieth-century cultural capital, a kind of rivalry in historical suffering that had been evident in black-Jewish relations since at least the era of the Russian pogroms now intensified dramatically. Victimhood became a desirable category and a source of strife between groups who had benefited to very different degrees and for different reasons from postwar American social change. In conversation with James Baldwin, screenwriter Budd Schulberg worried openly that comparing the suffering of slavery with the European Jewish experience of persecution and genocide "could become a careless attack on the Jews." Baldwin disagreed and opposed any downplaying of what American slaves and their descendants had endured. In a piece he wrote shortly after the dialogue with Schulberg, he wrote:

> One does not wish, in short, to be told by an American Jew that his suffering is as great as the American Negro's suffering. It isn't, and one knows that it isn't from the very tone in which he assures you that it is.... The Jew's suffering is recognized as part of the moral history of the world and the Jew is recognized as a contributor to the world's history: this is not true for the blacks. Jewish history, whether or not one can say it is honored, is certainly known: the black history has been blasted, maligned and despised.[34]

There was suffering, and then there was the recognition of suffering. Was there not something unfair, Baldwin seemed to be suggesting, in the fact that while crimes committed against blacks were forgotten in the country that had perpetrated them, American Jews were receiving sympathy from the attention increasingly shown to stories of Jewish suffering across the Atlantic. Especially when postwar America had by and large treated them so well. Indeed, was there not a certain worrying convenience in the fact that whereas any serious reckoning with slavery unavoidably raised awkward questions of the American present, a focus upon the Holocaust allowed the New World to complacently portray itself favorably in contrast with the Old. Yet one wonders how many American Jews would have agreed. For it was just in these years that they were coming to feel the sufferings of the Jews required more recognition, not less. Within the Jewish world, the Brooklyn-born Meir Kahane was a polarizing figure, an extreme Jewish nationalist who set up his notorious Jewish Defense League to fight antisemitism, in response to what he viewed as the excessive timidity of the ADL. Yet when Kahane insisted that the Jews were "the most victimized victim" in history, he was surely only articulating an assumption many American Jews shared. Black Americans had suffered slavery, the issue that above all others remained at the heart of American national life, but for American Jews there was the Holocaust.[35]

From Peter Novick's classic study *The Holocaust in American Life*, we learn that the leadership of the American Jewish community was initially deeply ambivalent about the idea of publicly commemorating wartime Jewish suffering. It was chiefly after the 1973 Arab-Israeli War—and what was perceived as Israel's narrow escape from defeat—that American Jews started to embrace the idea of the Holocaust not merely as history but as a warning for the future and an integral part of their sense of themselves.[36]

A bestselling history book, the 1975 *The War Against the Jews*, by Lucy Dawidowicz, a former AJC staffer, launched what became a sweeping redefinition of the Second World War, focusing attention on the Final Solution of the Jewish Question and thereby inaugurating a massive scholarly research effort that continues to the present. But what really galvanized public attention in the United States was the famous 1978 NBC TV series *Holocaust*: Neo-Nazis raged against it, cineasts loathed it, and many survivors found it vulgar and inaccurate, but *Holocaust* was an astonishing commercial hit. The series was supposedly watched in the United States by more than one hundred million viewers and in West Germany by an estimated half of the adult population, provoking agonized public discussions. By 1980 knowledge of the genocide was spreading rapidly; by the new millennium it had gone around the world.

The meaning of this transformation in global consciousness was quite evident to those who had worked hard to bring it about. Speaking to his colleagues in 1996, the president of the AJC, Robert Rifkind, extolled their part in securing "the centralisation of the Holocaust in the imagination of modernity." In his words: "We have stamped it indelibly on the mind of modernity.... We have seen to it that it has become one of the core cultural facts of the modern world, and that is a major contribution to the civilisation in which we live." As an overall assessment, this does not seem exaggerated. It was in a way a confirmation of James Baldwin's point: The recognition of suffering is a form of cultural assertion and validation. Such recognition involves commemorating powerlessness but it requires power to enact.[37]

The impact of what Rifkind called "the centralisation of the Holocaust" in modern consciousness was multiple. There was the effect upon the Catholic Church, which became outspoken against antisemitism as never before. There was its effect upon Holocaust denial, now combated in a much more systematic way than in the past. And there was also from the start a close connection between the rise of Holocaust commemoration, the increasingly respected status of American Jewry in the United States, and America's growing foreign policy commitment to Israel expressed in the form of soaring military aid. The US government emphasized the linkage. One month after *Holocaust* aired in the United States, President Jimmy Carter celebrated the thirtieth anniversary of Israel's founding at the White House. In the presence of Israeli Prime Minister Menachem Begin, he announced he was forming a commission for a memorial to "the six million who were killed in the Holocaust"; Elie Wiesel, a survivor and author, was to be the chair. The process that was to lead fifteen years later to the opening of the United States Holocaust Memorial Museum in a central location in Washington, DC, thus began with a presidential initiative designed to reassure the Israelis and American Jews that Carter's efforts for peace, and his recognition of Palestinian rights, went hand in hand with a "total absolute commitment to Israel's security" so that "the Jewish people will not be condemned to repeat the Holocaust." The old consensus had been reversed. American Jewish organizations, which had once resisted the calls for memorialization, now insisted on it; Israeli governments, which had once been loath to discuss the past, now pressed for it. And the Holocaust itself, a genocide perpetrated by Europeans upon other Europeans, had somehow become a guarantee of America's commitment to Israel.[38]

Not many commentators at the time seemed to think there might be anything at all odd about this. Historian Lucy Dawidowicz was one: She was appalled at the plans and resigned from the commission, arguing that a museum was "not an appropriate means to remember the Dead of the Shoah." In her view, it would have been better to have had nothing but a public memorial, which should have been located in New York City. A similarly dismayed response was registered by the Israeli historian Evyatar Friesel, who had fled Germany as a boy in 1939 and lost most of his family in the Holocaust. Reading that the planned new United States Holocaust Memorial Museum aimed to bring visitors into contact with the "experience" of the Holocaust, he was moved to record his dissent: "There was something deeply wrong...in the way American Jewry was trying to depict the destruction of European Jewry. Those museums...were contrary to the Jewish tradition of mourning and remembering: they would be little more than an hour of contrived sorrow, of gimmickry and make-believe. Worse...these plans indicated not sorrow for the destruction of European Jewry, but some darker and disruptive dimension in the soul of American Jewry itself."[39]

It was perhaps more than a coincidence that both Dawidowicz

(born in 1915) and Friesel (born in 1930) retained vivid personal memories of the world of European Jewry on the eve of destruction and as professional historians could gauge the disjunction with how it was proposed to now portray that world. But their misgivings were not widely shared. Over one dozen museums had been established in the United States by 2011 and more were on the way; the Association of Holocaust Organizations was formed and gained hundreds of members. Scholarly journals and academic programs sprang up. Educational centers preached universal moral lessons based on wartime events even as they simultaneously highlighted the specific suffering of the Jewish people. Polls indicated that the Holocaust was one of the episodes in world history most familiar to the average American: By 2011 it rivaled the US civil rights movement as a historical reference point for civic education in the country of chattel slavery and the American Civil War. Most striking of all perhaps for the historian of antisemitism and its shifting meanings, was how the memory of the Holocaust came to be combined with attachment to Israel across the increasingly diverse and secularized world of American Jewry as a marker of ethnic identity.[40]

"Ethnic identity": The very phrase was a new concept for new times. "Today we could hardly do without the word 'identity' in talking about...ethnicity," wrote the scholar Philip Gleason in 1983. *Identity politics*, a term coined by a black feminist collective in the mid-1970s, was on the rise in American life, registering the shift away from the old melting-pot ideal. With traditional "Americanism" losing its luster amid the strains of the Vietnam War, different groups embraced the possibility—indeed the desirability—of a hyphenated identity: A "new ethnicity" took over American politics. Black revolutionaries started it off. But after that an assertion of the virtues of ethnic identity went mainstream in the US and reshaped American Jewish life too. Within the community there emerged what one scholar has described as a "Jewish identity industry," which increasingly saw the question of "Jewish identity" as something to be defined, quantified, measured, and above all praised or (more usually) worried over. It was this "identity" whose survival so many American Jews were now told they should be worrying about, as they then did.[41]

This was something of a revolution in collective consciousness. Earlier generations of immigrant Jews, arriving (mostly) from the Yiddish-speaking world of the Old Country, had made the idea of America their own and contributed to the nation's sense of itself: George Gershwin had brought jazz into classical music; Israel Beilin had changed his name to Irving Berlin and given the country a favorite Yuletide song, "White Christmas." Those born either side of the Second World War were less observant and yet more unabashed about their Jewishness and much more inclined to take their Americanness for granted. By the 1980s American Jewry was a porous and diverse world in which more than four out of ten adults were married to a non-Jew and regular synagogue attendance was declining. Many commentators worried that this meant the end of Jewish life in the United States: As historian Lewis Namier had once done, they feared America's welcoming embrace as an existential threat. Yet at the same time, the overwhelming majority of American Jews said they were proud to be Jewish and three quarters felt a strong sense of belonging to the Jewish people. The sources of that pride and sense of belonging were twofold. One lay in an identification with Israel, which, in Glazer's words, had become "*the* Jewish religion for American Jews." By 2013 nearly half of all American Jewish adults had been to Israel, increasingly through the free travel grants of the Birthright Israel Foundation, and around one third said they believed the land of Israel had been given by God to the Jewish people. The other source of ethnic belonging, perhaps even more important, the polls suggested, was the Holocaust. Thus the Jewish state and the Jewish catastrophe had between them become for many American Jews the intertwined core

of a new identity: The Holocaust was commonly understood to rationalize the existence of Israel, which in turn seemed to enhance the
security and status of American Jewry.[42]

The historian Yuri Slezkine has satirized not only this transformation but also its competitive undercurrent. In *The Jewish Century*,
he describes how American Jews in the 1970s

> finally became regular American "ethnics," complete with an old
> country that was also a new state with a flag, an army and a bas-
> ketball team. More than that, they had become the first among
> American ethnics because their new old country was uniquely
> old, uniquely new, uniquely victorious and uniquely victimized.
> And of course its very existence and therefore the continued
> existence of all Jews... was (it turned out) a response to an event
> that was the "most unique" of all events that had ever occurred.[43]

With the secularization of American Jewry and its embrace of
ethnic politics, antisemitism was gradually becoming more and more
linked to the question of Israel. In the words of the historian Leonard
Dinnerstein, "the measuring tools for anti-Semitism may be in the process of changing. Whereas in the past, political, social and economic
barriers defined what anti-Semitism was, today many Jews equate
hostility toward Israel as the tell-tale sign."[44] Dinnerstein's explanation for this was that in the US discriminatory barriers had mostly
come down and social acceptance had been won almost everywhere.
As a result, only in their own minds did American Jews exist as a
"minority group" who needed the protection of the state; non-Jews did
not regard them in this way. And indeed it was generally understood by
Jews themselves that old-style discrimination within the US had
diminished and that the threat of violence from the far Right had
declined compared with the 1930s. "Nothing like [the Holocaust] will
happen in America," Nathan Glazer wrote. "It is inconceivable." Yet

many of them felt that prosperity and security in the US gave no grounds for complacency and often reacted negatively when told the outlook was relatively rosy. "It takes guts to bring good news to the Jewish community," observed Charles Silberman.

Threats to Israel's safety in particular, as Dinnerstein noted, were regarded by more and more American Jews as an attack on themselves. Henry Feingold put it thus: Since the ensuring of American support for Israel had become "an important tenet in the civil religion to which most American Jews adhere, by attacking it and the founding ideology of Zionism in which the Jewish state is rooted, the antisemite can easily get at the very center of contemporary American Jewish sensibility and concern." The question this begged, however, was how antisemitism was to be distinguished from reasonable political criticism of Zionism or Israel itself. It was easy to see how some people might end up regarding them as much the same thing, especially since unlike the ethnic homelands that Americans from other immigrant communities felt connected to—Ireland, for instance, or Italy—the country American Jews identified with was perpetually under threat.[45]

Was it in fact the waning of American antisemitism that made American Jews feel more at home and hence more able to support Israel openly and more inclined to worry on its behalf? Evidence for this came in 1985 when an American Jewish analyst, Jonathan Pollard, was convicted in the US of spying for Israel—the dual loyalty accusation come suddenly to life. Pollard's betrayal gave some American Jewish organizations pause for thought, and put them in awkward correspondence with the Israeli government for a time, while they did what they could behind the scenes in Washington; but others lobbied robustly on behalf of Pollard and his wife. "The spectre of dual loyalty still haunts our community," a senior American Israel Public Affairs Committee (AIPAC) official told members at the time. "But here, in this country of ours, we ought not to be shy about our interest in

Israel. This is a pluralistic society and our survival here is dependent upon that pluralism....We care to the depth of our souls about what happens to both the US and Israel—that caring is not inconsistent, it is not un-American and *it is not dual loyalty*. It is part of democracy." It took an Israeli political scientist to spell out what most American Jewish commentators still tiptoed around: A "new Jewish politics," wrote Peter Medding, had emerged in the US, characterized by the "militant public self-assertiveness" with which American Jews were now integrating the issues they cared about as Jews into mainstream American political life and assuming a new role as political insiders. Only a few openly wondered where this was leading. Admiral Sumner Shapiro, a former US director of naval intelligence, had met Jonathan Pollard before he was unmasked: He had gotten Pollard's security clearance reduced but failed to get him sacked. Shapiro, himself Jewish, was outraged at the support Pollard had received from American Jewish organizations following his conviction: "We work so hard to establish ourselves and to get where we are, and to have somebody screw it up... and then to have Jewish organizations line up behind this guy and try to make him a hero of the Jewish people, it bothers the hell out of me."[46]

THE RISE OF JEWISH ISRAEL

At the same time as these cultural shifts were taking place in the United States, inclining more and more American Jews to see attacks on Israel as threats to their own ethnic identity, a parallel anxiety about antisemitism was also emerging in Israel. To understand it, we might begin with a quiet conversation that took place in 1968 in the office of the political adviser to the Israeli prime minister. The adviser himself was the Dublin-born and rabbinically trained Yaakov Herzog, a lawyer and diplomat. His guest was the distinguished French political philosopher Raymond Aron. The two men were both European in origin but could not have been more different: While the former was a proud Zionist who had turned his back on his European home, the latter epitomized assimilated Jewish membership in the French Republican elite.

In polite but forthright terms, Aron opened their conversation by asking Herzog whether the very creation of Israel in 1948 had not been in opposition to modern notions of fairness and political justice. Did it not violate the basic rights of the Arabs who had already been living there? Unperturbed, Herzog told Aron to his face that he suffered from a kind of "spiritual schizophrenia" in thinking he could be a Jew and yet also a representative of France. Aron was deluding himself: The French would never truly accept him. Aron himself, Herzog alleged, had never really accepted what it meant to be Jewish. Had he done so, he would have realized that the Jews could not be understood in terms of twentieth-century concepts. Dismissing the very possibility or desirability of a Jew feeling at home elsewhere, Herzog's view of Israel as a Jewish state was one that rejected the very idea of normalcy. Even classical Zionists, Herzog said, had mistakenly thought that with the creation of Israel, the Jews would be turned into a normal people, accepted among the nations. What they had failed to realize was that the Jews were, in the biblical phrase, "a people that dwells alone."[47]

"A people that dwells alone": The very phrase conveyed an outlook that could be found along the spectrum from highbrow political philosophy to kitsch. On Israeli TV around this time, the Dizengoff Variety Ensemble could be seen performing their high-kicking rendition of a pop song called "Ha'olam kulo negdeinu"—"The Whole World Is Against Us." It was a "very ancient tune," ran the lyrics, one their forefathers had sung and their grandchildren would sing after them. They sounded almost cheerfully accepting of global hostility. But just like Herzog, the song registered the shift away from the classic Zionist presupposition that Israel would be "a light unto the nations" toward a fulfillment of the biblical prophecy that it had a unique destiny as "a people that dwells alone."[48]

In Ben-Gurion's time, Zionist leaders had mostly believed that antisemitism as a world problem would disappear. They were largely unconcerned about anti-Jewish prejudice in the diaspora and they thought that if Jews were really bothered by it, they should emigrate. When Ben-Gurion met one of the heads of the Anti-Defamation League in 1970, he greeted him with the cheerful query: "You still at it, saving Jews from the anti-Semites?" It was, for him, a fact of diaspora political life, not worth worrying about and easily solved by immigrating. But the bleaker and more introverted idea that Israel was doomed eternally to be alone was gaining ground and helped to pave the way for the ruling Labor Party's electoral defeat in 1977.[49]

The historian Eric Hobsbawm once famously stated: "Historians are to nationalism what poppy-growers in Pakistan are to heroin-addicts: we supply the essential raw material for the market." Israel bears out the truth of this claim as well as anywhere. As was suggested in chapter 1, the Jerusalem School of historians in Israel had been arguing since the 1950s that antisemitism was a form of antipathy more enduring and more serious than any other, which could not be compared with any other form of prejudice, and which stood, as it were, theologically apart. Their work posited a connection between history, faith, and politics that could scarcely have been tighter. Gentile hatred of Jews through the ages was the leitmotif of their approach.[50] Shmuel Ettinger's 1980 essay, "Hatred of Israel as an Historical Continuum," was among the first in a surprisingly successful genre; the British-educated historian Robert Wistrich penned *Antisemitism: The Longest Hatred* and popularized the idea that antisemitism was unique, endless, and ineradicable. To historians outside Israel—and increasingly to a younger generation of Israeli scholars too—such views seemed poorly argued, bizarre, even ahistorical: What kind of historian believes in any force moving unchanged through time in the way these historians portrayed antisemitism? Surely—some objected—historians have an obligation to detach themselves from the nationalism they study rather than to contribute to it? Scholarly debate moved in other directions, pointing out the ways in which antisemitism was not just one thing, nor disconnected from wider currents of the times, nor always indeed a matter of hatred precisely at all.[51]

Other historians might have treated the Jerusalem School's findings and presuppositions with reserve, but over time more of the public in Israel was coming to share their assumption that a Jewish people existing since biblical times, unchanged in its essential connection with God, incurred, as its necessary shadow, the eternal animosity of the world. As for the UN General Assembly, it simply—for this same public—mirrored a postcolonial world rife with new variants of antisemitism. After the 1975 General Assembly resolution, one writer in the Israeli press described the UN as "the carrier of Hitler's flag in our generation"; another claimed it should be called "United Nazis." It was a "racist anti-semitic organisation," and it was no coincidence its address was on New York's Forty-Second Street, "a street of pornography." The idea of a "new antisemitism" that threatened a repeat of the genocide of the Jews would not only come to be seen as compatible with Zionism but be taken up in official rhetoric and become second nature to many ordinary Israelis. It was a kind of approach, as Antony Lerman pointed out in 1985, which obviated any need to take criticisms of Israeli policy seriously: "Rather than concede the Arabs have an ideological case, we treat their anti-Zionism as prejudice. Rather than admit that Israel's mistakes fuel anti-Zionism, we prefer to brand critics as antisemites."[52]

This view of antisemitism, like the isolationist view of Israel's place in the world it underpinned, left very little space for real diplomacy; Yaakov Herzog had actually told Raymond Aron that he regarded international relations as no more than a matter of managing hatreds. Yet there were puzzling and unsatisfactory practical implications of following the theory too closely. If antisemitism was determinative among the Arabs, how had it not prevented Egypt's Anwar Sadat—a man who in his youth had collaborated with the Axis—from making peace? Clearly for Sadat, it was opposition to colonial rule, not antisemitism, that explained his pro-Axis sympathies in the war. Perhaps, therefore, antisemitism did not in fact explain everything and more importantly, allowing a stereotype to guide policy could turn into a self-fulfilling prophecy. And, to be honest, was Arab antisemitism not likely matched by another rather less studied phenomenon that was growing by the day: Israeli racist stereotyping of Arabs? Most of the Jerusalem School resisted going down that particular path, and the subject was virtually taboo in Israel for decades. But Yehoshafat Harkabi himself, near the end of his career, came to admit he had overlooked it and in 1988 he wrote that anti-Arab prejudice among Jews had grown so that "we can no longer find fault with Arabs without finding fault with ourselves."[53]

The Jerusalem School's view of antisemitism had not been embraced in Israel's early years either by the Labor Left or even by many on the secular Right. For one thing, the argument that Israel was needed as a safe haven for Jews worldwide sat oddly with the claim that the new Jewish state itself was doomed to face eternal hatred. For another, it seemed to imply that Jews themselves could not change. Yet in the mind of Ben-Gurion and many around him, the prime purpose of Israel had been to break with old-fashioned Jewishness and to create a new kind of secular Jew: Many would not have dissented from Arthur Koestler's prediction in 1949 that "within a generation or two, Israel will become an entirely un-Jewish country." Labor Zionists aspired to create a civic national identity, and to bring into being a new people: Israelis, unrecognizable from the Jews of the diaspora. In a far cry from today, an extreme version of this insisted that "whoever is a Hebrew [i.e., an Israeli] cannot be a Jew"; even much of the mainstream in 1950s Israel was strikingly uninterested in matters of faith or religiosity and—guided by the spirit of socialism—focused instead on the building of a functioning modern state, an army, and a new kind of society. Some devout Jews might wonder what this had to do with Judaism. But even Prime Minister Shamir as late as 1989 distinguished, in a way that was soon to seem old-fashioned, between the interests of Israel and those of world Jewry. In his view, it was the job of the Israeli government to keep the country safe and that of the world Jewish organizations to combat hate.[54]

It was thus the increasingly religious rhetoric of Israeli national politics that made politicians more receptive to the idea that Israel faced a fight internationally against antisemitism and that it fell to them to lead it. What might be called the Judaization of Israeli national identity began perhaps with the establishment of Jewish Consciousness programs in secular schools, but it was consolidated by the growth of the Orthodox communities and, even more importantly, by the spectacular growth of the country's non-Ashkenazi population. The result was not exactly that the country became more Jewish; it was rather that its politics came to rely more and more on the language of religion. "Secular authority appropriates for itself, when it can, the aura (which is also a weapon) of religion," writes the historian Carlo Ginzburg.[55] With the demise of the Left and the emergence of a new right-wing Zionism in 1977 under Menachem Begin, this process gathered pace. At an extreme there was Brooklyn-born right-winger Meir Kahane, for whom Israel was a divine mandate not subject to secular rules. In his view, Ben-Gurion had been creating nothing but "Hebrew-speaking *goyim*"; for Kahane, to be "religious *is* to be nationalist." Normalcy was for the rest of the world: "To be isolated is not to be alone."[56]

Once the Holocaust became enlisted in the transformation of Israeli civic consciousness, this view was reinforced. For Begin, the Holocaust was everywhere, and the Israeli prime minister, who had lost his father, mother, and eldest brother in the Shoah, invoked it constantly. In the 1982 invasion of Lebanon, a war that left both Israel and Jews worldwide deeply divided, Begin was widely criticized for his propensity to bring up the Nazis: The French classicist Pierre Vidal-Naquet, whose own parents had died in Auschwitz, assailed "the daily use made of the great slaughter by the Israeli political class." "Hitler is already dead, Mr. Prime Minister," novelist Amos Oz wrote in a famous article. "Again and again, Mr. Begin, you reveal to the public eye a strange urge to resuscitate Hitler in order to kill him every day anew in the guise of terrorists." The analogy could be used in different ways of course, and the taboo against publicly likening government policy to the Nazis was broken as commentators mulled over the possibility that Begin's tendency to see everything through the lens of his own family's wartime experiences was becoming responsible for enduring harm. "Here lies the international stature and moral integrity of a wonderful people. Died of a false analogy," wrote Ze'ev Mankowitz in *The Jerusalem Post*. "At what point does a devotion to history," asked Roger Rosenblatt in *Time*, "cease to be a weapon against present and future error and begin to cripple those who seek its protection?" Yet at the same time, there were plenty in the nationalist camp who embraced the idea of what philosopher Yeshayahu Leibowitz famously criticized as Begin's "Judeo-Nazi" policy: "Better a living Judeo-Nazi than a dead saint," one outspoken Israeli nationalist insisted, defending the invasion of Beirut and the massacres that followed.[57]

When the Labor Party returned to power in the 1990s, the martial rhetoric subsided for a time. Once a go-it-alone warrior, Yitzhak Rabin eschewed the Holocaust analogies and aimed to make Israel "a normal nation." He registered some success: The number of countries recognizing Israel internationally rose appreciably. But his assassination by a right-wing zealot brought back the Right and the instrumentalized language of the Holocaust as well. Voters were greeted in the 1996 elections with the slogan: "Only Netanyahu is good for the Jews." The choice was clear: the old secular Israel, or the new Jewish nationalism. When Shimon Peres was defeated, he was supposed to have remarked: "The Israelis lost, the Jews won." The commentator and peace activist Uri Avnery wrote: "We have not only two political blocs, but two cultures, and in reality two separate nations." There were the "Israelis," whom he regarded as part of modern international culture; against them there were the "Jews," with the beleaguered outlook of "an oppressed minority."[58]

But the minority was becoming dominant and not merely dominant but increasingly domineering. As Israeli society became more overtly polarized, the presence of a racist Right—and of racist attitudes stretching beyond it—was tracked in social scientific surveys. Against Arabs, above all, prejudice was rampant. Poll findings published in 1999, on the eve of the Second Intifada, showed that no fewer than 77 percent of Israelis opposed the idea of a romantic relationship with an Arab, and more than half opposed granting Arabs equal social rights to Jews. (As so often, the very categories were problematic: *Arab* referred to Muslim or Christian Arabs and not to Arabic-speaking Jews from the Middle East; *Israeli* tacitly excluded Israeli Arabs.) "The grim past of the Jewish people has not checked hate," concluded the authors of the survey. "On the contrary, past suffering may have contributed to the diffusion of xenophobic attitudes.... A vast majority of Israelis would like to close the state's gates and leave 'others' outside its borders." For many of those Israelis who were old enough to remember the hatreds of Europe, seeing similar prejudices emerge in Israel was shocking. The Holocaust survivor and former Knesset Speaker Shevach Weiss wrote bitterly:

> Your average Jewish racist hates "the goyim" especially when they're Arabs. He's xenophobic, a sworn hater of foreigners. He hates Jews who don't hate Arabs. He shatters glass because he's never heard of Kristallnacht.... [He] draws a distinction between Jewish blood and Arab blood.

Such views, Weiss went on, were most reprehensible when found among Jews—who of all people should have known better—and needed to be "cast out of society" by those who have been "schooled in suffering" and "victims of racism."[59]

But this felt increasingly like the wisdom and the worldview of an older generation watching as the country they had built changed out of recognition. In the 1950s, the vast majority of the population comprised newcomers from countries where they had once faced persecution themselves. By the early twenty-first century, more than four fifths of Israelis had been born in Israel, where they had grown up with the occupation, discrimination against the Arab minority, and an increasingly empowered settler movement as facts of life. As Weiss wrote, the peace camp was becoming beleaguered and—in Israel as elsewhere in the world—the Right was in the ascendant. The number of settlers in the occupied territories rose a hundredfold, from 4,400 in 1977 to 427,800 forty years later, which meant that the most successful political movement in the country was among the least supportive of a peace deal with the Palestinians. In 1988 the right-winger Meir Kahane had been barred from running for parliament by a special anti-racism law—it was perhaps around then that the taboo against acknowledging that Israel had a racism problem was broken—but his funeral two years later was attended by huge crowds and his ideas were taken up by growing numbers. Today the settlers remain a violent and, to many in Israel, unpopular fringe. But the views they hold are not theirs alone: The anti-Arab racism of hardcore fans of soccer teams such as Beitar Jerusalem and Maccabi Tel Aviv is no secret in Israel and has recently erupted in fighting overseas. Thirty years on, Rabin's 1994 pronouncement—"The whole world is not against us. The world is with us"—seems like an ever-fainter echo from the past.[60]

One of the founders of the field of American Jewish history, the rabbi and scholar Jacob Marcus, noted in 1964 that the rise of the United

States to global power created the opportunity of a new international role for American Jewish organizations. The country, after all, possessed what was by then easily the largest, wealthiest, and most successful Jewish community anywhere, at least twice the size of the population of Israel. More Jews lived in New York City alone than in the whole of Western Europe. Marcus imagined the formation of an "overall international Jewish agency" under American Jewish leadership, unifying the efforts of Jews everywhere and saving what could be saved of Jewish life in the Old World.[61]

Marcus's vision raises the thorny question of international power and the Jews. It is thorny because it is a leitmotif of conspiratorial antisemitic thought but it is at the same time a real topic too since Jews have been both powerless and powerful at different points in their history. "If American Jews bridle at the notion of 'Jewish power,' they have good reason," wrote the author of a book with that very title. Yet as he showed, American Jews provide a model of politically consequential mobilization and have built up not only a widely feared lobbying apparatus to enlist politicians in support of Israel, but also a vast, sprawling network of communal philanthropic organizations. Irrespective of cause or issue, the size, scale, and political sophistication of Jewish philanthropic life in the United States has no peer among any other immigrant ethnic group. The question these days is no longer whether American Jews enjoy some political power; it is rather which individuals and groups among them wield it, and to what ends.[62]

As for Marcus, he turned out to be both wrong and right. The unifying agency of his dreams was never created and certainly neither the Jewish Agency for Israel nor the World Jewish Congress ever came close to playing the role he envisaged: Coordination among Jewish groups always remained a priority for community leaders precisely because they were often both allies and rivals at the same time. Despite this, American Jewish organizations were to become significant players on the international stage in much the kind of redemptive vein he anticipated. Pre-1914 Jewish groups had lobbied the diplomats of the Great Powers as we have seen, but their position was marginal and bore no comparison with that of their successors in the Cold War and after, by which time the United States had achieved a position of unrivaled prominence in world affairs and had also come to regard Israel as an important ally. The issue that marked their coming-of-age and showed their clout was the campaign to help free Soviet Jewry, by far the largest of the surviving Jewish communities in Europe and the most in need of aid. It was to turn into what its historian has called "among the most effective transnational human rights mobilizations of the twentieth century."[63]

The plight of Soviet Jews had been evident ever since Stalin's embrace of antisemitism in the late 1940s. But only in the 1960s was the issue adopted by American Jewish activists. Following the rise of black nationalism, and the disintegration of the civil rights movement, Jewish activists shifted their humanitarian energies abroad; their battle was now with the Soviet system. "If injustice cannot be condoned in Selma, USA, neither must it be overlooked in Kiev, USSR," they insisted.[64] Fired by the example of the Black Power movement that many of them regarded as a model of the benefits to be gained from campaigning for one's own, grassroots American Jewish groups took up the cause publicly and left the more established organizations following in their wake. They eventually won support from the US government, which under Presidents Jimmy Carter and Ronald Reagan showed willingness to help. The result was activist social protest, modeled on the civil rights movement, which would transform American Jewish advocacy thereafter.[65]

One consequence was the marginalization of an older generation of Jewish human rights experts who had devoted their lives to the pursuit of universal rights. Jewish internationalists who had grown up in the dark times of the 1930s had helped to reshape postwar international organizations and international law. For many years they had sought to avoid conflict between their universalism and their specifically Jewish commitments, whether toward Israel or diaspora communities. But their universalism was under attack from two sides: from former allies, for whom any sympathy they might feel for Zionism or for Israel was increasingly questionable and, at the same time, from much of American Jewry itself, for whom rights increasingly implied Jewish rights. The movement to free Soviet Jewry called on the Kremlin to "Let My People Go," but only one people was meant: Jewish activists were largely silent on the plight of Germans, Armenians, and others who were similarly seeking to flee the Soviet Union or the Baltic. A Chicago rabbi objected when it was suggested he should change the slogan outside his synagogue from "Free Soviet Jews" to "Free People from the USSR"; that would, he retorted, be "absurd universalism." Things had moved a long way since the 1950s.[66]

The enormous success of the Soviet Jewry movement offered proof of what American Jewish advocacy, discreetly coordinated with Israeli agencies, could achieve when harnessed to the formidable power of the late–Cold War United States. The Soviet authorities began sporadically loosening emigration restrictions, allowing more than 30,000 people a year to leave for Israel in the early 1970s. But the issue became a political football: Leonid Brezhnev's slogan of "neither antisemitism nor Zionism" was a virtually impossible balancing act in the Soviet context and during his lifetime many refuseniks were jailed. With the sudden disintegration of the USSR, however, Jewish emigration soared: 185,000 people left for Israel in 1990 at the peak, 148,000 the following year. Recent estimates suggest that a staggering total of close to 2 million Soviet Jews left between 1970 and 2018, around 1.3 million of whom went to Israel. No Jewish emigration had occurred on such a colossal scale since the First World War. By the start of 2019, barely 200,000 Jews remained in Russia, Belarus, and Ukraine; Israel itself was fundamentally changed in consequence.

With this last wave of Russian Jewish emigration, a major chapter in the history of antisemitism closed. The end of the nineteenth century had initiated the reversal of the long course of Jewish movement from western Europe to the east: The vast emigration from the Pale of Settlement had turned American Jewry into the chief protector of those who remained and made New York a major center of Jewish life. Now the centuries-old Jewish presence in the Russian world, which Soviet rule had helped to shield from complete extinction in the Holocaust, had been massively and definitively reduced. Even in 1970 Russia still had the largest Jewish population in Europe; by 2020 it had shrunk to 155,000. Only a handful of other countries in Europe had sizable Jewish populations any longer: Nearly as many Jews were settled in the occupied West Bank as were living in France. And for the first time, thanks to the influx from the Russian lands, Israel seemed set to surpass the United States as home to the largest Jewish population in the world.[67]

The struggle to free Soviet Jewry was also important for another reason. The activist template that proved so effective in that case provided inspiration for what became one of the key international campaigns of the new century: the fight against antisemitism. Decades had passed since the swastika epidemic of 1959–60—the last time there had been an effort to mobilize diplomatically against antisemitism—and much had changed in the world. The European empires had all but vanished, the Soviet Union had collapsed, and the USA enjoyed global supremacy. Yet while Europe itself had reunified peacefully, peace appeared more remote than ever for Israel and the Arabs.

It was at this moment that a number of American Jewish organizations, American policymakers, and Israeli officials began to focus on raising international awareness of antisemitism. The scale of this effort dwarfed anything seen before on the issue. In the first two decades of the twenty-first century, they lobbied national governments and intergovernmental institutions; they fought for the creation of new monitoring agencies that would compile lists, collect data, and issue statistics and reports; they proposed initiatives and drafted laws. As they did so, the challenge of identifying the scale of the problem inevitably raised some basic questions. What exactly was antisemitism and, equally pertinent, what was it not? Was it ethnic prejudice? Was it a singling out of Israel for blame? Were these conceptions related and where was the boundary between them to be drawn? And perhaps the most important question of all: Who got to decide?

CHAPTER 8

Word Weapons

"The question is," said Alice, "whether you can make words mean so many different things."

"The question is," said Humpty Dumpty, "which is to be master—that's all."

LEWIS CARROLL, *ALICE'S ADVENTURES IN WONDERLAND*
AND *THROUGH THE LOOKING-GLASS*[1]

Words can be used in different ways. They can charm and they can repel. They can open up debate and they can close it down. After the demise of white rule in South Africa in 1994, *apartheid* went from being a descriptor of a specific historical situation to becoming a crime under international law that was defined in a way that did not mention South Africa at all. Floating free of the specifics of time and place, the concept was universalized. The French philosopher Jacques Derrida, for instance, called apartheid the "ultimate racism in the world." The term has been deployed by Israel's critics against it in the hope perhaps that it would have the same delegitimizing effect that had once helped the anti-apartheid movement. A detailed historical comparison suggests something unexpected: To equate the Palestinians' situation with apartheid South Africa is misleading not because it exaggerates their predicament but because in reality it downplays the much more lethal oppression they face at the hands of the Israeli state. A weaponized word is one that is relatively impervious to the complexity of historical realities.[2]

Zionism and *racism* became word weapons as well, and with similar consequences. *Zionism*, not least when used as a term of opprobrium, is an abstraction from a wide range of ideas (as is *anti-Zionism*, as we shall see in chapter 10). Those who call themselves Zionists have meant surprisingly different things by the term over the years, initially arguing over where the Jewish homeland should be (alongside Palestine, Uganda as well as locations in the British dominions and the Americas were also mooted), and later debating often radically diverse constitutional visions. As for *racism*, although the term was popularized internationally in a context overshadowed by the Nazi persecutions, in fact, of course Jews are by no means incapable of expressing racist views and Zionist racism exists. Yet there have been plenty of Zionist anti-racists too, including in both the American civil rights movement and the anti-apartheid struggle. Thus, if we must opt for a single overarching rubric, Zionism is probably better described not as racism but—more consistently with its origins—as a form of nationalism. This is how many interwar critics—ranging from Communists to the American Jewish Committee to Orthodox rabbis—understood it, and it is what formed the basis of their objections to it. In 1944, a London rabbi, Harold Reinhart, wrote in a letter to *The Times* that Zionism was "bred on despair and disillusion—naked nationalism—contrary to the whole Jewish tradition." It would not have occurred to Reinhart, nor would he have likely thought it necessary or appropriate, to describe Zionism as racist in order to oppose it. But although *nationalism* as a term helps us better understand Zionism's ambiguities and range, it lacks the stigmatizing quality of the charge of racism. It is not—at least not yet—a word weapon.[3]

Which brings us to our principal concern. From the 1970s, as we have seen, antisemitism was coming more and more to be viewed, notably in the United States and Israel, in a frame that regarded much of the criticism of Israel as a disguised form of prejudice. It was not, however, until the early 2000s that this reframing turned into a significant factor in global political discourse. What ensued was a kind of rhetorical jousting with real-world consequences. Let critics of Israel attempt to equate Zionism with racism, or Israel with apartheid-era South Africa: The response would be to recast the meaning of antisemitism in a way that would put the critics themselves on the defensive.

The end of the Cold War was a time of American triumph and liberal euphoria and simultaneously of rising nationalism and racism. In a Europe celebrating its peaceful reunification and integration, long-established center-Right parties were increasingly outflanked by far-Right rivals. Parties such as the National Front in France, the Freedom Party in Austria, and the National Alliance in Italy, which were once regarded as electorally extreme, performed well at the polls. In eastern Europe, new nationalist right-wing movements tapped into a history that associated Soviet rule with "Judeo-communism"; some ran as apologists for wartime collaborators. A wave of violence across the Continent targeted immigrants and asylum seekers. "A new specter is haunting Europe: racist, ethnocentric xenophobia," *Die Zeit* warned in July 1989.

The turbulence was even greater in the Middle East. Initially the ending of the Cold War seemed to presage peace, ushering in the first (and to date the last) decade in the history of the Israel-Palestine conflict to pass without any large-scale eruption of violence between the two sides. But in 2000 the Camp David peace talks between the Israelis and the Palestinians collapsed in mutual recriminations, Ariel Sharon made a provocative visit to the Temple Mount in Jerusalem, and the Second Intifada broke out, an uprising that was far bloodier than the first one.

It was against this background that a UN-organized world conference against racism was held in Durban, South Africa, in the autumn of 2001, intending to spotlight the Global South's demands for reparations for slavery and colonialism. Some participants also aimed to emphasize the Palestinian cause as the last great anti-colonial and anti-racist struggle, but with antisemitic vitriol rife on the conference sidelines, the United States and Israel withdrew. Three days after the conference ended on September 8, al-Qaeda made its dramatic attack on the United States: The "global war on terror" that was the West's response saw violence surge not only across the Middle East but around the world.

Antisemitism and Islamophobia both grew worse in the following months and Jewish sites such as synagogues, cemeteries, and communal centers were targeted. Often they were selected as proxies for the United States or for Israel and in fact it was hard sometimes to tell motives of classical antisemitism apart from retaliation for the US-led invasions in the Middle East or from anger at the plight of the Palestinians. The "recent rise in anti-Jewish acts and sentiments in Western Europe was often influenced by Middle Eastern events or conflated with anti-Israeli views," noted the US State Department: "Traditional far-right groups still account for a significant proportion of the attacks against Jews and Jewish properties; disadvantaged and disaffected Muslim youths increasingly were responsible for most of the other incidents."[4] Public opinion across the Continent generally was overall significantly less supportive of Israel's handling of Palestinian protest than in the United States, and many American onlookers were inclined to link this too to an increased threat to Jewish life.[5] Several went so far as to claim that hatred of Jews had become "politically correct" in Europe and analogies with the Holocaust proliferated as anxiety rose; commentators talked about a "Second Holocaust" or another Final Solution. Yet Leon Wieseltier, the literary editor of *The New Republic*, himself a staunch supporter of Israel, saw this constant evocation of the Nazi genocide as deeply problematic:

> It is a political argument disguised as a historical argument. It is designed to paralyze thought and to paralyze diplomacy. All violence is not like all other violence. Every Jewish death is not like every other Jewish death. To believe otherwise is to revive the old

typological thinking about Jewish history, according to which every enemy of the Jews is the same enemy, and there is only one war, and it is a war against extinction, and it is a timeless war.[6]

The truth was that Europe in the early twenty-first century bore little resemblance to the Europe of the 1930s, for much had happened in the intervening decades. The memory of the Second World War and the passing of generations had reshaped social norms and public culture. Polls indicated that those possessing a real ideological commitment to old-style antisemitism were but a small minority—the end of the Cold War had not changed this—while most people said they had positive associations of Jews. Reflecting the real impediments in Europe to any simple return to the antisemitic politics of the past was the ideological shift of the far Right. It had indeed made a comeback in political terms since the end of the Cold War, but few if any major parties on the European scene any longer overtly espoused antisemitism. The reason was clear: It had in fact become obvious to ambitious far-Right politicians that antisemitism was a barrier to electoral success. Anti-immigrant talk might win votes but antisemitism generally lost them. As one political analyst at that time noted: "Antisemitism has a completely different structure and motivation from xenophobia."[7]

This development took many militants on the Right by surprise and remained under constant challenge from party cadres. Political realism came most naturally to a younger generation of leaders keen to move into the mainstream: When Marine Le Pen wrested control of the French National Front from her unrepentant father, she broke decisively with him over this issue. As a senior party official explained: "Antisemitism stops people voting for us. Only that." Le Pen's strategy of "de-demonisation" by decrying antisemitism allowed the party to continue to preach its anti-immigration message at minimal electoral cost. Other parties of the Right followed the same course, helping them get closer to government. Those that clung to versions of neo-Nazism found success more elusive. Repudiating antisemitism thus became a twenty-first-century form of political sanitization for the political Right.[8]

The sincerity of the move might have been questionable but the political payoff was not, and over the years one far-Right party after another came out against Holocaust denial or talked positively about Israel. The times favored their shift. The post-9/11 spread of intense Islamophobia, enhanced suspicion of immigrants, and growing fear of Islamicist terrorism encouraged the European Right to embrace Israel as an ally. There was backing too from some sympathetic Jewish voices, such as the German writer Henryk Broder, who claimed the Continent was in thrall to Islam, paralyzed by political correctness, and unwilling to confront the anti-liberal sentiments of its own Muslim immigrant population. Under her pen name Bat Ye'or (Daughter of the Nile), the Anglo-Swiss writer Gisèle Littman penned *Eurabia: The Euro-Arab Axis*—described by the Israeli historian Robert Wistrich as a "Protocols of the Elders of Brussels"—a ferociously Islamophobe fantasy that alleged European and Arab states were conspiring to flood the Continent with Muslim immigrants.[9]

This far-Right turn to Israel elicited an unexpectedly warm reaction from the Right in Israel itself. Between Netanyahu and Hungary's autocratic leader, Viktor Orbán, for instance, the links were close: Orbán used his friendship with the Israeli prime minister to defend himself against accusations his party was antisemitic, and when he targeted the Hungarian Jewish billionaire George Soros, a favorite bugbear of the Right, in an advertising campaign that many Hungarian Jews regarded as dangerous and demagogic, Netanyahu defended him, ignoring criticism from the Hungarian Jewish communal leadership. This was not an isolated case: Israeli politicians went on to embrace other European politicians on the far Right over the protests of diaspora Jewish communities. The Israeli diaspora affairs minister, Amichai Chikli, remarked on the eve of the 2024 French presidential election that it would be "excellent for Israel" if National Front leader Marine Le Pen won. He also shocked Romanian Jews by seeming to favor an extreme nationalist with a soft spot for the prewar fascistic Iron Guard. Chikli, also serving as Israel's "minister for the struggle against anti-semitism," evidently saw no incongruity between this role and overtures to far-Right parties across Europe. His stance makes little sense according to a traditional understanding of antisemitism but falls into place once antisemitism is redefined as hostility to Israel. Indeed, Chikli's two ministerial portfolios—the fight against anti-semitism and diaspora affairs—seemed to be at odds: His stance, and that of his prime minister, suggested that in their minds Israel's national interest trumped genuine concern for the security and the opinions of the Jewish diaspora. Fighting antisemitism apparently meant embracing neofascists and authoritarian leaders who supported Israel even when they were associated with antisemitic extremists and decried by local Jewish leaders. When Chikli's ministry sponsored an international conference on antisemitism in 2025, there was nothing on the program to have worried anyone on the far Right, and notables from Europe's far-Right parties were officially invited and evidently saw kindred spirits in their hosts.[10]

The European Left too had changed since the days when a broad antiracism had brought together Jews and non-Jews under the banner of socialism. Now the unity of the Left was strained as an often ill-defined anti-Zionism turned into a kind of litmus test of progressivism that pushed away Jewish leftists sympathetic to Israel. Seeing the world in crude binaries of oppressor and oppressed or privileged and unprivileged made it harder to see Jews as needing protection. Yet Jews could be a target of prejudice too. After Jeremy Corbyn became leader of the British Labour Party, an episode from his own past revealed some of the complexities. He had once written an introduction to a classic Edwardian-era text on imperialism by the radical thinker John Hobson. Sensitive to, and articulate about, the antiblack racism present in Hobson's text, Corbyn had said nothing about the way it also stressed the role of international financiers in imperialism, figures Hobson described as "men of a singular and peculiar race." Corbyn was no antisemite. Perhaps he had simply not registered Hobson's antisemitism, or perhaps he had not thought it worth mentioning. Yet Hobson had expressed the prejudices of his time against both the exploited Africans and Jews: the former portrayed as an exploited class, the latter as a cabal of wealthy exploiters. Historically, both targets of bigotry had suffered catastrophe, and the disparity in Corbyn's treatment of the two was the more striking from someone on the Left precisely because of its general concern with racism. The underlying issue was how antiracism was to be defined, and whether it allowed or precluded registering concern about prejudice against Jews.[11]

If American commentators had a tendency to misread European attitudes and to read the worst of the past into a rather different set of dynamics in the present, it was because the Atlantic divided two communities that differed more than was immediately apparent in their recent historical experience and tradition. In the former European colonial powers, many people were sympathetic to the idea that the Palestinians had ended up as victims of colonialism. Other historical experiences of oppression too were fresh enough to produce greater sensitivity to the Palestinian plight than was generally encountered in the United States. In Ireland, for instance, there were the memories of British rule: These, much more than any indigenous antisemitism, explained widespread support for Palestinians. Memories of Nazi occupation that had underpinned European admiration and support for Israel in its early years could—especially once the occupation of Palestinian territories dragged on after 1967—in turn generate feelings of solidarity with the Arab side. And there were also the relatively recent experiences of the south European dictatorships of the 1960s or of Cold War East European Communism, which had politicized many European leaders and remained vividly alive in the popular imagination. None of these had equivalents in the US political consciousness. Historical memory thus helps explain why military occupation was seen by Europeans as a genuine problem, international law as an achievement to build on and not question. Perhaps too these experiences help explain why terrorism was not the automatically disqualifying label it was in the United States. Indeed, the Northern Ireland peace offered a kind of precedent for ending terrorist violence through negotiation, as did the peaceful ending of decades of Basque separatist terrorism in Spain.

Critics in Europe therefore pushed back against what they saw as an American alarmism that talked a little too readily of existential peril and misrepresented the risks to Jewish life in the Old World. There were threats, to be sure, especially in the shape of a resurgent racism, but Jewish cultural life was on the upswing in central and eastern Europe and interest in the Holocaust stood at an all-time high. Annual visitor numbers for Auschwitz, which had hovered around the half-million mark since the late 1960s, soared to over a million early in the millennium and kept rising, topping two million in 2016. These were the very years when aging survivors finally felt able to tell their stories in public, and an immense collective labor created an archive of victim testimonies that underpinned consciousness-changing historical research.[12] Europe's political leadership derived an ecumenical message from the Holocaust and interpreted "Never Again" to mean standing against xenophobia in general. By expressing solidarity with Jews, as prominent politicians did in the early years of the millennium, they were defending Europe as a protector of minorities and an opponent of ethnonationalism. Many European Jewish leaders embraced this outlook. The general secretary of Germany's Central Council of Jews declared in 2009 that "as a Jew I know that anyone who attacks a person because of their race, nationality or religion is not only attacking the minority, they are attacking democratic society as a whole."[13] Talk of an unprecedented surge of antisemitism, critics argued, exaggerated the danger to Jews and overlooked the much greater threat to other ethnic and confessional minorities. Rabbi David Goldberg in the UK said that warnings of a rise in antisemitism were "paranoid and exaggerated....At the present time it is far easier and safer to be a Jew than a Muslim, a black person or an east European asylum seeker." Speaking in 2004, European Commission President Romano Prodi was emphatic: "Today's Europe is not the Europe of the 1930s and 1940s and it would be false to claim it were." There was no organized antisemitism to compare with the past, he insisted: To invoke the Shoah was to insult its victims.[14]

The discrepancy in assessments—some deeply pessimistic, some relatively sanguine—was itself striking. According to an official of the World Jewish Congress, things had never been so bad since the war; yet the director of the International Center for the Study of Antisemitism at the Hebrew University refuted this. British Chief Rabbi Jonathan Sacks warned antisemitism was returning in a frightening way; yet only a few years earlier, his predecessor Lord Jakobovits had stated emphatically that never before in their history had Jews inhabited a world where they faced no official persecution. Shocking incidents made for disturbing headlines, but the underlying trends were not easy to discern. Rabbi Arthur Hertzberg, consistently among the most perceptive American commentators on the issue, noted that the existence of such a wide divergence of views among Jews about antisemitism was itself "a new and very serious development."[15] For many people, the answers were to be found in hard facts, and data and statistics were tossed to and fro. But these could not resolve the argument either because the collection and presentation of data, far from offering a haven of objectivity and calm, had become a political minefield too.

Hate crime was in some ways a very old problem and in others it was surprisingly new. The term itself had begun to circulate widely only in the 1980s in the context of fears about anti-gay and racist prejudice in

North America: After the 1990 Hate Crimes Statistics Act mandated US federal crime agencies to collect such data, experts debated the usefulness of the response. Some pointed out that there was a fundamental problem: The media consensus that the United States was undergoing a hate crime epidemic was based on data provided by the very advocacy groups calling for more legislative action. The media made the headlines but scientifically they were on shaky ground: A lack of historical perspective and the self-interest of the organizations involved could easily produce an "epidemic" where none existed. In the words of two leading criminologists, James B. Jacobs and Kimberly Potter, in 1997:

> The "epidemic hypothesis" asserts that *all forms* of prejudice-motivated crime are rising alarmingly.... We believe that there is reason to be skeptical.... Indeed, it is almost certainly true that there is far less prejudice and intergroup violence now than at most previous points in our history. For example, does anyone really believe that black Americans are now in as much danger from attack by white racists as they were during the Jim Crow era...? Is it plausible that there is more virulent anti-Semitism (not to mention anti-Catholicism) now than in the heyday of Father Coughlin...? And could it likely be shown that there is more xenophobic violence against immigrants today than during the Sacco and Vanzetti era...? The rediscovery of hate crime is probably best explained not by an epidemic of prejudice-motivated violence but by our society's far greater sensitivity to prejudice.[16]

Reviewing their work, the commentator Jim Sleeper similarly urged caution. Hate crime laws were not the solution people seemed to believe they were, he suggested: They might "advance their sponsors' political status and moral self-importance yet diminish tolerance and justice." Statistics were supposed to present a picture of reality. But what they really reflected was the authority of numbers and their political usefulness. The ADL was the main Jewish defense organization involved at this time in shaping the expanding hate crime bureaucracy and it has since become well-known as a disseminator of antisemitism data. It was clear that its twin missions of advocacy on the one hand and supposedly objective data collection on the other made for an uneasy pairing. In the words of Jacobs and Potter: "Advocacy groups that collect and report hate crime statistics use those statistics to further their claims that the racial/religious/sexual orientation group they represent is experiencing unprecedented victimization at the hands of prejudiced criminals. Such claims are used to raise funds and to obtain government support on a whole range of issues." Despite such concerns, ADL statistics are widely used to this day. But the history of the debate over antisemitism and what to do about it was to raise identical issues.[17]

It was likely the 1980 Rue Copernic synagogue bombing in Paris, which killed four people and left more than forty injured, that marked an important shift in official Israeli attitudes and policies toward antisemitism. In its wake, Menachem Begin arranged for security advice to be provided to Jewish communities abroad, and the Israeli intelligence agency, Mossad, began to collect data on antisemitic incidents and threats. An Israeli interministerial forum was created in 1988 to monitor antisemitism; four years later, the government set up the Project for the Study of Antisemitism at Tel Aviv University to provide an academic outlet for its work. At first not much attention was paid to the initiative or its activities but the governmental impetus behind the data collection efforts was to have a marked impact on the data itself.

Demand for statistics was growing. With the rise of computerized systems transforming policymaking across a wide range of areas, tackling antisemitism—like other "hate crimes"—became an objective that depended upon quantifiable inputs, and the collection of information accelerated. But the shortcomings of much of the antisemitism data were a problem from the start. When the London-based

Institute of Jewish Affairs (IJA), publisher of a well-respected scholarly journal, began planning an Amnesty International–style country-
by-country annual report that would assess antisemitism in post–Cold
War Europe, it encountered a difficulty. "We were already aware of
a general problem with the quality of the data available," wrote its
director, Antony Lerman, whose memoir is an invaluable behind-the-
scenes source. "The overall picture was muddied by a stream of raw data
distributed throughout the world by Israeli government sources....
Most antisemitism researchers knew full well that this material was
of very poor quality. It comprised lists of so-called 'antisemitic incidents' but in very many cases there was no evidence at all that the
incidents were antisemitic. Even known antisemitic incidents were
often distorted, exaggerated or wrongly described."[18]

Some of this reflected a difficulty inherent in anti-hate data generally: knowing how to attribute motives to incidents without making
unwarranted assumptions. But the bigger impediment in this case was
political. Lerman, no newcomer to the charged world of antisemitism
research, found his measured approach was being challenged from two
directions: first, by large American Jewish organizations expanding
their operations in newly reunified Europe and demanding sensational
material that would get their names in the headlines, and second, by
the Israeli authorities. The former read the European situation in the
light of an oversimplified history and were wont to exaggerate the
severity of the situation. The Israeli state wanted not only to help
Jewish communities abroad but also to encourage aliyah: The more
alarming the picture, the more young Jews from abroad might be
tempted to move to Israel. This meant that there was a problem of hate
crime data being used as "a Zionist recruiting tool." In 1994 Lerman
wrote that

> the ethos behind the [Israeli] antisemitism work... is that only
> Zionism provides the answer to the problem of antisemitism.

Thus the tone of much of their work is highly alarmist and exaggerated.... What is most important is a rigorous and objective
approach. Only such an approach will command the respect of
governments, international organisations and so on.[19]

In short, data was not neutral and raised basic questions about
framing, perspective, and intent. What was at stake may easily be
seen by comparing the *Antisemitism World Reports* that were published
annually from 1992 by Lerman's Institute for Jewish Affairs, with *Anti-
Semitism Worldwide*, the rival volumes produced by Tel Aviv University's Project for the Study of Anti-Semitism. Even though they were
ostensibly concerned with the same phenomenon and often relying to
a large extent on the same data, the tone and the outlook of the two
series are completely different. Lerman's London-based organization
reflected the perspectives of many European Jewish communities who
were anxious to understand the scale of the problem without wishing
to be needlessly panicked by it. This led to a fundamentally different
approach from those who were more ready to write off Europe as a
haven of antisemitism and more inclined to see its Jewish populations
as pawns in a larger struggle. But Europe had become a poor relation
and the IJA could not operate on the same scale as its rich American
cousins. And because nuanced stories made for poor headlines, the
consequence was that figures for trends in antisemitism—like other
"hate crimes"—seemed by and large only to register in the media when
they provoked alarm. In frustration Lerman noted: "We found that
the message that antisemitism was declining was not one that many
people wanted to hear."[20]

What compounded the problem was that the landscape of US-
based advocacy for Israel was changing and starting to overlap with,
and affect, the fight against antisemitism. In the 1980s the dominant
organization had been the American Israel Public Affairs Committee,
the main lobbyist active on behalf of Israel in Washington. Focusing

on the military alliance and fostering close diplomatic ties, AIPAC was scarcely involved in discussing antisemitism at all: Its core concerns were strategic in nature. As for the domestic American Jewish defense organizations, their interest in Israel advocacy was actually on the wane at a time when peace negotiations held out the hope of a settlement with the Palestinians, and American Jews were by and large supportive of this prospect. Domestic concerns like rising rates of intermarriage seemed to many people an existential threat to American Jewish life far more pressing than either the future of Israel or antisemitism. But after the ending of the Cold War, the major Jewish defense organizations sought a place for themselves in Europe.

In a moment of US predominance globally, they carved out a new role as intermediaries with post-Communist central and east European governments in particular. These countries understood that US support was conditioned on how they tackled such matters as antisemitism and human rights, Holocaust remembrance and diplomatic relations with Israel. American Jewish organizations could offer advice on such matters, and put in a good word, testifying, for instance, in Congress to admit them into NATO and other bodies. Lerman told his own directors in 1993 that such organizations "regarded it as their right, even duty to initiate some kind of activity in Europe." The World Jewish Congress was the first: It had played a prominent role in helping Soviet Jewry and then in exposing the Nazi past of the former UN Secretary-General Kurt Waldheim. It was soon followed by others. In Lerman's words, Europe "became the battleground that provided all these organizations with a seemingly endless supply of material that was used to give legitimacy and appeal to their organizational goals." If Europe was their battlefield, the fight against antisemitism was their rallying cry.[21]

After surmounting an internal financial crisis, the American Jewish Committee was finding a new voice abroad, combining its long-standing concern for European Jewish life with greater involvement with Israel.

Abandoning its old suspicion of Jewish nationalism, from the early 1990s it opened official functions by playing the Israeli national anthem; most of its peer organizations already did. An internal split became evident between those AJC staffers faithful to its older tradition of research and impartiality and a new leadership drawn from the Soviet Jewry movement that was worried about fundraising and keen to assert its primacy as a pro-Israeli advocacy group.[22] The ADL, which specialized in tackling antisemitism domestically, had taken a leading role in lobbying for federal hate crime action, and had moved faster than the AJC to identify itself with the cause of Israel: It forged its own partnership in antisemitism research with the Tel Aviv program. The newest player in this arena was the Simon Wiesenthal Center, based in Los Angeles, which had been founded by a rabbi, Marvin Hier, who seemed to have been photographed with everyone from Clint to "Bibi" and several popes. A fundraising phenomenon, Hier's organization was said to have raised between $600 and $700 million in just three decades since its founding in 1977. True to the vocation of its namesake, it was still focused on hunting Nazis, eventually hailing the conviction of a 101-year-old German man with the headline: LATE JUSTICE IS BETTER THAN NO JUSTICE. It ran a Holocaust center in Los Angeles; it was also constructing a Museum of Tolerance in Jerusalem over a medieval Muslim cemetery.[23]

All these organizations were products of the American Jewish philanthropic tradition and—with annual revenues of tens of millions of dollars each—far better resourced than any European equivalents. Although they tended to speak (and were often treated by officialdom abroad) as if they acted on behalf of American Jewry as a whole, of course they did not: No single body did. In reality, American Jewry, while united over the need to fight antisemitism, was sharply and often bitterly divided regarding Israeli policy toward the Palestinians. So far as generalization is possible—and American Jewish life was, and is, characterized by enormous diversity—American Jews as a whole tended to be more progressive and liberal than these organizations, whose leadership and main donors tended to relative conservatism and to show deference to whichever Israeli government was in office.[24]

This globalization of the major American Jewish advocacy groups coincided with an effort by Israeli governments to push the fight against antisemitism up the diplomatic agenda. The turning point came when the Right returned to power in 2001. Among the ministers most closely identified with the effort was the former Soviet dissident Natan Sharansky. Enjoying quasi-heroic status among many American Jews as a refusenik who had stood up to Soviet power, Sharansky was decorated by the White House, feted by the press, and embraced by America's neoconservatives. In the Cold War he had mobilized support from both grassroots groups and high-level figures in US administrations; in Israel he had entered the Knesset as a voice supporting recent Russian immigrants. Now he played a key role in publicizing a new understanding of antisemitism as delegitimization of Israel. Sharansky wrote that Israel was being assailed by a "new, historically unprecedented antisemitism of the political Left" that was a direct successor of Stalinist and Soviet anti-Zionism. As a minister in the Sharon government, he created an official Forum Against Antisemitism and announced that "the State of Israel has decided to take the gloves off and to implement a coordinated counter-offensive against antisemitism." Yitzhak Shamir's sense that global antisemitism was not Israel's business lay in the past.[25]

A new level of coordinated international mobilization around the issue was soon visible, thanks to the backing this initiative received from US politicians and diplomats who folded the fight against antisemitism into their democracy-promotion efforts around the world. In 2004, the year after Sharansky's announcement, US Secretary of State Colin Powell spoke at a conference on antisemitism in Germany. "In the opening decade of the twenty-first century," stated Powell, "we, 55 democratic nations of Europe, Eurasia and America, have come to Berlin to stamp out the new fires of anti-Semitism within our societies, and to kindle lights of tolerance so that future generations will never know the unspeakable horrors that hatred can unleash." He announced plans for the Organization for Security and Co-operation in Europe to establish a bureaucracy that would collect hate crime statistics, track antisemitic incidents, and advise members on legislative reform and anti-hate education. A new international bureaucracy dedicated specifically to countering antisemitism was being conjured into existence.[26]

That same year the US Congress passed the Global Anti-Semitism Review Act, obligating the State Department to report on antisemitism around the world. The department, which already reported on religious freedoms across the board, initially resisted the demand that it should single out one confessional group above the rest. But its objections were overridden; the act passed and led to the creation of the Office of the Special Envoy to Monitor and Combat Antisemitism, which was supposed to advance "US foreign policy on antisemitism." Not only did this imply that antisemitism had become institutionalized as a foreign policy matter of state, but the law stated that the term *antisemitism* now encompassed "vilification of Israel," thereby suggesting that American diplomats had an obligation to act on behalf of another nation. It does not seem there is any other country that State Department officials are required to look out for in this way: The anti-antisemitism campaign was creating not only a bureaucracy but a diplomacy all its own. Fighting antisemitism no longer meant combating racial prejudice; now it could also mean fighting back against critics of Israeli policies.

As a result, there was another, perhaps even less noticed but equally revealing, connection being forged: Those engaged in this campaign were now arguing not merely that antisemitism meant to be against Israel; some were going so far as to argue that it meant being anti-American too. The Tel Aviv antisemitism researchers, who worked closely with the Israeli government in assessing the ongoing campaign, noted approvingly that the US government was now underscoring "a major aspect of antisemitism today, the linkage between antisemitism and anti-Americanism... hinging specifically on America's support for and efforts to safeguard Israel." Such a remarkably instrumental redefinition of antisemitism passed unnoticed at the time; twenty years later, it would help forge the coalition between Jewish and American nationalists, two groups divided in their views on classical antisemitism but brought together by their shared backing for the Jewish state.[27]

Where the United States led, others followed: By the end of 2023, at least twenty-four countries around the world had set up similar posts, creating a new cadre of antisemitism watchdogs, mostly career civil servants with little specialist knowledge of the issues, often lobbied by and brought together under the aegis of organizations like the World Jewish Congress. Their emergence had the consequence of splitting antisemitism campaigning from the larger world of antidiscrimination activism. Antisemitism was now being treated as a unique problem, as the historians of the Jerusalem School had always insisted it was.

Campaigners also homed in on the United Nations. Since the General Assembly's 1975 anti-Zionism resolution, Israel's defenders had regarded the UN and its human rights activities as irredeemably biased against it. Irwin Cotler, a Canadian professor and politician who was active in promoting the idea of a new antisemitism directed against Israel, had long inveighed against the UN as a key site of this phenomenon, and a new NGO, UN Watch, was formed in 1993 with the backing of the AJC, likely the very first of what would become numerous groups "monitoring" for anti-Israel bias.[28] Entering office in 1997, the new UN secretary-general, Kofi Annan, was determined to end the standoff. The 2001 Durban Conference—"a frenzy of antisemitic rhetoric and vicious anti-Israel resolutions"—certainly did not help, but Annan signaled his desire to lower the temperature. A UN seminar was convened on antisemitism, plans were laid to reform the controversial Human Rights Council (which eventually happened), and in 2005 the UN General Assembly marked the sixtieth anniversary of the Red Army's liberation of Auschwitz by voting to establish the International Holocaust Remembrance Day. As several dozen countries established annual commemorative ceremonies of their own, Holocaust remembrance was internationalized and came to be regarded as an integral part of the official identity of reunified Europe in particular.

The memory of the Holocaust could serve as a reminder not only of the evils of xenophobia but also of the recuperative power of nationalism. So perhaps it was not surprising that the idea for the General Assembly resolution seems to have come from the Israeli Ministry of Foreign Affairs; in Israel itself an analogous memorial ceremony had been held annually since shortly after the country's creation. It was Ben-Gurion who had insisted back in 1950 (despite the protests of the American Jewish Committee) that "the whole Jewish people" were "the business of the state of Israel." His minister of education, the historian Ben-Zion Dinur, had gone further, arguing that Israel was entitled to speak not only for the Jewish living but for the dead as well—notably those who had died in the Holocaust. For Dinur, the creation of the Yad Vashem memorial center in 1953 aimed at "the ingathering of memory into the homeland." It was in line with this logic that the law establishing Yad Vashem bizarrely conferred what it termed a retrospective Israeli citizenship upon the millions who had died in the Holocaust "as a token of their having been gathered to their people."[29]

The assumption behind this law was that there was a simple unity between Judaism as an ancient faith, the state of Israel as a modern polity, and the entirety of Jews past, present, and future. But in reality there was nothing simple about it: This was a highly contentious claim on a matter of the first importance to Jews everywhere. Indeed, a vigorous and often charged debate over Israel's relation to Judaism had erupted from the very moment the new state was established. In 1948 the scholar Simon Rawidowicz, for example, had told David Ben-Gurion directly that the decision to call the state "Israel" made a mockery of traditional Jewish belief: Judaism, as enshrined in the many age-old associations of the name "Israel," encompassed both the new state and the diaspora and could and should not seek to deny the latter's long history or for that matter the spiritual value for the Jewish faith of the very idea of living in exile. Their correspondence went to and fro. Ben-Gurion could scarcely have disagreed more profoundly. He wrote bluntly to Rawidowicz that the diaspora was doomed and could not support a Jewish cultural life: For the Israeli prime minister, *Israel* as a word was henceforward to lose its own general connection to the collectivity of the Jewish people and be identified solely with the new state, which had effectively subsumed into it all the associations of the old term, past and present. The centuries of minority life were to be effaced and with them the languages of Jewish exile: They offered shameful memories of powerlessness and should not be celebrated. This was a theologically novel and even shocking position but one that was to become accepted without question by many later on.[30]

Dissent to this nationalist view of Judaism's relationship to the new state came from all sides. For another Zionist dissenter, the Anglo-Jewish philosopher Leon Roth (1896–1963), the Jewishness of Israel could never be merely a question of demographic numbers or political power; it implied an ethical standard that existed before and beyond the state and was not bound to it. The Orthodox Israeli philosopher Yeshayahu Leibowitz regarded fetishization of any state, including a so-called Jewish one, as tantamount to Fascism; the doctrine of Return to Land was idol worship. Among ultra-Orthodox Jews, many even regarded Zionism itself as a blasphemy because, in their view, the decision to found a state without obeying the age-old injunction to await the coming of the Messiah flouted God's will and violated the covenant "between Israel and its Father in Heaven." For Rabbi

Joel Teitelbaum, Zionism was "the greatest form of spiritual impurity in the entire world." Some of these positions reflect their proponents' Zionism; some their anti-Zionism or "post-Zionism." Some are concerned with matters of faith; others are more concerned with the importance of the idea of exile and diaspora in Jewish thought and history. All of them, however, under whatever label, take issue with the premise that to challenge today's Jewish state is necessarily to challenge the Jews or Judaism itself.[31]

Yet this was exactly the premise that was being reasserted and acquiring new force as Israel's government moved rapidly to the Right. The question of what would be lost by equating all Jews everywhere with a political entity calling itself Israel was precisely the problem to which Rawidowicz had tried to alert Ben-Gurion. But the conflation of the Jewish state with Jews in general was pushed far harder half a century later when phrases like "the Jewish people" and "Jewish peoplehood" became a voguish shorthand for a new ethnonationalist conception of worldwide Jewish unity. They emerged in the mid-1990s at a time of concern about Jewish political and religious *dis*unity in the aftermath of the assassination of Israeli prime minister Yitzhak Rabin. In the space of only a few years, there was a new Commission on the Jewish People and a Jewish People Policy Institute. A foundation was established to "support and advance Jewish peoplehood"; a book appeared entitled *The Case for Jewish Peoplehood: Can We Be One?*. Once known for his work on democracy, Natan Sharansky justified ethnic particularism in his 2008 book *Defending Identity*, and as leader of the Jewish Agency for Israel he propagandized for *peoplehood*, a term described by a journalist who profiled him in 2012 as "the buzzword du jour among Jewish communal leaders." Precisely at the moment, therefore, that the campaign to redefine antisemitism in a way that connected it to Israel was emerging in the United States and Europe, a parallel tendency sought to emphasize the connection between "Jewish people" and "Jewish state."[32]

The political valence of these phrases first became apparent when legislators submitted to the Knesset the draft of a law that proposed to define Israel as "the nation-state of the Jewish people." Back in 1960 Alan Stroock, chair of the AJC's Committee on Israel, had insisted on the point that "Israel speaks only for its citizens and in no way speaks for the Jews of other lands." But in the twenty-first century such views had gone the way of the dinosaurs. No major American Jewish organization restated anything like this position when the Basic Law was voted through in the Knesset in 2018, affirming explicitly that Israel belonged chiefly *not* to its citizens but to "the Jewish People": The AJC, for instance, confined itself to warning of the impact the law would have on Israel's claim to be a democracy. For despite the Netanyahu government's insistence that the country's democratic commitments remained unchanged, it was obvious that the law further compromised the already diminished position of Israel's non-Jewish minorities. Less dramatically or severely, it also unmistakably compromised the position of diaspora Jewry too. "[Israel] is the national state, not of all its citizens, but only of the Jewish people," said Prime Minister Netanyahu, in remarks intended to clarify what the new legislation meant. "Other peoples, other nationalities and other minorities—have national representation in other states. The national representation of the Jewish people is in the State of Israel. Israel is the national state of the Jewish people and of it alone." Such ideas recalled nothing so much as the sentiments of those right-wing nationalists of Weimar Germany nearly a century earlier, another demographically obsessed group who claimed the allegiance of ethnic Germans everywhere. In its assumption that there was a "community of the nation" that transcended borders, the 2018 law thus resembled a vein of central-east European ethno-nationalistic thought that had been repudiated by most of Europe itself after the Second World War. It was as though under Netanyahu Israel was bent on turning itself politically into a reminder of what postwar Europe had left behind.[33]

In Israel, the Left was in decline, and the peace movement too. Nonetheless, many Israelis opposed the 2018 Basic Law fiercely, and some declared they no longer wished to be registered as Jews in official documents. One of them was the former Speaker of the Knesset, Avraham Burg, who protested that the law imposed an inferior status on non-Jewish citizens that was "similar to what Jews suffered for untold generations." Among American Jews, the direction being taken by Netanyahu's government was generally unpopular because it threatened the cherished assumption that Israel could be both Jewish and democratic. Had not an astute commentator noted back in 1992 that the "new Jewish politics" in the United States rested upon an assumption that Israel shared the same moral and democratic values as the United States itself? This was also the very moment when Europe was declaring for multiculturalism and support for minorities. ISRAEL POSES A SERIOUS DILEMMA FOR EUROPE'S JEWS ran a headline in *Haaretz*. The writer, Diana Pinto, asked: "Are Israel's actions truly protecting the Jewish people? Or is it forcing Jews outside Israel to defend a state that has abandoned the post-war values that define Europe and the West, values that lie at the heart of their own legitimacy as Jews in democratic countries?"[34]

The passing of the 2018 Basic Law seemed almost designed to encourage a confusion between Israel and Jews in general. "The identification of all Jews with Israel," the intellectual historian Martin Jay has written, "which seems to be an excuse for anti-Semitism in some quarters, is as troubling as the menacing insistence on the part of some of Israel's defenders that all Jews must rally behind it, right or wrong." Indeed, the 2018 law could be interpreted as implying that Jews who radically opposed Israeli policies were not really part of "the Jewish people" and perhaps thus in some sense not really Jews at all. As we shall see in the next chapter, this kind of accusation was to become more common. In these and other ways, the always complex balance within Zionism itself was being changed in ways that made dissent within as well as outside Jewish circles seem both more necessary and more difficult.[35]

The fundamental problem is that an Israel-centered notion of "Jewish peoplehood" challenges the standard diaspora view that one can be Jewish, owe allegiance to the country of one's birth, and retain the freedom to define one's own stance toward Israel—be that positive, negative, or neutral—in the same way as to any other state. That Jewish political allegiances were not defined by ethnicity or faith was an axiom that formed the grounds of Jewish emancipation itself: The challenge posed by the 2018 Basic Law was thus a continuation of a much longer-standing debate between Zionists and their opponents. The big difference was that now the point was being argued over in the age of an actually existing Jewish state whose policies had become increasingly controversial, including among Jews themselves. Moreover, it was dragging into its vortex the concept of antisemitism, for it raised the prospect of replacing the traditional diaspora paradigm of antisemitism—understood as prejudice or bigotry against Jews as an ethnicity—with one shaped to serve the interests of the Jewish nation-state. According to this new paradigm, an attack on Israel was by definition antisemitic because it implied criticism of "*the* Jewish people." But could antisemitism really be so radically redefined?

CHAPTER 9

The Very Nature of the Thing

For the errours of Definitions multiply themselves, according as the reckoning proceeds.

THOMAS HOBBES, *LEVIATHAN*

Some people, when they see a word, think the first thing to do is to define it.

RAYMOND WILLIAMS, *KEYWORDS*[1]

Nothing, wrote the Tudor scholar-statesman Thomas Wilson in 1551, is more important than a clear definition that allows us to show in words "the very nature of the thing." He listed three rules of definition. First, it must be bounded: "The definition should contain no more than the thing defined." Second, it must sum up the essentials: "We must heed that the definition express the very nature and substance of the thing defined, or else it is no good definition." And third, it must be "plain and open, without ambiguity."[2]

The prevailing consensus among scholars over the past thirty or forty years has generally been that any attempt to come up with a hard-and-fast definition for antisemitism is bound to run into problems because as a concept it is impossibly multifaceted, varying in time and place. "We are left with a highly confused, emotionally loaded term from which serious, mutually opposed consequences are drawn not only by polemical antagonists but by purportedly disinterested analysts," wrote an expert in 1981. "The term antisemitism, especially in its American setting," noted Henry Feingold a few years later, "is so inclusive and therefore imprecise, that the student can classify under it almost

anything which involves conflict with Jews from the perennial con-
tretemps over Christmas crèches to the question of alternate side park-
ing on Jewish holidays." A panoply of theorizing by social scientists,
philosophers, and theologians has done nothing to alter the sense of
complexity, and the rich recent scholarly exploration of antisemitism's
history confirms these doubts even as it has transformed our knowledge of the Jewish past. Indeed, a leading scholar questions whether
the concept of antisemitism adds very much to serious historical inquiry
at all. To assert the existence of antisemitism is to follow a semantic
convention, suggests the historian David Engel, which does "not describe
anything actually in the world." Drawing attention to the distortions
that can be produced by bringing together under the one term different kinds of incidents from epochs with very different values, Engel
concludes that it would be helpful for historians to minimize or even
give up using the word in order to try to understand episodes of anti-
Jewish hostility or prejudice on their own terms and in their proper
context. This book, it is perhaps needless to say, does not go so far: The
concept of antisemitism can surely, when deployed with sensitivity, help
illuminate aspects of the past. Yet concern about its potential to sow
confusion and misunderstanding is warranted. If proof is needed, we
have the cautionary tale of what has come to be known as the IHRA
definition.[3]

Let us begin with a question: At what date did the idea of promoting
a particular definition of antisemitism begin to be identified by the
Israeli government as a foreign policy objective? The answer is almost
certainly in the first years of the new millennium. For that is when, as
one agency after another piled into antisemitism research, representatives of the large American Jewish defense organizations active in
Europe along with Israeli officials were upset to learn that a cog in the
EU machine, the European Monitoring Centre on Racism and Xenophobia (EUMC), had supposedly held back a report because it would

have revealed that many antisemitic incidents had been the work of young Muslims. Whether or not the accusation was warranted is disputed, but it led to a discussion of the technical issue of how to compare data across countries absent a standardized understanding of what acts count as antisemitic. This is a known problem in compilations of hate crime data generally. In the case of antisemitism, it is compounded by the complication that police forces differ on whether antisemitism should be counted as a religious or racial matter. Now there was an additional source of confusion: In the case of many incidents that seemed connected in one way or another with Israeli policy and the situation in the Middle East, it was not easy to disentangle political motives from anti-Jewish prejudice. As we have seen, between European campaigners against antisemitism on the one hand, and their American and Israeli counterparts on the other, there was already an incipient divergence of views on the question of whether this was even a meaningful distinction. A barrage of books and articles from the United States arguing that Europe was roiled by antisemitic antipathy to Israel was met by critics who riposted that the very idea of a "new antisemitism" was confused. An AJC expert, Kenneth Stern, was brought in to help reach a consensus by drafting guidelines that would help say when the line into ethnic bigotry was crossed. The end result was a two-sentence definition accompanied by several illustrative examples. It was intended for internal administrative rather than public use, and it was a low-key beginning for what was quickly to become a powerfully fought effort to enforce international compliance with the premises of the "new antisemitism."[4]

The EUMC was scarcely a well-known or a major organization but nonetheless Dina Porat, a Tel Aviv historian involved in the drafting process, hailed the result as a momentous achievement. In her words: "An international working definition of anti-Semitism was accepted for the first time since the term was coined in the late 19th century." She then, however, went on to ask a good question: "Why was a

new...definition needed?"[5] Why indeed? After all, previous generations had not needed one in order to recognize the problem, and the
fight against antisemitism had shown remarkable success in the decades
after 1945 without policymakers utilizing a standardized definition at
all. To Porat's question, there were two answers.

One was technical: With the rise of quantitatively-based hate crime
monitoring, there was a vogue for formal definition-making driven by
bureaucrats and dataset technicians seeking to monitor antidiscrimination policies and hate crimes and needing to classify information in
hard-and-fast categories. "From history we always get ideas of...con-
stant development, of instability," a late-nineteenth-century legal thinker
once noted. "But in law, at any rate for the purposes of the practical
lawyer, what we need are ideas of fixity, of uniformity." Above all,
one might add, in an age of computerization. Besides administrative necessity and the demands of technology, however, there was a
second answer to Porat's query. As the cultural theorist Raymond
Williams observed, what he called "temporarily dominant groups"
like to fix definitions in order to legitimize some meanings of a word
and prohibit others. Williams warned that this was especially problematic for value-laden terms where absolute definition was in fact "not
only an impossible but an irrelevant procedure" that involved trying
to obscure "a history and complexity of meanings." To enjoy the privilege of fixing the meaning of potentially justiciable terms such as
antisemitism could be tempting not so much in order to enhance
understanding of them but precisely to be able to exclude certain views
as unwanted and perhaps even unacceptable. The answer to Dina Porat's
question about why a definition was needed was thus not just technical but also ideological.[6]

The postwar generations of campaigners against antisemitism had
not needed a hard-and-fast definition partly because theirs was a less
data-driven age, partly because they were not bothered about Zionism—
before 1967 Israel had simply not been part of the antisemitism

problematic—and partly because they were operating with a contextualized understanding of antisemitism that they sought to link to other social phenomena (such as psychology, racism, poverty, and education) instead of emphasizing what might set it apart. The results had been an unquestionable success: Antisemitism had declined. But by the early twenty-first century that mode of looking at the problem was gone, and the politics had changed: Anti-antisemitism campaigning had become detached from the broader struggle against racism; it had migrated from being associated with the Left to targeting the Left; and it had become connected to Israel, which was both asserting its prominence in Jewish affairs worldwide and subject to increasing international criticism.

As we shall discuss in the next chapter, this new framing of antisemitism has turned out to do little or nothing to improve the efficacy of campaigning against the problem itself: It is a lot better at producing headlines than results. But what was immediately obvious to those monitoring it for the European Union was that while some of the illustrations that accompanied Stern's definition—such as those that covered Holocaust denial—were uncontentious, the ones that dealt with Israel begged many questions. Aware of this, the EUMC first watered down and then gradually abandoned the formula that Stern and his colleagues had produced. Despite being described subsequently as having been adopted by the European Union—there were many false claims in an effort to bolster the definition's credentials—EU bodies remained wary of it; even the EUMC itself ultimately failed to adopt it officially, and the successor agency dropped it entirely.

In another world, this whole attempt to define antisemitism would have ended there. But that is not what happened. Instead, in a development that highlighted the overriding political impulse behind the entire exercise, its originators cast around for another body to lend the definition its imprimatur, presumably because sponsorship by a major Jewish organization or by Israel itself would more likely be discounted as partisan and struggle for general acceptance than one that had been blessed by an international agency. As it happened, a whole alphabet soup of sponsoring authorities was potentially available because some of the staffers from the American Jewish organizations involved not only held observer status in intergovernmental agencies but served in them too. An AJC representative at the Organization for Security and Co-operation in Europe, for example, doubled as the chairman's Personal Representative on Combating Anti-Semitism. And a colleague from the Simon Wiesenthal Center chaired a committee on antisemitism in a lesser-known intergovernmental body, the International Holocaust Remembrance Alliance (IHRA). In existence since 1998, the IHRA worked in the field of Holocaust education in a low-key way, and had managed until then without a definition since it was neither a monitoring body nor a center of scholarly research. But in 2016, lobbying on behalf of the orphaned "working definition" resulted in the members of the IHRA voting to adopt it: The so-called IHRA definition of antisemitism was up and running.[7]

In order to understand what the IHRA has actually put its name to, we might compare its version with the work of professional lexicographers. The *Oxford English Dictionary* (*OED*), for instance, defines antisemitism as:

> *Prejudice, hostility, or discrimination towards Jewish people on religious, cultural, or ethnic grounds.*

The IHRA "working definition" says it is:

> *A certain perception of Jews, which may be expressed as hatred toward Jews. Rhetorical and physical manifestations of antisemitism are directed toward Jewish or non-Jewish individuals and/or their property, toward Jewish community institutions and religious facilities.*

Using nearly three times as many words as the *OED*, the IHRA says less and does so less clearly. In just its first sentence, the word *certain* is not needed; *perception* is an imprecise term; *may be* is odd since a definition generally tells us what something *is*; and *hatred* is not the only and not necessarily even the most important expression of antisemitism. Indeterminate, repetitive, and incomplete, the IHRA formula fails to convey what Thomas Wilson called "the very nature of the thing." In fact, compared to the *OED* version, the IHRA definition is poorly crafted and not really a definition at all. That it has been taken seriously is a conundrum to which we shall return.[8]

Perhaps because of these fairly evident deficiencies in its wording, the main work of the IHRA formula is primarily done not by the two sentences given above but by a number of illustrative examples that follow them. These are couched in conditional terms—which is to say that they give examples of things that may but need not necessarily count as antisemitism. In fact, such illustrations only confuse things further.

For instance, the IHRA says it may be antisemitic to apply "double standards [to Israel] by requiring of it a behavior not expected or demanded of any other democratic nation." It may, but then it may not: We are not told how to spot the difference. Such unfairness has happened, of course, and in the 1970s and 1980s the egregiously one-sided UN Human Rights Council saw tyrannical regimes, often equally bad if not worse abusers of human rights than Israel, picking on it. Yet the chief criticism of Israel today from the international community is not of this kind. It stems not from holding it to a different standard from other democratic states but from applying the same standard. The most frequent and telling criticism is made not despite Israel's policies being akin to those of other democratic states but because, say, its approach to military occupation and international law now diverges significantly from them.

Moreover, organizations are one thing; individuals another. The political scientist Peter Beattie has thoughtfully sorted out the different kinds of reasons why people may focus upon Israel. One of these may indeed be antisemitism, in other words, a desire to find fault with the Jewish state because it is Jewish. But this is not the only one. There is also Third Worldism—a desire to show solidarity with what may be seen as a weaker non-Western people in a struggle with a stronger Western one. A third may be simple ignorance: in other words, lack of knowledge of what is going on elsewhere in the world. One might add a fourth reason too, namely that people can feel a special sense of political responsibility around a specific issue; this may reflect an ethnic, confessional, or familial tie or perhaps just a sense of "not in my name" such as might be felt by a US taxpayer unhappy about the extraordinarily high level of American support for Israel's military. These last three motives—Third World solidarity; ignorance; "not in my name"— do not imply antisemitism. What Beattie shows us is that strong criticism of Israel often has nothing to do with antisemitism at all. He concludes: "Inaccurate charges of anti-Semitism are not merely calumny but threaten to debase the term itself and weaken its connection to a very real, and very dangerous, form of prejudice."[9]

The IHRA generates more confusion when it suggests it can be antisemitic to deny "the Jewish people their right to self-determination, e.g., by claiming that the existence of a State of Israel is a racist endeavor." Here the IHRA unhelpfully runs together two distinct issues. Accusing Israel of racism through and through is obviously contentious; on the other hand, many other countries today are also decried as racist in their very origin—countries in the Americas, for instance, or New Zealand or Australia. We do not prevent people from expressing a debatable view in these cases, and if there are reasons why Israel should be exempt from normal free speech concerns, the IHRA does not give them.

As to the so-called right to self-determination, this is an issue often invoked by proponents of the "new antisemitism" who like to say that antisemitism has simply shifted levels since the end of the Second World War: In the words of Irwin Cotler, for example, "all that has happened is that there was a move from discrimination against the Jews as individuals to discrimination against the Jews as a people."[10] Natan Sharansky makes much the same point. From this angle, denial of "the right of the Jewish people to live as equal members of the family of nations" is said to denote a form of antisemitism: Jews are being denied their right to self-determination.

Yet the argument rests upon a false analogy. For whereas individual rights are bestowed by states upon their citizens, the recognition of a state in international society is granted by the members of that society. International recognition is certainly not granted to all nations and there is in fact no such universal right: Many ethnic groups in the world have never won statehood and likely never will. Responding back in the mid-1960s to loose talk at the UN General Assembly about a general right of self-determination for "all peoples," Harvard political scientist Rupert Emerson concluded his lengthy analysis unambiguously: "All people do *not* have the right of self-determination; they have never had it, and they never will have it."[11]

As it is, the whole discussion is oddly beside the point given that Israel has in fact enjoyed international recognition since it was admitted to the UN as a full member back in 1949; by the late 1960s it had been recognized by most countries in Western Europe, the Americas, and sub-Saharan Africa, and by the twenty-first century by the large majority of UN member states. Some states refuse to recognize it, it is true, more of them than for any other member of the UN. But they are not necessarily motivated by antisemitism; their refusal may stem from political disagreements over territory or history (as with nonrecognition of Taiwan or Armenia). The African states that withdrew recognition after the 1973 war had not suddenly become antisemitic but were taking a political stand, just as they had not suddenly become pro-semitic when they restored diplomatic relations later. What is more, as an essentially political matter, nonrecognition can only be resolved through politics—as Prime Minister Yitzhak Rabin demonstrated in his time in office. To describe nonrecognition as an expression of antisemitism, absent evidence, is thus not only an assumption and a confusion of categories, but also a view that ignores the possibility of a solution.

Equally beside the point is the commonly made claim that it is antisemitic to deny Israel's "right to exist." The Soviet diplomat Andrei Gromyko put the matter succinctly long ago: "As regards the Jewish State, its existence is already a fact; whether or not anyone likes that State, it is actually there."[12] Even more dismissive of talk of a "right to exist" was Menachem Begin. On taking office as prime minister in 1977, he said:

> The right to exist? it would not enter the mind of any Briton or Frenchman, Belgian or Dutchman, Hungarian or Bulgarian, Russian or American, to request for his people recognition of its right to exist. Their existence per se is their right to exist. The same holds true for Israel. We...do not expect anyone to request, on our behalf, that our right to exist in the land of our fathers, be recognized. It is a different recognition which is required between ourselves and our neighbours: recognition of sovereignty and of the mutual need for a life of peace and understanding. It is this mutual recognition that we look forward to: For it we shall make every possible effort.[13]

"Their existence per se is their right to exist." There is little more to be said. As Begin made clear, what matters is international recognition, which is an affair of states, diplomacy, war, and peace. Like other concepts that cluster around the IHRA redefinition of antisemitism, therefore, the meaning of "the right to exist" obscures more than it clarifies. It blurs key distinctions such as that to be made between calling for the very extinction of Jewish life in Israel, on the one hand, and demanding an end to the denial of equal rights to the country's Arabs on the other. It is not to the IHRA definition that we should look for assistance in drawing such sensitive and important distinctions. Fortunately, there are alternatives that provide more meaningful guidance.

The confusing nature and sheer conceptual inadequacy of the IHRA approach is an open secret among scholars. In fact, since the definition's creation and dissemination involved shunning much of the mainstream expertise on the question, it is not surprising that an array of respected researchers took issue with its basic assumptions from the outset. Alternative definitions were produced in response, two of which are fairly close to each other and more in line with most contemporary expert understanding: the so-called Nexus definition and the Jerusalem Declaration on Antisemitism. The latter offers a particularly useful discussion of the central issue—when criticism of Israel is and is not antisemitic—that avoids many of the traps of the IHRA approach and manages to offer tools for combating prejudice while safeguarding political debate and free speech.[14]

Under the category of examples of discussion of Israel that it suggests *would* appear on the face of it to be antisemitic, the Jerusalem Declaration lists the following:

> [a] applying the symbols, images and negative stereotypes of classical antisemitism to the State of Israel; [b] holding Jews collectively responsible for Israel's conduct or treating Jews, simply because they are Jewish, as agents of Israel; [c] requiring people, because they are Jewish, publicly to condemn Israel or Zionism (such as, at a political meeting); [d] assuming non-Israeli Jews, simply because they are Jews, are necessarily more loyal to Israel than to their own countries; [e] denying the right of Jews in the

State of Israel to exist and flourish, collectively and individually, as Jews, in accordance with the principle of equality.

Under the category of examples that would appear *not* to be antisemitic, it lists:

[a] supporting the Palestinian demand for justice and the full grant of their political, national, civil and human rights, as encapsulated in international law; [b] criticizing or opposing Zionism as a form of nationalism, or arguing for a variety of constitutional arrangements for Jews and Palestinians in the area between the Jordan River and the Mediterranean; . . . or to support arrangements that accord full equality to all inhabitants "between the river and the sea," whether in two states, a binational state, unitary democratic state, federal state, or in whatever form; [c] evidence-based criticism of Israel as a state; [d] boycott, divestment and sanctions, which the Declaration notes are commonplace, non-violent forms of political protest against states; [e] political speech—which need not be measured, proportional, tempered, or reasonable to be protected under international law.[15]

A few of its specific observations are helpful and detailed. Thus the Declaration states that it is not antisemitic to point out or assert the existence of systematic racial discrimination in Israel. Just as we do in debating other states, we can accept a position as contentious—for instance, the view that Israel is practicing a form of apartheid or settler colonialism—without deeming it antisemitic. Antisemitism is not the same as mere unreasonableness; and merely because a view on Israel is felt by some to be outrageous or disconcerting does not make it a matter of prejudice.

All this is laid out straightforwardly in a quite different spirit to the IHRA formula and constitutes a clarifying response to it. Emerging out of a series of workshops convened by an Israeli institute of advanced studies—the Van Leer Jerusalem Institute—this Declaration has been signed or endorsed since its appearance in 2020 by many of the world's leading scholars. Benefiting from the advantage of having appeared after the IHRA text, it is able to dispel a number of confusions that the former has fostered. Yet remarkably, neither it nor any other definition has enjoyed anything close to the same political support or international success as the IHRA's. In fact, in a back-handed acknowledgment of their existence and perhaps their merits, the 2023 antisemitism bill that passed the US House explicitly rules out the use of rival definitions. Likely in the face of scholarly criticism, the IHRA's website now flags that its definition is supposed to be not only a "working" one but also "non-legally binding." But that is like shutting the stable door after the horse has bolted: It is no longer up to the IHRA to determine what shall be legally binding and what not.

The IHRA definition has been internationally embraced on a scale vastly disproportionate to its merits. In December 2016, the US Senate passed the Anti-Semitism Awareness Act, which made reference to it. An executive order signed by President Trump in 2019 also referred to it.[16] To date more than forty governments have endorsed it in one way or another, including almost all the members of the EU, as have thirty-four US states and most of the provinces in Canada. In the UK, universities have come under pressure to adopt it, and most have done so in one form or another; hundreds of other organizations across Europe and North America have incorporated it into their training programs. Others, however, notably the UN itself, have so far held off.[17]

Lemmings may not in fact commit mass suicide, but lemming-like behavior by international actors and official institutions often leads to poorly considered and counterproductive results. As a result of adopting the IHRA formula, some countries—notably the United States—now in effect find themselves attempting to dictate what their own nationals may or may not say about another country. There seems to be little if any precedent for this, and the potential consequences for freedom of expression are profound. For, as a shield deflecting foreign policy criticism while presenting itself as a means to combat hate crime, the IHRA definition of antisemitism provides the kind of armor many countries would like to have. One can easily imagine, for instance, how advantageous the Kremlin would have found it to have been able to watch the US clamp down on anti-Russian speech in 2022. The slippage this conception of antisemitism offers between the domestic level (abhorring violence against an ethnicity) and the international level (ruling out-of-bounds certain criticisms of another country) makes it extraordinarily powerful. And while the case of antisemitism remains to date unique, Hindu nationalists have already been inspired by the IHRA example and some hope to define "Hinduphobia" and have it enshrined in US antidiscrimination law in ways that will effectively silence critics of Hindutva in the United States. Behind them may be others, awaiting their turn in the lobbying queue. What will be left of free speech then? The answer may be found by exploring in greater detail what adoption of the IHRA's definition of antisemitism has meant for political dissent, public debate, and cultural life more generally on both sides of the Atlantic.[18]

CHAPTER 10

Hunting the Wrong Elephant

It has been said that the British Empire was lost and won on the play-ing fields of Eton. The crown of Judaism and Jewishness will be won and lost on the campuses of America.

RABBI IRVING GREENBERG, "JEWISH SURVIVAL AND THE COLLEGE CAMPUS," 1968[1]

Any criticism is anti-semitic; every opponent is an enemy; every enemy is Hitler; every year is 1938.

AVRAHAM BURG, FORMER SPEAKER OF THE KNESSET, JULY 26, 2022[2]

It is easy to tell the story of the past few years either as a conspiracy theory—a story of the deliberate exploitation and weaponization of a term—or as a clash of cultural and ideological beliefs, moral norms, and mutual incomprehension. What is harder is to do justice to it as a blend of all these things and more. It would be naive to ignore the ways in which the IHRA definition has been used politically. At the same time, Western societies are demonstrably more sensitive to ques-tions of bias and discrimination than ever before, and an age inclined to see feelings as truth is one that gives emotions and perceptions new weight in matters of prejudice. These factors vastly complicate any effort to assess the scale and significance of antisemitism in our time.[3]

The essential geopolitical fact is that a highly contentious and problematic definition of it has been promoted and disseminated in a time when polls have consistently shown a long-term hardening of global opinion against Israel. Claiming—and over time, no doubt, having largely come to believe—that antisemitism was largely the reason for this, the country's foreign policy and military elite appears for a long while mostly to have reconciled itself to this worldwide trend, regarding the alliance with Washington, and behind that, American public opinion, as the vital factors. Yet cracks in the latter are appearing, for although public support in the United States has remained robust since 1967, there are signs it is beginning to follow the international pattern, to express greater concern about the direction of the hard-line policies pursued by the Netanyahu government, and to show far more sympathy toward the Palestinians. This is not an either/or matter: Most people remain supportive of Israel even as they criticize its use of indiscriminate and overwhelming force. But the trend is unmistakable, especially among young Americans, and a generation gap in attitudes has opened up.

That American campuses have turned into a key arena for the resulting tensions is not surprising: They have, after all, been a site of Jewish ambivalence for decades. Dreaming of their children succeeding in college, many Jewish parents simultaneously feared what might become of them there. The old anxiety was the lure of assimilation and secularization: The siren call of the blond shiksa haunted the nightmares of Jewish mothers from the moment quotas disappeared. "College is a disaster area for Judaism, Jewish loyalty and Jewish identity," wrote Rabbi Irving Greenberg in 1968, warning that academia preached a "universal, secularist life-style" that looked down on "ethnic tribalism."[4] The rise of identity politics allayed this particular concern—ethnic tribalism has flourished on American campuses—but brought new worries about left-wing indoctrination, antipathy to Israel, and latterly even antisemitism itself.

These things have been associated in many people's minds for some time now, and the belief that universities have become centers of political correctness has unfortunately made those worried about antisemitism more accepting of attacks on them. Academics have their own jargon, it is true, and postmodernism has not helped. But the political correctness argument is often based more on hearsay than on a real sense of what universities are like. To describe them as "essentially factories of Maoist cadres," as one pundit did recently, suggests real ignorance of the work they do: If there is one thing American society does not have to fear from its universities, it is the mass production of Maoists. (Most students, including those protesting, would probably have difficulty finding, let alone recognizing, one, and Maoist faculty these days are about as common as the dodo.) In their anxiety, the worriers typically misjudge the forces that shape the outlook of young people: Campuses reflect larger changes in the culture more than they generate them. Just as American society's shift toward ethnic politics belied the concerns of Rabbi Greenberg, young Americans across the board in the early twenty-first century were changing their minds about the Israel-Palestine question. College students were scarcely unusual in following social trends: If they protested, it was because they chose to and not because they were being told what to do by their professors.[5]

The growing generational divide between student protesters on one side and parents, alumni, donors, and trustees on the other was graphically illustrated in the spring of 2024 (see also the Epilogue). While university encampments made headlines, newspapers revealed that a group of billionaires had quietly got together to urge a police clampdown against pro-Palestinian demonstrators on campuses in New York City. Products of a different era, these men were accustomed to seeing Israel as a plucky and beleaguered underdog and felt outraged by the protests. Many of the students, for their part, were equally outraged by US support for an occupying force that was systematically evicting Palestinians from their ancestral homes and obliterating much of Gaza. The older generation understood the Holocaust to enjoin undying solidarity with Israel; the younger believed it meant standing up to be counted in the face of state-organized mass violence. As the businessmen were mostly around sixty years old or above, the students were young enough to have been their grandchildren. Or more precisely their granddaughters, for passing almost unnoticed at the time was the fact that the billionaires were all men while a preponderance of the students were female. Religion itself was irrelevant, for Jewish student opinion was itself divided, and there were plenty of protesting students who, like the billionaires, were Jewish and who also invoked this fact as the reason for their activism.[6]

To understand the role played by competing ideas of antisemitism in this struggle, we need to go back in time to the early 2000s. For it was then that those anxious to combat what they saw as a new antisemitism began to look to American universities and colleges to take the fight there. On the one hand, they sought to garner academic backing for their own approach by setting up programs and institutes; on the other, they hoped to combat the shifts in student opinion that disturbed them through clampdowns and other forms of pressure. But because advocacy and academia are actually less easily integrated than is often thought, because the scholarly mainstream had long contested the premises of the new antisemitism paradigm, and because the paradigm itself involved a misjudged response to student activism, what followed was a story of increasingly painful entanglements.

In 2006—amid intense international discussion about antisemitism in the post–Cold War world—Yale University proudly hailed the launch of the first ever interdisciplinary research initiative into antisemitism at an American university. Only five years later, however, it closed the initiative down. Some onlookers criticized the program's lack of scholarly rigor; others commented upon the dangers of advocacy masquerading as scholarship. The initiative's founder—who had never been a member of the tenured faculty—left Yale to focus on running the Institute for the Study of Global Antisemitism and Policy (ISGAP). Although ISGAP's website makes it look rather like yet another academic research center, it is committed to "fighting antisemitism on the battlefield of ideas" and the sort of "research" it does includes allegations that secret Gulf State government donations have been corrupting academic work in the United States. In fact, ISGAP is funded by the Israeli government and its advisers include ex–government minister Natan Sharansky as well as a former intelligence officer, Sima Vaknin-Gil, who was director-general of the Israeli Ministry of Strategic Affairs and Public Diplomacy. Put simply: We seem to be somewhere between the world of academia and the shadow realm of what are known today as "influence campaigns."

Organizations like ISGAP, which originated around the time of the first efforts to forge a new working definition of antisemitism, should be seen in the context of the larger semi-public Israeli government effort to improve the country's image abroad and to try to curb the impact of pro-Palestinian groups. Vaknin-Gil herself told the Knesset in 2017—the year after the dissemination of the IHRA definition really began—that Israeli government agencies were working together to solve the problem of the country's plummeting global reputation. Rebranding had been tried and failed; curbing criticism abroad was the new priority. Faced with the growth of the Boycott, Divestment, and Sanctions (BDS) movement, Vaknin-Gil described activist protest abroad as an existential threat to national survival. The strategy she outlined implied getting the BDS movement outlawed as antisemitic, and in general seeking to shape the international debate over antisemitism—in short an intervention in the cultural, intellectual, and academic life of other countries in the form of a countermobilization against supporters of the Palestinians. The "battlefield of ideas" thus formed part of a larger war to be waged far beyond the Middle East. Such a militarized view of intellectual and academic life in the West has today become commonplace among competing external political actors. Campuses are the "second front of the war," Natan Sharansky wrote after October 7: "Student activists are our infantry.... May our soldiers on both fronts continue to be strong."[7]

This is of course basically an activist view of education and no doubt it was shared by some on the opposing side of the argument over the Middle East. But the discrepancy in the relative power and influence of the two sides was unmistakable, especially in the US, where the concept of antisemitism could be made to do so much work. For it was the IHRA's conflation of antisemitism with criticism of Israel that opened the way to depict student protests as predominantly antisemitic and thus allowed outsiders a plausible basis for intervention in university life. Already by the time Israel's government embarked upon the initiative described by Vaknin-Gil, the potential for misuse of the antisemitism definition was worrying some people. One of the first to express alarm was the man who had originally drafted it. Back in 2010, Kenneth Stern learned about plans to invoke his definition in civil rights litigation against American universities. He knew better than anyone that it had not been intended for that purpose; a long-time free speech advocate, he held the view that even hateful talk ought to be allowed on campus. As he put it: "I can say I think Israel is Nazi-like and shouldn't have to worry about being prosecuted." Inside the AJC at that time, other staffers shared Stern's concern about the dangers the definition they had helped draft now posed, and Stern took the step of issuing a statement opposing its misuse. "By trying to censor anti-Israel remarks," he warned, "it becomes more, not less, difficult to tackle both antisemitism and anti-Israel dogma." But this letter, which Stern authored jointly with the president of the American Association of University Professors, set off a firestorm of criticism from right-wing Jewish groups that was so fierce that the letter was disavowed by the AJC president, David Harris. Stern eventually quit the organization where he had worked for twenty-five years and would become a leading critic of the abuse of the IHRA definition. Harris later joined the board of ISGAP. The split within American Jewish life over whether the IHRA definition actually helps or hinders the fight against antisemitism was reflected in their divergent paths.[8]

Since then, the problem Stern feared has become far greater. American Jewish groups that once opposed anti-discrimination measures on free speech grounds have come out demanding similar action against antisemitism. Faced with the accusation they were more concerned with certain kinds of prejudice than others, universities found themselves on the back foot. Their ability to appeal to the principle of free speech was limited because they were already policing potentially offensive discourse. Rather than treating their students as adults and thinking subjects, they seemed more and more to regard them as easily wounded loci of feelings. Some of this reflected a new cultural sensitivity to trauma, a category with an ever-widening ambit; some reflected a subjectivist turn that made the recipient's feelings about a potential injury the test of whether injury had occurred. But there was another reason too: Thanks to US federal antidiscrimination law, university administrators faced the threat of being charged with creating a "hostile environment" for specified groups.

It was this that now opened the way for people to argue—for more or less the first time with some prospect of success—that criticism of Israel might itself be said to create a hostile environment. Previously no one had thought to use antidiscrimination law in this way. But assisted by the blurry ambiguities of the IHRA definition, civil rights attorneys started to file Title VI cases with the Department of Education against universities they said were tolerating antisemitism. A pioneer of this approach, Kenneth Marcus, was appointed in 2018 to direct the department's Office for Civil Rights (OCR). It was the thin end of the wedge. By 2024 dozens of American colleges and universities found themselves the subject of OCR inquiries, which could be triggered by complaints brought not by students or their representatives but by politicized advocacy groups. At risk were not only institutional reputations but millions of dollars in federal funding. Even as the US government began rolling up the larger antidiscrimination apparatus, it flagged campus antisemitism as a special case. A mechanism that had been designed originally to defend the victims of social injustice was being turned into a means of censoring debate and cowing universities. Those who had once fiercely attacked cancel culture now became its most ardent advocates; those who had demanded viewpoint diversity now sought to close debate down. And at the heart of this effort, enjoying an almost totemic significance, was the IHRA definition of antisemitism.[9]

Even before private universities like Harvard bowed to political pressure and incorporated the IHRA formulation in crafting their own internal antidiscrimination policies, a number of US state legislatures were introducing bills against antisemitism which mandated that public colleges or state agencies adopt the IHRA definition. Several of them made matters worse by ignoring the conditionality in the IHRA examples—the IHRA text says only that the cases it lists *may* count as antisemitism—and referring to them as if they constituted proof of it. A New York bill proposes outlawing any event promoting antisemitism on campus—surely a laudable aim—but then cites the IHRA in a way that leaves it entirely unclear what is covered and what is not: A literal reading of the bill would imply that any criticism of an individual Israeli politician, for example, would risk running foul of the law. In response, PEN America has argued that "ill-considered proposals regarding antisemitism" risk restricting protected speech, while Stern himself has described efforts to legislate "something that's inherently political speech" as a "total travesty."[10]

Some activists with the campuses in their sights have taken a more direct route, preferring forms of rent-a-mob intimidation that see any speaking out on behalf of the Palestinians as antisemitism. The history of this practice goes back forty years to the aftermath of the 1982 invasion of Lebanon, when the ADL and other groups circulated lists of scholars they alleged "use their anti-Zionism as merely a guise for their deeply felt anti-Semitism." But in those days such McCarthyite actions were still new and shocking: Indeed, the ADL disavowed one such list, after being accused of thus defaming academics, writing it off as "an unfortunate incident." Innocent times by today's standards, when such tactics have broadened and coarsened and become a ubiquitous feature of anti-antisemitism activism. Online blacklists, doxing trucks, and vitriolic social media shaming campaigns spray accusations of antisemitism against professors and students alike. Although it is hard to credit, some of those responsible are themselves students and faculty who not only record campus life but collaborate with intelligence or police services to inform on their fellows. In a well-known example from 2025, Palestinian student activist Mahmoud Khalil was first harassed online and then seized and threatened with deportation: Those involved vaunted their achievement. One can only imagine what early campaigners—men such as Louis Marshall in the United States or the German Jewish émigré Alfred Weiner (whose library still testifies to the seriousness of his approach) would have made of what is now being perpetrated in the name of fighting antisemitism.[11]

Nearly half a century ago, Nahum Goldmann, the founder of the World Jewish Congress, warned "of the greatest danger for a people that, after centuries of persecution and lack of power, comes to a position of strength, wealth, and power within one short generation." What is done today purportedly to combat antisemitism suggests he was right and shows the sea change that has taken place since those days—one Goldmann's generation had lived through—when Jews feared the arbitrary power of the state and understood all too well the dread of a knock at the door. Now, in the United States, some are so at ease with their own access to power and feel their interests to be so happily aligned with those of the American state that they publicly brag about their role in getting others defamed, expelled, dismissed, or arrested. One might write them off as misguided extremists. But what does it tell us about the deep hold of the values and assumptions now animating such actions that far from condemning the distress they are causing to innocent people, and their corrosion of the trust needed for learning to take place at all, the major American Jewish organizations have stayed silent or actively supported such tactics, either because they genuinely share their concerns or because they worry about being outflanked by the hotheads. Indeed, rather than acknowledging the dangers of abusing anxiety about antisemitism, they have seemed to want only to heighten it. The ADL, for instance, has devised what it calls a Campus Antisemitism Report Card to grade universities on how well they are doing. In the small print we read: "Just because a school has received a letter grade A or B based on the above method-ology does not mean that the school does not have an antisemitism problem." With caveats like this, it is not surprising to learn that the ADL's "methodology" raises serious questions and is weighted to making things seem as grim as possible. Lauded by politicians and criticized by many students, such gimmicks show how far leading Jewish advocacy organizations have fallen from the commitment to truth and public purpose that guided their predecessors in tackling serious issues of discrimination in the past. A Jewish student recently analyzed the shortcomings in ADL "research" methods and concluded that "it seems like part of a larger pattern of outsiders off-campus claiming to have the answers to the problems of students, staff and faculty of a university, while speaking over us in the process." Another wondered openly why external activists seem to be so keen to encour-age fighting rather than learning.[12]

The short answer is that it is politics, of course, but the politics is not all of one kind. For flying under the banner of fighting antisemi-tism and standing up for Israel, there has emerged a coalition of three overlapping groups. On the one hand, there are those whose primary concern is Israel itself and who desire to defend it from criticism by all means necessary. Overlapping with them is a significant portion of American Jewry, some of it organized, some of it not, supportive no doubt of Israel but animated primarily by anxiety about the effect of campus antisemitism upon students. These two groups have been now joined by a third, quite different segment of American political life—a broad coalition of conservative culture warriors for whom the question of antisemitism matters little in itself but serves instrumentally to advance a broader agenda. The anti-liberal Heritage Foundation, for instance, with roots in Christian conservatism, is keen primarily to promote free-market economics and to roll back big government and programs of social amelioration. For like-minded pressure groups on the Right, the issue of antisemitism facilitates their drive to police the universities, end long-standing anti-discrimination and diversity initiatives, reassert "Western values," and reaffirm the role of religion in American life. That such groups may traffic in conspiracy theories and have indeed been accused of being antisemitic has not blinded them to the advantages of co-opting the war on antisemitism. For it turns out to be an issue that neutralizes most Democrats who would otherwise oppose them, and is ideally suited to fuel a sweeping assault on the ideological enemy that they have always seen in the Left.

The long-standing presumption of "the new antisemitism" that anti-Jewish prejudice was a problem of Marxist culture has thus turned out to offer the American Right the opening it sought for its own cultural counterrevolution. This all makes perfect sense in political terms and it exploded into public view early in the second Trump administration. Whether so closely linking the fight against prejudice to the forces of Christian nationalism and anti-liberalism actually helps fight antisemitism or makes Jews safer is highly debatable, and a question we shall return to later in the chapter. Meantime, we might remember Chenevix Trench's warning: When a term with a once-precise meaning comes to be used "in a wider, vaguer, more indefinite way...[it] has lost its place in the army of words and become one of a loose and disorderly mob."

"What puts the 'new' into 'new antisemitism'?" asked scholar Brian Klug. "The answer in a word is anti-Zionism." The equating of anti-semitism with anti-Zionism has been extraordinarily successful politically in that it enabled pro-Palestinian protests to be labeled as antisemitic. After the 2019 presidential executive order on antisemitism was issued, with its reference to the IHRA definition, a White House adviser remarked that the administration was adopting a "definition of antisemitism... [that] makes it clear what our administration has stated publicly and on the record: anti-Zionism is antisemitism." In fact, the IHRA text does not mention the term *anti-Zionism* and makes few hard-and-fast assertions of any kind and certainly none supporting this view. Despite this, a formula that was originally intended to demarcate the line between permissible and impermissible criticism of Israel is now often cited to rule out any criticism of it at all.

If we really want to figure out the relationship between antisemitism and anti-Zionism, the first thing to note is that the latter is a capacious term that can mean quite different things to different people: To talk about being against anti-Zionism is thus to say little. Anti-Zionism may, for instance, be based upon a principled dislike of ethnonationalism of all kinds—whether Jewish or non-Jewish—and there is certainly nothing antisemitic in that unless it is antisemitic simply to believe nationalism is bad, as many people do. For others it may connote radical disapproval of the outcome of 1948 or maybe a desire for a polity with equal rights for all on either side of the pre-1967 borders. Some espouse the dream of an earlier generation of idealistic Zionists, namely a single federated state for both Arabs and Jews, and some may indeed dream of a state without Jews at all. But these are all different from one another in their implications. Ethnic cleansing is deplorable whatever the intended target, whether it is carried out by Arabs or for that matter by Jews; as the Jerusalem Declaration clarifies, calling for violence against Jews is a different matter from hoping to see the existing Jewish state turn into one that gives all its citizens equal rights irrespective of their faith. To all these, one might add what Antony Lerman once called forms of "fictive anti-Zionism" that bear no relation to anything in the real world. Thus

"Zionist" has been used as a slur to denounce enemies as various as Chinese Communists (by Radio Outer Mongolia) or Papa Doc (by Haitian exiles). In right-wing circles in the United States, the prefix "Zio-" is used to denote foes, much as "Judeo-" did for the Nazis. And of course there is the Stalinist precedent for using anti-Zionism as a thinly disguised way of talking nastily about Jews.

In short, anti-Zionism carries the risk of its own form of intolerance and prejudice, as history makes clear. But that is a very different matter from saying it is *equivalent* to antisemitism, which it clearly is not. In what is perhaps the most thoughtful discussion of their interrelation, the historian David Myers sees anti-Zionists as making a crucial contribution to a "debate over issues of key import to the Jewish future," namely the basic character of Israel. From that perspective, he advises, shutting down speech purely on the grounds that it is couched in the language of anti-Zionism is not simply wrong but harmful.[13]

But let us assume for a moment—as a thought experiment—that anti-Zionism really does equal antisemitism. Does that mean that because Israel is a Jewish state no criticism of it at all is possible without being antisemitic? Although rarely articulated so starkly, no doubt because the premise might then start to seem questionable, we can find examples of recent political reasoning that move in this direction. The British Chief Rabbi Jonathan Sacks, for example, once testified to a parliamentary committee that accusing Israel "of racism, ethnic cleansing, attempted genocide, crimes against humanity" was not merely inaccurate but itself antisemitic. And in 2024 some Labour MPs in the UK criticized their own government's decision to withdraw arms export licenses from Israel because of the fighting in Gaza. They were quoted as saying that while "we have been tackling antisemitism in our party, [the Foreign Secretary and the Prime Minister] seem to be taking sides in a conflict that involves the world's only Jewish state." Their implication appeared to be that the British government should back "the world's only Jewish state" or at least abstain from criticizing it if it wished to avoid the charge of antisemitism.[14]

Yet Kenneth Stern's original effort—at the very start of the IHRA definition saga—did not for a moment presuppose that antisemitism and anti-Zionism were the same. On the contrary, his assumption was that they were distinct discourses with an overlap that needed to be demarcated. For someone like Stern as for others in the AJC at the time, criticism of Israel was both permissible and (on free speech grounds) desirable: The objective was to help figure out where it drifted over the line into antisemitism. In fact, as we have seen, the definition that he drafted and that was taken up with minor modifications by the IHRA failed to achieve this. Instead, it has created a confusion that means many of those who cite it appear to believe there is simply no line at all, or at any rate, none they can plausibly identify.

A definition is supposed to be clear, which the IHRA "working definition" is not. But is it perhaps precisely here—in its very lack of clarity— that the explanation for its remarkable political career lies? Could it be that its chief recommendation as a definition in the eyes of those who have most ardently promoted it lies in its *failure* to define? After all, as Jacques Derrida once pointed out: "The more confused a concept, the more it lends itself to opportunistic appropriation." Scholars can protest its shortcomings. But if organizations are told that contravening the IHRA definition will expose them to legal or bureaucratic jeopardy, and if they are unsure what exactly *does* contravene the definition, they will likely err on the side of caution. It is in this way that the definition threatens intellectual freedom. Shoddy drafting can actually be useful because it allows words to mean different things to different people and hence to expand the range of their impact. PEN America has noted the problem of lawmakers relying on the IHRA in drafting legislation and warns of the consequences: "By forcing schools to consider criticism of Israeli policies as possible 'crypto' antisemitism, the likely outcome here will be schools overreacting.... Such an approach would impair free expression and open the door to efforts to curtail other forms of speech that specific groups may regard as inherently offensive."[15]

These free speech concerns are far from imaginary; indeed, they are already having an impact well beyond universities thanks to busy politicians, unconcerned about what they may see as mere semantics, who have been adopting the IHRA formula as an easy form of virtue signaling. This is not only a problem confined to the United States. During the furor in 2017–18 over allegations of antisemitism in the British Labour Party, for instance, it was the party's embrace of the IHRA definition that served as a signal to the public that the issue was being dealt with.[16] For others in public life—arts bodies, festival organizers—it may provide a convenient court of appeal given the general uncertainty over what antisemitism really is. As a result, the definition is doing on an extensive scale what some of its supporters clearly intend it to do: shutting down protest on behalf of the Palestinians. A recent survey of western European countries reveals dozens of cases between 2017 and 2023 in which the IHRA definition was invoked to the detriment, almost exclusively, of speakers on Middle Eastern issues. The old worry of antisemitism campaigners, the threat of violence from the Right, seems to have turned into a secondary concern.[17]

Although the free speech fallout has been visible in many countries in Europe, nowhere perhaps has it been greater or more disturbing than in Germany, where the IHRA definition was adopted by decision of the federal cabinet. Because reunification in 1990 aroused historical memories of the last time a powerful Germany was at the heart of Europe, signaling the country's complete break from the past on the Jewish question has been regarded as essential by its political elite for many years. This has meant the adoption of a variety of measures from Holocaust education to formalizing support for the official communal leadership, the Central Council of Jews in Germany, and providing help for the large number of Russian Jews who settled in the country after the collapse of the USSR. Close ties with Israel date back to the time of Ben-Gurion and Chancellor Adenauer, who brokered a reparations agreement in 1952. Since 1990 there has been a quasi-alliance between the two countries through military cooperation and arms sales, solidarity in international forums, and even occasional joint cabinet meetings. Under Chancellor Angela Merkel, Israel's security was even declared a German "reason of state" (though whether that meant the same thing as unconditional support remained uncertain for a long time). Since 2018 it has also involved combating antisemitism through specially appointed commissioners of whom there are now several dozen in various echelons of government.[18]

What then does it mean to tackle antisemitism while standing, in the words of Merkel's successor, "by Israel's side"? It means for one thing relying heavily on the new anti-antisemitism commissioners and their conception of their role. Despite evidence from German police data that identifies perpetrators of violence against Jews as coming overwhelmingly from the Right, these new commissioners have seemed reluctant to single out right-wing antisemitism as a problem, preferring to cite the IHRA definition against left-wing critics of Israel and clamping down on nonviolent expressions of support for Palestine.[19] Felix Klein, the Federal Commissioner for Jewish Life in Germany and the Fight Against Antisemitism, was quoted in 2021 as saying: "It is important that we do not hierarchize which form of antisemitism is currently the most dangerous, but rather examine all three sources of antisemitism, the left, the right and the religious, in an unbiased manner."[20] In fact, the problem is not bias but prioritizing the suppression of legitimate speech over the threat of racist violence. Commissioners have unhesitatingly branded distinguished intellectuals as antisemites (including well-known Jewish thinkers) because they criticized the Netanyahu government, and at least one commissioner has even cast doubt on whether German Jews critical of Israel are really Jewish at all.

But the commissioners in their partiality merely reflect the problematic attitude of the German political class as a whole, which has allowed a sense of historical guilt to lead it astray. A telling case concerned the German historian, Peter Schäfer, a respected scholar of early Judaism. The author of a masterly study of anti-Jewish hatred in the ancient world, Schäfer left Princeton University in 2013 to become director of the Jewish Museum in Berlin. Five years later, the Israeli prime minister took the remarkable step of complaining about an exhibition about Jerusalem at the museum on the grounds it was biased against Israel. The head of the German Jewish community chimed in, though it transpired he had not visited the exhibition. Although on that occasion the German culture minister defended the museum, the barrage of complaints was incessant. The following year the Bundestag passed a resolution deeming the BDS movement antisemitic. The debate was acrimonious and even some of those who voted for the resolution feared it was unconstitutional and expressed concern about the free speech implications. Their worries were borne out a few months later when the Jewish Museum's spokesperson tweeted critically about the BDS resolution. A storm of vitriolic criticism was directed both against the museum and against Schäfer personally and he decided to resign. In this way, one of the world's most respected authorities on antisemitism was hounded from office as an antisemite. "The accusation of antisemitism is a club that allows one to deal a very rapid death blow," Schäfer commented later. "Political elements who have an interest in this used and are using it."[21]

The Schäfer affair should have been a wake-up call that the fight against antisemitism risked discrediting the term itself. What it unfortunately illustrated was the susceptibility of the German political class to moral blackmail. Jewish opinion in Germany and abroad was sharply divided but only one side seemed to count politically. A barrage of unhinged accusations of antisemitism that should have been self-evidently absurd in the case of a figure like Schäfer proved sufficient to outweigh the counterprotests of cultural and academic leaders in Germany and abroad. Privately, German politicians and diplomats complained about the abuse of the antisemitism accusation; some even warned that Germany's tolerance for supporting Israel abroad would wane if such things continued. But they were the ones retreating to legalism and enforcing censorship on arts managers, museum directors, and academics. Meanwhile, organizations such as the Simon Wiesenthal Center, possessing no special academic credentials, felt justified in complaining to Chancellor Angela Merkel when antisemitism researchers at the Technical University Berlin supported scholars whose views on Israel and Zionism they found wanting. Far from things improving, Germany's antisemitism commissioners set about enforcing the IHRA line yet more stringently. Some tragic-comic limit of absurdity was perhaps reached in 2021 when the Simon Wiesenthal Center even denounced one of Germany's anti-antisemitism commissioners as an antisemite, ranking him number seven in its Global Anti-Semitism Top Ten list for the year. It took this attack on one of her own colleagues to elicit a rare rebuke from the EU's coordinator for fighting antisemitism, Katharina von Schnurbein.[22]

Not that there are many signs of a reassessment. On the contrary, the fallout following the Hamas attack on Israel in October 2023 has hardened the climate, introducing an unpleasant anti-immigrant note into the entire debate. In November 2024, the Bundestag passed another resolution on "Protecting, Preserving and Strengthening Jewish Life in Germany," which reaffirmed the BDS ban, and once again conflated the fight against antisemitism with "hostility to Israel." What was clear was the extent to which the German political class believed itself obliged to provide Israel extensive immunity in the face of criticism; altogether less clear was what this approach would actually do to protect Jewish life in Germany.[23]

What this whole debate forces us to confront, in fact, is the possibility of a fundamental clash between the interests of Israel as defined by its political leadership and those of the Jewish diaspora. For the awkward truth is that concern for the flourishing of Jewish life in Europe is not only distinct from a policy of outlawing criticism of Israel; it may in some ways even be at cross-purposes with it. As the writer Ian Buruma has noted: "In today's political environment, being pro-Israel and antisemitic is not a contradiction." Indeed, more and more antisemites on both sides of the Atlantic find in Netanyahu's Israel a mirror of their own right-wing aspirations and a potential partner. It is in this vein, for instance, that the far-Right Alternative for Germany has hailed Israel as a role model for Germany. The problem does not only lie on the far Right, however. There is the deeply problematic nature of mainstream Germany's quasi-official philo-semitism (perhaps more accurately, philo-Israelism), which has a long history dating back to the earliest years of postwar West German reconstruction, and which today offers a means, as one cultural theorist has shown, for much of the country's political elite to performatively demonstrate their love for Jews. Yet this approach, which was supposed to provide the answer to antisemitism, can uncomfortably resemble it in its basic assumptions.[24] "A philosemite," a leading historian of Germany has written, only partly tongue-in-cheek, "is an antisemite who loves Jews." Especially perhaps when they are living in Israel. For in fostering the view that tackling antisemitism means defending Israel, the German authorities come close to implying that Israel is in some sense where Jews truly belong. Nor is Germany the only case of a country whose politicians apparently accept at face value Israel's claim to be the ultimate guarantor of Jewish life. President Biden remarked more than once—provoking some consternation within liberal

American Jewish circles—that "if there weren't an Israel, every Jew in the world would be at risk." Antisemites want Jews out of their country; philo-semites suggest their real protector is not their own state but rather Israel; Israeli governments say they are the safeguard for Jews all over the world. The space between these three positions is not broad. Not one of them helps to nurture Jewish life in the diaspora.[25]

It is time to ask a fairly basic question that is not asked often enough: Where fighting antisemitism is concerned, what works? For today two paradigms of antisemitism coexist, confusingly offering competing views of what it is and implying very different kinds of responses. The dominant version, the one that has landed us where we are, insists, as the Jerusalem School did before it, that prejudice against Jews is in some important sense eternal, independent of context, and unique. It posits a close connection in modern times between antisemitism and hostility to Israel, which it sees as the newest form of the ancient hatred. At root, it doubts the existence of much of a remedy beyond endless watchfulness, and (with the possible exception of American Jewry, which is often seen as a case apart) it regards the existence of Jewish minorities outside Israel as precarious and perhaps even ultimately doomed. The only solution to antisemitism by this logic is (as it has always been) to support a Jewish state and to defend it against all those who attack it, in words or deeds. The other view, which emerged out of the experience of Nazism and the Second World War, and was once far more influential than it is now, sees antisemitism as time—and context—dependent, capable of being studied and understood and tackled. It sees it as affecting the life of Jewish minorities in nation-states, existing in close relation with other forms of racism. It regards these diaspora minorities as having the same right to exist as any other section of the Jewish world, it is by the nature of its outlook suspicious of the extremes of nationalism, and it regards any linkage with Israel in a much more contingent light.

It is, needless to say, the former of these two positions that has spurred the vigorous campaigning against antisemitism of the past few years, underpinned by the IHRA definition. Yet for the first time even some of its best-known advocates are beginning to admit it has not worked. Speaking before the Israeli Knesset in January 2025, for instance, the ADL's chief executive, himself one of its most ardent proselytes, confessed failure and called for fresh thinking. Such a revealing admission of defeat may not bother those who have merely used the fight against antisemitism for their own ends. But anyone who does care about antisemitism must be wondering by now where the evidence is that the current approach is productive when by the ADL's own reckoning the problem keeps getting worse and worse.

One place to start perhaps would be by questioning the idea that antisemitism is sui generis and best tackled apart from other forms of bigotry. There is, after all, long-standing empirical support for the idea that prejudice against Jews is connected to other factors, most obviously to other forms of racial prejudice. A 1964 analysis of nearly thirty years of AJC-sponsored poll data noted that "when hostility toward Jews showed an increase . . . so did hostility toward other minorities." FBI statistics show a similar correlation in recent years between trends in antisemitic and other hate crimes. The practical implication is that a broad anti-racist strategy is more likely to identify the ideological roots of antisemitic violence—and hence the likely perpetrators—than an approach taking antisemitism in isolation. "Antisemitism and Islamophobia are two sides of the same coin, and stem from the same root," the Runnymede Trust—the UK's leading racial justice research organization—has noted.[26]

If reliable sources of data thus point to one major source for antisemitic violence today in racism, they point unequivocally to the other as well: turmoil in the Middle East. Analysts from the well-respected Center for the Study of Hate and Extremism at California State University have found a close correlation between spikes in conflict there and in antisemitic incidents in the United States. According to researcher Brian Levin, three decades of data "clearly show huge percentage spikes in anti-Jewish hate crime in the US when there is war in the Holy Land." "There's been no factor that explains increases in antisemitism greater than when Israel is engaged in violent conflict with its neighbors," reports Ayal Feinberg. Much the same has been observed with incidents of Islamophobia. Such findings, which apply to Europe as well as to the United States, help explain why there is no evidence that the new framing of antisemitism implicit in the IHRA definition has actually helped either to diminish prejudice or to shift attitudes toward the Middle East. Indeed, they shed light on the two main reasons behind its profound failure. The blanket condemnation of Israel's critics as antisemites overlooks a major long-standing source of antisemitic violence around the world today, which is the racist Right. And when attitudes toward the Middle East produce bigotry, prejudice, and antisemitic violence, the spur is often less eternal hatred of Jews than what is happening in Israel.[27]

In ignoring these realities, the recent politicization of the antisemitism debate, far from aiding Jews, has arguably left them more vulnerable, not less. A 2025 report evaluating the fight against antisemitism in the UK states unequivocally that the current approach has itself become "detrimental to Jewish communities' safety and well-being." For the United States itself, a recent survey of more than four thousand students comes to an equally stark conclusion: Equating antisemitism with criticism of Israel leads to no useful practical outcome because it has relatively little purchase on the reality that most students are not antisemitic, including most students who strongly oppose Israeli policies. Those who do hold antisemitic views, it finds, are more likely to support rather than to oppose Israel and to position themselves on the Right rather than the Left of the political spectrum. Not only is it possible—indeed commonplace—to be anti-Zionist (in many senses of that overused term) and not antisemitic, but it is equally possible to be antisemitic *and* pro-Zionist. In fact, right-wing supporters of Israel in Europe and on the Christian far Right in the United States are *more* likely to espouse antisemitic ideas than Israel's critics are.[28]

These findings, needless to say, run counter to the prevailing anxiety—shared by conservative anti-woke crusaders and much of the American Jewish mainstream alike—about the purported growth of antisemitism on campuses and in cultural life and suggest it has been not only overblown but actually counterproductive. They serve as a further reminder—were one needed—that the question of where and how precisely antisemitism overlaps with political speech about Israel is something that needs to be elucidated with discrimination, care, and impartiality rather than simply assumed or settled by decree. There has been little sign of these things to date either from those advocacy groups lobbying hardest on the matter or from the legislators entrusted with crafting a response. On the contrary, the fight against antisemitism has been hindered by the way it has been instrumentalized first for foreign policy ends and then for a domestic culture war with its own quite distinct concerns.

It is obvious today that the IHRA definition has become very useful to politicians who wish to use the issue of antisemitism to clobber dissent and assail civil liberties. For them, its flaws, confusions, and internal contradictions not only do not matter; they are in fact helpful, offering them cover to pursue their larger goals indefinitely. Other politicians are no doubt genuinely concerned and anxious about anti-Jewish feeling. Yet the manifold ambiguities of the IHRA approach ensnare them too. As government bureaucrats and civil servants have gotten more involved, we have ended up with an inquisition in which the inquisitors themselves have trouble defining the target. A 2024 congressional committee report on antisemitism on college campuses provides a striking example. At one point the report describes some students as "revealing antisemitic attitudes," and it criticizes one of them for saying: "There's no way that you can make a critique of the country that brands itself as the premier state for Jewish people without somebody being able to somehow claim that you're targeting Jewish people." Actually, as a statement of a genuine difficulty, the way this student is reported to have put the issue seems pretty close to spot-on: As we have seen, the identification of Israel as "the nation-state of the Jewish people" is indeed said by some to make any criticism of it tantamount to antisemitism, a position that would exempt Israel from any criticism at all. Yet in the eyes of the authors of this congressional report, merely to point out this self-evident difficulty is apparently itself evidence of antisemitism. Is pointing out *this* difficulty antisemitic too? An infinite regress looms: We have entered the realm of the absurd.[29]

In an article entitled "Israel and Its Elephants," Steven Beller, the author of the most sensible brief guide to the whole subject of antisemitism, suggests the fundamental problem is that the concept these days has come to be a "term that is trying to mean too many things for too many people." He asks if it is plausible to use the same word—one derived from nineteenth-century racialist thought—to lump together the policies of Egyptian pharaohs with postwar American real estate exclusions.

Evoking the analogy of the blind men trying to figure out the nature of the elephant, Beller questions whether antisemitism is one elephant at all as opposed to a single label mistakenly applied to two or more quite distinct kinds of animals. One of these is the well-known version that is associated with age-old stereotypes about Jews. Another is what he calls the "Israel-related elephant," which has some quite specific characteristics of its own. For while classic antisemitism, post-Auschwitz, is viewed as the embodiment of unmitigated evil, the Israel elephant involves matters at the heart of modern ethics such as human rights, international law, and democratic values. How can a term proudly embraced by Fascists and Nazis really be usefully applied when liberals or Leftists raise concerns of this kind in the case of the

Israel-Palestine dispute? The strain of the effort to describe what they are doing as antisemitism produces a sort of incoherence. The reason, says Beller, is simple enough: "Antisemitism was historically built around the 'Jewish Question.' What we have in Israel/Palestine today is not so much a Jewish Question as a Palestinian Question." People have been hunting the wrong elephant.[30]

Just as our understanding of the Holocaust has shaped our conception of antisemitism in the past, Israel increasingly overshadows our understanding of it today. That shadow is likely to grow. In 2010 there were an estimated 13.9 million Jews globally, a mere 0.2 percent of the world's population. Looking ahead to 2050, the overall number is forecast to rise to around 16 million. As now, two countries, Israel and the United States, will make up more than 80 percent of the total, but there will be one important difference. Whereas in 1950 the American Jewish population vastly outnumbered Israel's and in 2010 still outstripped it, by the middle of the twenty-first century Israel will likely be home to more than half the world's Jewish population.[31]

If that is a demographic prospect that would surely have made David Ben-Gurion proud, it needs to be placed in a context that might leave him squirming. In 1950, shortly after Israel's establishment, there were some 1.2 million Jews living there, almost 90 percent of the population: The prospects for nation-state normality in those first years were not implausible. Today things are very different. According to the 2021 estimates of the leading Israeli demographer, Sergio Della Pergola, there are approximately 6.2 million Jews within Israel's pre-1967 borders, some 77 percent of the total, and some 6.9 million Jews in an overall population of over 14 million in the combined landmass of Israel and the Palestinian territories. Thus, even as the government proclaims Israel's Jewish national character, its appetite for land, driven by the settler movement, is undermining that claim and creating a situation in which the so-called Arab minority is no longer a minority at all. As the concept of antisemitism drifts untethered from its historical origins, it will probably be ever more deeply affected by what Israel says and does in response to these trends.[32]

How the country could help to fight antisemitism was a question that weighed heavily on the formidable mind of Haim Cohn, a former Israeli attorney general and supreme court justice. Born in Lübeck, Germany, in 1911, Cohn belonged to a generation that brought their personal experience of Fascism in interwar Europe to their life and work in the new Jewish state. From a family of rabbis, he was a self-professed "old-fashioned Zionist and an ardent patriot of the state of Israel." He had fled Germany when the Nazis seized power, setting up a practice in prewar Palestine before becoming one of the architects of the Israeli legal system after 1948.[33]

In 1985 he was invited to take part in a seminar convened by the Israeli president on the subject of contemporary antisemitism. American campaigners from the ADL mixed with social psychologists, Sovietologists, and specialists with expertise ranging from Argentina to Scandinavia. Politically, they ran the gamut from anti-Communists to the feminist Betty Friedan. One after another, the speakers—who included some of the leading thinkers and scholars of the day—warned of the threat posed by antisemitism, its mysterious expansion around the world, and the need to understand it in all its manifold incarnations. The only dissenting note was struck by Cohn. He questioned how it was that the creation of a Jewish state, instead of bringing antisemitism to an end, had led it to assume new forms. What, he asked, had gone wrong? Had their very assumptions been mistaken? If so, what was Zionism, really?

What worried him was not the mistakes they had made. These had been inevitable, and after all they had not done badly in the circumstances. No, the problem that concerned him was the growing tendency in Israel to fixate upon antisemitism. Instead of rushing to decry the prejudices of others, would it not be best to "make sure we ourselves are entirely free of any such prejudices"? It was one thing to have hated the goyim (non-Jews); in the diaspora in the past that could be forgiven as an expression of self-respect in the face of daily humiliation. But with the establishment of Israel, things had changed: "The self-respect and dignity of Jews are no longer in jeopardy." He deplored the propensity of Israelis, as he put it, to see every Arab as a potential murderer in just the same way "every Jew had been a potential murderer" for the Germans. Cohn's conclusion was simple. In his words: "For Jews in Israel there is only one way to combat antisemitism. That is not to imitate."[34]

What I Saw

For men believe their reason governs their words. But it is also true that words have their own power under which the understanding may buckle and bend.

FRANCIS BACON, *NOVUM ORGANUM*

On October 7, 2023, a Hamas raid from Gaza into southern Israel led to a bloodbath: Over one thousand people were killed and more than two hundred, among them infants and the elderly, were abducted as hostages. The shock of these events—the deadliest terror attack in the country's history—prompted the Israeli government to launch a military assault upon the densely populated Gaza Strip. A bombardment unprecedented in its severity wiped out entire families and left tens of thousands dead beneath the rubble. Around the world, an extraordinary debate erupted that reflected the existential fears on both sides.

At Columbia University, where I teach, arguments spilled over into demonstrations, counterdemonstrations, sit-ins, encampments, and occupations. Student protests became a national spectacle and sparked an international movement before being halted in a show of force by the New York Police Department, whose riot squads stormed the lawns and pathways in order to arrest several dozen protesters. Later, the university president spoke on camera from a campus usually full of life but now eerily deserted. The gates were padlocked and guarded by private security guards; students and faculty were shut out; the community of learning I knew and loved had vanished. Alongside the unfolding tragedy in the Middle East, another drama thus played itself out in the spring of 2024 before my eyes, one far less acute in terms of human suffering or violence but with its own political and cultural reverberations. The two were connected but the nature of the connection was far from obvious and it seemed important to try to figure out what it was.

Over the preceding months, some of the protesters had flown red-green-white-and-black flags, camped out in tents, affirmed solidarity with Gaza, and called on the world to heed the rising toll of Palestinian dead. Counterprotesters sought sympathy for the Israeli victims: They planted blue-and-white flags on the campus lawn and posted flyers with the faces of hostages. The shorthand of political contestation— symbols, slogans, and chants—is designed for impact, not semantic clarity; ambiguities were inherent and arguments flared. Was the call for "Intifada" incitement to genocide or simply encouragement to Palestinians to rise up and fight for their rights? Did a banner with the Star of David signal solidarity with Jews, Israel, or Zionism? "From the river to the sea" mirrored old slogans for a Greater Israel but was here understood as the opposite: Yet was that an Arab Palestine without Jews, or freedom for Arabs alongside them? Some people said what these things meant was clear and demanded action; others insisted they could mean different things to different people. I thought what they meant was probably not always evident even to those using them, and that using them was often the beginning of a process of figuring it out. I saw the arguments around me as a form of education, unruly but also admirable. But in the world outside many viewed them differently.[1]

Nowhere was the tension greater than over the meaning of antisemitism. No one wanted to be called an antisemite, and yet if you believed the pundits, antisemites were everywhere, and it sounded like Manhattan was Berlin on the eve of Kristallnacht. The spike in hate crimes around the country and beyond was real: Worsening conflict in the Middle East was putting Jews at risk and Muslims too.

Outside the campus, a motley array of ideological extremists jostled for the attention of the cameras, and some days there was a line of photographers three blocks long hoping to gain admission and glimpse something that would make the news. But inside the gates, things were mostly quiet, and with the notable exception of the student newspaper, which proved to be the only reliable source of eyewitness reporting, what I read and heard in the press was a distortion of what I saw. Antisemitic name-calling had increased, and I had students and friends who had been ostracized because they were Israelis, which did not strike me as antisemitic exactly (something similar had happened to Russian students after the invasion of Ukraine), but I felt sure was also wrong. But the name-calling was going both ways, and I failed to understand the maligning of students of all backgrounds and creeds for speaking out against the terrible things that were happening in Gaza, the killing week after week of innocent people on a scale that dwarfed anything seen previously in the history of the conflict. This had become by any measure one of the great issues of our time. Were the protesters and the faculty defending them seriously thought to be antisemites? The claim that American universities were hotbeds of institutionalized antisemitism I knew from my own experience to be an accusation as preposterous as it was damaging. In response to the demands of politicians, trustees, and donors, task forces were set up to investigate and stamp out "this ancient scourge." Only first they had to figure out what it was.[2]

I had been teaching, writing, and thinking about persecution, violence, and nationalism in European history for many years, and if one thing was clear to me, it was that the lines dividing antisemitism from opposition to Israeli policies and criticism of Zionism had become hopelessly blurred. Things some felt had to be said in a moment of catastrophe were deemed beyond the pale by others. Could you deny Israel's "right to exist" without being labeled an antisemite? Could you talk about Gaza as a genocide and if not, why not? I wondered who the Zionists were whom some now talked about with such loathing. For that matter, what was anti-Zionism, and was that now antisemitism too? Magnified and distorted in the echo chamber of an inflamed public opinion, the charge of antisemitism seemed to cover a range of sins—some serious, some venial, some nonexistent.

Rare indeed were the incidents on the Columbia campus that involved any physical violence at all.[3] Yet only six years after the massacre in the Tree of Life synagogue in Pittsburgh and five after the murderous rampage by a neofascist in the German town of Halle, no sensible person could believe the threat of force against Jews has vanished into history. The extreme Right was flourishing on both sides of the Atlantic, and old-style conspiracy theories had taken wing once more. Racist populism was in the ascendant. A hostage crisis at a Texas synagogue in 2022 that could easily have resulted in fatalities served as a reminder of the continued risk from al-Qaeda sympathizers. In short, there seemed to be good reason to target antisemitism where it posed a threat to life and limb. Yet it was the campus that got the attention of American media and politicians. In Washington, DC, members of Congress not previously known for their solicitude either for Jews or for universities developed a keen interest in both, conducting hearings that were McCarthyite in tone and occasionally surreal. One lawmaker asked whether God would curse universities that did not take action. Another was troubled by the word *Ashkenormativity*, an ungainly neologism that likely no one on Capitol Hill had come across until a researcher turned it up in a student handbook, whereupon everyone acted outraged for the cameras. As it transpired, the word had nothing to do with antisemitism. If it involved any kind of offense, it was against the English language. But that was the last thing people were worrying about.[4]

As I watched, two questions struck me. I wondered first what it was that these denunciations of antisemitism were preventing us from talking about. Because it seemed increasingly clear to me that the constant invocation of antisemitism needed to be understood as a refusal to acknowledge other things: I sensed that if the demand is that antisemitism must always be dealt with first, and if more or less any pro-Palestinian advocacy provokes shouts of antisemitism, then you have created a formidable obstacle to seeing the other side of the struggle that is at the heart of all this—that is to say, the existence of a suffering Palestinian people and their desire for freedom—as something worthy of real attention at all. The sense of collective victimhood that has beset contemporary Israel's understanding of itself and its place in the world is a stunning reversal of what Zionism's founding fathers expected or desired. Antisemitism offers a rationale for this: Invoking the old curse has become a kind of refusal to face the facts and accept the meaning of criticism. But today much of the world refuses the refusal: It says you can mourn the Israeli dead and the Palestinian dead too.[5]

Which led to the question behind this book: What *had* happened to the concept of antisemitism? Trying to comprehend the contradictions it contains today is like entering a hall of mirrors. A term that began as a way to describe the hostility faced by Jews as a minority struggling for their legal rights is now used to defend a Jewish majority state depriving the minority within it of theirs. Fighting antisemitism once meant battling ethnonationalism; now it often justifies ethnonationalism's excesses. For some, anti-racism and human rights are the solution; for others, they are the problem. Anti-Zionism is antisemitism, say some; Zionism is, say others. Even racists these days say they are fighting antisemitism, something that would have been unimaginable when the term was coined and should itself be a kind of signal that it is now being abused.

In his 2020 encyclical *Fratelli tutti* (*We Are All Brothers*), Pope Francis echoed his medieval namesake's call for a renewed sense of universal fraternity, and he expressed his concern at the rise of nationalist hatreds in recent years and warned they were being made worse by a growing lack of historical awareness and by the ease with which words could be manipulated as a result. As he wrote: "One effective way to weaken historical consciousness, critical thinking, the struggle for justice, and the processes of integration is to empty words of great significance of their meaning or to manipulate them" so that they can be "bent and shaped to serve as tools for domination, as meaningless tags that can be used to justify any action." Forty years ago, Antony Lerman had already warned that it would scarcely serve the fight against antisemitism if the word came to be used "so widely that at one and the same time it means everything—and nothing." While the term manages for now to encompass its present-day contradictions, we cannot know how it will fare in the years ahead. Despite efforts to fix their meaning, words are recalcitrant things, and it is the future course of events and not administrative fiat that generally determines what happens to them. Will the current confusion of meanings and associations survive, or will some of them be transformed, discarded, or superseded? The philologist Victor Klemperer noted the process "whereby a currently highly fashionable expression, one apparently never destined to be expunged, suddenly goes silent [and] disappears with the context that gave birth to it." Could antisemitism perhaps even become one of those terms that—as he wrote—remain "like a fossil" to testify to the preoccupations of a bygone era?[6]

All we can say is that contention over antisemitism is unlikely to end soon. The point of trying to clarify terms like it is not to help resolve the conflicts that underlie them: That lies beyond the power of such an analysis. It is rather to become more conscious of the hidden depths of the ideas, associations, and implications we have inherited, to see that meanings may vary with the circumstances that prompted them, and in finding our own way with words to thereby make ourselves participants in the process of change in the world.

Although much general writing these days on the subject of anti-semitism is second-rate polemic, there is also plenty of first-rate scholarship. A good place to start is Steven Beller, *Antisemitism: A Very Short Introduction* (Oxford University Press, 2015), followed by David Feldman, "Toward a History of the Term 'Anti-Semitism,'" *American Historical Review* 123, no. 4 (Oct. 2018): 1139–50, as well as the essays in Scott Ury and Guy Miron, eds., *Antisemitism and the Politics of History* (Brandeis University Press, 2024). The insider accounts by Antony Lerman, *Whatever Happened to Antisemitism?* (Pluto Press, 2022), and Kenneth Stern, *The Conflict over the Conflict: The Israel/Palestine Campus Debate* (University of Toronto Press, 2020) are indispensable. Derek Penslar, "Who's Afraid of Defining Antisemitism?," *Antisemitism Studies* 6, no. 1 (Spring 2022): 133–45, is levelheaded. This book's approach was influenced by three great works on words and their political debasement: George Orwell's essay "Politics and the English Language" (1946), Victor Klemperer's *The Language of the Third Reich: LTI—Lingua Tertii Imperii* (Bloomsbury Academic, 2021), and Raymond Williams's *Keywords: A Vocabulary of Culture and Society* (Oxford University Press, 1976). The era that produced them also inspired what remains one of the outstanding books ever written on the subject of antisemitism,

Hannah Arendt's *The Origins of Totalitarianism* (Harcourt Brace, 1951). Also useful are the essays collected in Arendt, *The Jewish Writings*, ed. Jerome Kohn and Ron H. Feldman (Schocken Books, 2007).

A representative selection of the brilliant scholarship produced on the subject in recent years might include David Sorkin, *Jewish Emancipation: A History Across Five Centuries* (Princeton University Press, 2019); Laura Engelstein, *The Resistible Rise of Antisemitism* (Brandeis University Press, 2020); David Feldman, *Englishmen and Jews: Social Relations and Political Culture, 1840–1914* (Yale University Press, 1994); Ruth Harris, *Dreyfus: Politics, Emotion, and the Scandal of the Century* (Metropolitan Books, 2011); Eugene M. Avrutin and Elissa Bemporad, eds., *Pogroms: A Documentary History* (Oxford University Press, 2021); William W. Hagen, *Anti-Jewish Violence in Poland, 1914–1920* (Cambridge University Press, 2018); Mark Levene, *War, Jews, and the New Europe: The Diplomacy of Lucien Wolf, 1914–1919* (Oxford University Press, 1992); Jeffrey Veidlinger, *In the Midst of Civilized Europe: The Pogroms of 1918–1921 and the Onset of the Holocaust* (Metropolitan Books, 2021); Elissa Bemporad, *Becoming Soviet Jews: The Bolshevik Experiment in Minsk* (Indiana University Press, 2013); Alexander Stille, *Benevolence and Betrayal: Five Italian Families Under Fascism* (Picador, 1991); Thomas Weber, *Becoming Hitler: The Making of a Nazi* (Basic Books, 2017); Alon Confino, *A World Without Jews: The Nazi Imagination from Persecution to Genocide* (Yale University Press, 2014). On the Final Solution, a good place to start is anything by Christopher Browning, including most recently "Hitler, Antisemitism, and the Final Solution," *Antisemitism Studies* 7, no. 1 (Spring 2023): 80–99. His *The Origins of the Final Solution: The Evolution of Nazi Jewish Policy, September 1939–March 1942* (University of Nebraska, 2007) is unsurpassed. The elements of a new synthesis of the Holocaust are in Florent Brayard, *La "solution finale de la question juive"* (Fayard, 2023). Two literary works of lasting value are Mihail Sebastian, *For Two Thousand Years* (Other Press, 2017), and Curzio Malaparte, *Kaputt* (New York Review Books, 2005). Also worth reading is Gregor von Rezzori, *Memoirs of an Anti-Semite* (New York Review Books, 1981).

For the postwar era, there is Nathan Kurz, *Jewish Internationalism and Human Rights After the Holocaust* (Cambridge University Press, 2021); Joshua Rubenstein and Vladimir Naumov, eds., *Stalin's Secret Pogrom: The Postwar Inquisition of the Jewish Anti-Fascist Committee*, trans. Laura Wolfson (Yale University Press, 2001); and Robert Levy, *Ana Pauker: The Rise and Fall of a Jewish Communist* (University of California Press, 2001). As a survey, François Fejtö's *Les juifs et l'antisémitisme dans les pays communistes* (Plon, 1960) has never been surpassed. For France, see Alexandre Bande et al., eds., *Histoire politique de l'antisémitisme en France: De 1967 à nos jours* (Robert Laffont, 2024).

The Middle East context is discussed in Daniel J. Schroeter, "'Islamic Antisemitism' in Historical Discourse," *American Historical Review* 123, no. 4 (Oct. 2018): 1172–89. Jonathan Gribetz, *Reading Herzl in Beirut: The PLO Effort to Know the Enemy* (Princeton University Press, 2024), is fascinating; unfortunately, we do not yet have the equivalent for the analogous efforts from the other side. For Jewish anti-Arab racism, see Shaul Magid, *Meir Kahane: The Public Life and Political Thought of an American Jewish Radical* (Princeton University Press, 2021). Yaacov Yadgar, *Israel's Jewish Identity Crisis* (Cambridge University Press, 2020), is gripping, as is Idith Zertal, *Israel's Holocaust and the Politics of Nationhood* (Cambridge University Press, 2005). For the larger questions posed by Israel and by Zionist attitudes to Jewish life outside its borders, see Arnold Eisen, "Zionism, American Jewry and the 'Negation of Diaspora,'" in Michael A. Meyer and David Myers, eds., *Between Jewish Tradition and Modernity: Rethinking an Old Opposition; Essays in Honor of David Ellenson* (Wayne State, 2014), 175–191, and Amnon Raz-Krakotzkin, "Exile Within Sovereignty: Critique of the 'Negation of Exile' Within Israeli Culture," in Zvi Ben-Dor Benite, Stefanos Geroulanos, and Nicole Jerr, eds., *The*

Scaffolding of Sovereignty: Global and Aesthetic Perspectives on the History of a Concept (Columbia University Press, 2017), 393–420.

For the United States, an article that offers a glimpse into a vanished world is Marshall Sklare, "Lakeville and Israel: The Six-Day War and Its Aftermath," *Midstream* 14, no. 8 (Oct. 1968): 1–18; also relevant is Frederic Cople Jaher, "The Search for the Ultimate *Shiksa*," *American Quarterly* 35, no. 5 (Winter 1983): 518–42. Leonard Dinnerstein's sunny *Antisemitism in America* (Oxford University Press, 1995) is challenged by Pierre Birnbaum, *Tears of History: The Rise of Political Antisemitism in the United States* (Columbia University Press, 2023). Arthur Hertzberg, *The Jews in America* (Columbia University Press, 1997), is balanced and wry. Peter Novick's classic *The Holocaust in American Life* (Houghton Mifflin, 1999) and Eric Goldstein's *The Price of Whiteness: Jews, Race, and American Identity* (Princeton University Press, 2006) are essential and readable, as is Amy Kaplan's *Our American Israel: The Story of an Entangled Alliance* (Harvard University Press, 2018). The dissenters are covered in Geoffrey Levin, *Our Palestine Question: Israel and American Jewish Dissent, 1948–1978* (Yale University Press, 2023). There is much of value in David Leeming, *James Baldwin: A Biography* (Alfred Knopf, 1994). American Jewish power is discussed by J. J. Goldberg, *Jewish Power: Inside the American Jewish Establishment* (Basic Books, 1996), and Henry Feingold, *Jewish Power in America: Myth and Reality* (Transaction Publishers, 2008). Best of all is a short essay by Peter Medding, "The 'New Jewish Politics' in the United States," in Zvi Gitelman, ed., *The Quest for Utopia: Jewish Political Ideas and Institutions Through the Ages* (M. E. Sharpe, 1992). A sharp, myth-busting analysis of the state of thought around antisemitism in the United States in 2023–24 is Musa al-Gharbi, "Misunderstanding Antisemitism in America," *Slow Boring*, Jan. 11, 2024. Equally insightful is Samuel Catlin, "The Campus Does Not Exist: How Campus War Is Made," *Parapraxis*.

Two institutional histories of the AJC that are of much wider interest than their subject might suggest are: Naomi W. Cohen, *Not Free to Desist: The American Jewish Committee, 1906–1966* (Jewish Publication Society of America, 1972) and Marianne R. Sanua, *Let Us Prove Strong: The American Jewish Committee, 1945–2006* (Brandeis University Press, 2007). Lila Corwin Berman's work on the history of American Jewish philanthropy is path-breaking. The real story of American Jewry has probably best been tackled by novelists such as Philip Roth. For those with an interest in data, the back issues of the *American Jewish Year Book* are invaluable sources, a fantastic reminder of the extraordinary research that was once supported by the American Jewish Committee. For more recent times, the reports of the Pew Research Center are reliable and revealing. FBI hate crime statistics are useful and enable comparison to other targeted groups; the ADL data should be taken with a pinch of salt.

To end back where we started, with words: Richard Chenevix Trench, *On the Study of Words* (Macmillan, 1878), is a classic. In this philological spirit, surprisingly little attention has been paid to antisemitism as a member of the clan of *anti-* words. See Allen Walker Read, "The Scope of the American Dictionary," *American Speech* 8, no. 3 (Oct. 1933), 10–20. Walker Read remarks, "In the field of politics, where feeling has run high, the ANTI- words have been particularly prevalent" (p. 14). Another of them is of course anti-Zionism, on which far and away the best introduction is by James Loeffler, "Anti-Zionism," in the outstanding volume of essays, S. Goldberg et al., eds., *Key Concepts in the Study of Antisemitism* (Palgrave, 2021), 39–51.

INTRODUCTION: CONFUSION

1. Lewis Carroll, *Alice's Adventures in Wonderland* and *Through the Looking-Glass* (Oxford University Press, 2009), 191.

2. Victor Klemperer, *The Language of the Third Reich: LTI–Lingua Tertii Imperii; A Philologist's Notebook* (Bloomsbury Academic, 2021).

3. Salo Baron, foreword to *Essays on Antisemitism*, ed. Koppel S. Pinson (Conference on Jewish Relations, 1942), vii. On Marr and the rise of the movement, see Moshe Zimmermann, *Wilhelm Marr: The Patriarch of Anti-Semitism* (Oxford University Press, 1986), and Frederick C. Beiser, *The Berlin Antisemitism Controversy* (Routledge, 2024).

4. Feldman cited by Antony Lerman, *Whatever Happened to Antisemitism? Redefinition and the Myth of the "Collective Jew"* (Pluto Press, 2022), 1, 19; on anti-antisemitism, see Elad Lapidot, *Jews Out of the Question: A Critique of Anti-Anti-Semitism* (State University of New York Press, 2020). On the hyphen, see Jonathan Judaken, "Rethinking Anti-Semitism," *American Historical Review* 123, no. 4 (2018): 1125–27; cf. Robert Musil, *The Man Without Qualities* (Picador, 1988), bk. 1, ch. 8, for an earlier hyphen dispute. My view on the hyphen is it doesn't much matter either way: There are more important things to worry about.

5. For a very thoughtful consideration of how the Holocaust changed historians' framing of antisemitism, see David Engel, *Historians of the Jews and the*

Holocaust (Stanford University Press, 2010), 202–6; on the 1939 survey: Tony Kushner, *We Europeans? Mass-Observation, "Race" and British Identity in the Twentieth Century* (Ashgate, 2004); on the 1940s research: Thomas Wheatland, *The Frankfurt School in Exile* (University of Minnesota, 2009); Stephen Frosh, "Studies in Prejudice: Theorising Antisemitism in the Wake of the Nazi Holocaust," in Daniel Pick and M. ffytch, eds., *Psychoanalysis in the Age of Totalitarianism* (Routledge, 2016), 29–42; Norman Cohn, *Warrant for Genocide* (Eyre and Spotiswoode, 1981), 12. The best entry points to the current state of scholarship are "AHR Roundtable: Rethinking Anti-Semitism," *American Historical Review* 123, no. 4 (2018), and Scott Ury and Guy Miron, eds., *Antisemitism and the Politics of History* (Brandeis University Press, 2024). Also useful is Jonathan Judaken, *Critical Theories of Anti-Semitism* (Columbia University Press, 2024). On "thinking with history," see Carl Schorske, *Thinking with History and Other Essays: Explorations in the Passage to Modernism* (Princeton University Press, 2014).

6. Evyatar Friesel, *The Days and the Seasons: Memoirs* (Wayne State University Press, 1996), 184–85.

7. Edward Rothstein, "Bearing Witness Beyond the Witnesses," *New York Times*, Mar. 24, 2011; the poll of rabbis is in "Freedom for Russian Jews, Less Anti-Semitism Predicted for Year 2000," *Jewish Telegraphic Agency*, Oct. 21, 1960; Eric Alterman, *We Are Not One: A History of America's Fight over Israel* (Basic Books, 2022), 84–85; Leon Wieseltier, "Hitler Is Dead," *New Republic*, May 27, 2002.

8. Uriel Heilman, "Abe Foxman Looks Back at Changing—and Declining—Face of Anti-Semitism," *Forward*, Feb. 19, 2014.

9. European Union Agency for Fundamental Rights [FRA], *Antisemitism: Summary Overview of the Situation in the European Union, 2001–2010* (Working Paper: Apr. 2011).

10. Yehoshafat Harkabi, "On Arab Antisemitism Once More," in *Antisemitism Through the Ages*, ed. Shmuel Almog (Pergamon, 1980), 228.

11. Josh Richman, "State Department Opposes New Antisemitism Office," *Forward*, Aug. 6, 2004, forward.com/news/5089/state-department-opposes-new-antisemitism-office; H.R. 4230 (108th): Global Anti-Semitism Awareness Act of 2004, govtrack.us/congress/bills/108/hr4230/text; S. 2292 (108th): Global Anti-Semitism Review Act of 2004, https://www.congress.gov/108/plaws/publ332/PLAW-108publ332.pdf.

12. Charles S. Kamen, review of *Jews in the Mind of America*, by Charles Herbert Stember et al., in *Sociological Analysis* 28, no. 1 (Spring 1967): 44–48, here 46;

Stuart Svonkin, *Jews Against Prejudice: American Jews and the Fight for Civil Liberties* (Columbia University Press, 1997). Good overviews are Jack Wertheimer, "American Jews and Israel: A 60-Year Retrospective," *American Jewish Year Book* 108 (2008): 3–79, and Britt Tevis, "Trends in the Study of Antisemitism in United States History," *American Jewish History* 105, nos. 1/2 (Jan.–Apr. 2021): 255–84.

13. Nancy Sinkoff, *From Left to Right: Lucy Dawidowicz, the New York Intellectuals and the Politics of Jewish History* (Wayne State University, 2019), 111; Kenneth Stern, *The Conflict over the Conflict: The Israel/Palestine Campus Debate* (University of Toronto Press, 2020), 11; Lila Corwin Berman, "Jewish Philanthropies Acted as if Their Work Was Above Politics. Until Now," *Washington Post*, Dec. 12, 2019; Corwin Berman, *The American Jewish Philanthropic Complex* (Princeton University Press, 2022); usnews.com/news/best-countries/articles/us-news-unveils-best-countries-rankings; Peter Beinart, "Has the Fight Against Antisemitism Lost Its Way?," *New York Times*, Aug. 26, 2022.

14. Cnaan Liphshiz, "EU Official Says the Simon Wiesenthal Center's Annual Antisemitism List Has Gone Too Far," Jewish Telegraphic Agency, Jan. 10, 2022.

15. James Jacobs and Jessica Henry, "The Social Construction of a Hate Crime Epidemic," *Journal of Criminal Law and Criminology* 86, no. 2 (Winter 1996): 366–91; "ADL Officials Say Anti-Semitism Rampant Throughout the World," Jewish Telegraphic Agency, Mar. 6, 1974; Arthur Hertzberg, "Is Anti-Semitism Dying Out?," *New York Review of Books*, June 24, 1993; Lerman, *Whatever Happened to Antisemitism?*, 21. See also Mari Cohen, "A Closer Look at the 'Uptick' in Antisemitism," *Jewish Currents*, May 27, 2021; Shane Burley and Jonah ben Avraham, "Examining the ADL's Antisemitism Audit," *Jewish Currents*, June 17, 2024; Emmaia Gelman, "The Anti-Defamation League Is Not What It Seems," *Boston Review*, May 23, 2019; and Jonathan Guyer and Tom Perkins, "Anti-Defamation League Staff Decry 'Dishonest' Campaign Against Israel Critics," *Guardian*, Jan. 5, 2024. More basically, see Smith and Schapiro, "Antisemitism," 122. On antisemitism prompting donors, see P. M. Rooney et al., *American Jewish Philanthropy 2022: Giving to Religious and Secular Causes in the U.S. and to Israel* (Indiana University, Dec. 2023), 36–37; Jodi Rudoren, "Calling Everything a Crisis Is Bad for the Jews," *Forward*, March 7, 2025.

16. This book is not concerned with theorizing antisemitism, an endeavor that has lasted for decades with few enduring results. See Judaken, *Critical Theories*, and "A Brief Guide to Further Reading" for more on the subject.

17. Shlomo Bergman, "Some Methodological Errors in the Study of Antisemitism," *Jewish Social Studies* 5, no. 1 (Jan. 1943): 43–60; Yehuda Bauer, "Problems of Contemporary Antisemitism," 2003, humanities.ucsc.edu/JewishStudies/docs/YBauerLecture.pdf; Ben Halpern, "What Is Antisemitism?," *Modern Judaism* 1, no. 3 (Dec. 1981): 251–62; David Engel, "Away from a Definition of Antisemitism: An Essay in the Semantics of Historical Description," in *Rethinking European Jewish History*, ed. Jeremy Cohen and Moshe Rosman (Oxford University Press, 2008), 30–53.

18. A good recent scholarly analysis is Derek Penslar, "Who's Afraid of Defining Antisemitism?," *Antisemitism Studies* 6, no. 1 (Spring 2022): 133–45.

19. See A. Lange et al., eds., *An End to Antisemitism!*, vol. 1, *Comprehending and Confronting Antisemitism* (De Gruyter, 2020), for essays by many of the IHRA's proponents. Another advocate of the IHRA is Kenneth Marcus, "The Definition of Antisemitism," in *Global Antisemitism: A Crisis of Modernity*, ed. Charles Small (Brill, 2013), 97–109; cf. Erica Green, "Wider Definition of Judaism Is Likely to Aid Crackdown on Colleges," *New York Times*, Dec. 11, 2019, and Vimal Patel, "The Man Who Helped Redefine Campus Antisemitism," *New York Times*, Mar. 24, 2024. H.R. 6090 (118th): Antisemitism Awareness Act of 2023, introduced on Oct. 26, 2023, Section 3 (5), https://www.congress.gov/bill/118th-congress/house-bill/6090/text; Eyal Press, "The Problem with Defining Antisemitism," *New Yorker*, Mar. 13, 2024. For a reasoned critique, see Jan Deckers and Jonathan Coulter, "What Is Wrong with the International Holocaust Remembrance Alliance's Definition of Antisemitism?," *Res Publica* 28, no. 4 (2022): 733–52. The 1981 piece is Halpern, "What Is Antisemitism?"

20. For the distinction, see the discussion in Ben Gidley et al., "Labour and Antisemitism: A Crisis Misunderstood," *Political Quarterly* 91, no. 2 (Apr.–June 2020): 413–21.

21. Raymond Williams, *Keywords: A Vocabulary of Culture and Society* (Oxford University Press, 1985); Richard Chenevix Trench, *English Past and Present* (Macmillan, 1870), 275–76; George Orwell, *Politics and the English Language* (Bodleian Library, Oxford, 2022), 53, 56.

CHAPTER 1: GOD, NATION, ETERNITY

1. Dr. Judah L. Magnes, quoted in Max Grossman, ed., *A Tribute to Professor Morris Raphael Cohen, Teacher and Philosopher* (New York, 1928), 24.

2. Abram Leon, *The Jewish Question: A Marxist Interpretation* (Ediciones Pioneras, 1950), 174.

3. *La question juive en Allemagne: Extrait du Correspondant* (J. Gervais, 1881), 7–8.

4. Josef Hayyim Brenner, "Self-Criticism" (1914), in *The Zionist Idea*, ed. Arthur Hertzberg (Jewish Publication Society, 1997), 308; in general, see Michael Stanislawski, *Zionism: A Very Short Introduction* (Oxford University Press, 2017).

5. Leo Pinsker, "Auto-Emancipation" (1882) in Hertzberg, *Zionist Idea*, 187, 198.

6. Pinsker, "Auto-Emancipation," 186; David Feldman, "Toward a History of the Term 'Anti-Semitism,'" *American Historical Review* 123, no. 4 (Oct. 2018): 1139–50, here 1147; on Zionist alternatives, see Dmitry Shumsky, *Beyond the Nation-State: The Zionist Political Imagination from Pinsker to Ben-Gurion* (Yale University Press, 2018); on difficulties with the term *Ottoman Palestine*, see Jonathan Marc Gribetz, *Defining Neighbors: Religion, Race and the Early Zionist-Arab Encounter* (Princeton University Press, 2014), ch. 1.

7. Henryk Erlich, "Is Zionism a Liberating Democratic Movement? An Answer to Simon Dubnow," *Di Tsukunft*, Oct. 1938, translated at foroys.wordpress.com/2017/06/20/is-zionism-a-liberating-democratic-movement. My thanks to Molly Crabapple for the reference.

8. William Zukerman, *Voices of Dissent* (Bookman Associates, 1964), 74. For more on Zukerman, see chapter 6.

9. David Vital, *A People Apart: A Political History of the Jews in Europe, 1789–1939* (Oxford University Press, 2001); Robert Wistrich, *Antisemitism: The Longest Hatred* (Pantheon, 1991); Olga Litvak, "The God of History," in *The Social Scientific Study of Jewry: Sources, Approaches, Debates*, ed. Uzi Rebhun (Oxford University Press, 2014), 290–302; Michael Berkowitz, "Robert S. Wistrich and European Jewish History: Straddling the Public and Scholarly Spheres," *Journal of Modern History* 70, no. 1 (Mar. 1998): 119–36. See David Myers, "'Was There a Jerusalem School?' An Inquiry into the First Generation of Historical Researchers at the Hebrew University," *Studies in Contemporary Jewry* 10 (1994): 66–92.

10. Jean Daniel, *La prison juive* (Odile Jacob, 2003), 133; Shmuel Ettinger, "Jew-Hatred in Its Historical Context," in *Antisemitism Through the Ages*, ed. Shmuel Almog (Pergamon, 1988), 1–12.

11. Martin Lockshin, "Sinat Yisrael [Hatred of Jews]," in *Key Concepts in the Study of Antisemitism*, ed. Sol Goldberg et al. (Palgrave, 2021), 273–85. Abraham Besdin, ed., *Reflections of the Rav: Lessons in Jewish Thought Adapted from Lectures of Rabbi Joseph B. Soloveitchik* (KTAV, 1993), 1:110; see also, Adi Ophir

and Ishay Rosen-Zvi, *Goy: Israel's Multiple Others and the Birth of the Gentile* (Oxford University Press, 2018).

12. Adam Sutcliffe, *What Are Jews For? History, Peoplehood and Purpose* (Princeton University, 2020), ch. 4; Yosef Yerushalmi, "Modern Dilemmas," in *Zakhor: Jewish History and Jewish Memory* (University of Washington Press, 1996), 89.

13. Ettinger cited in Scott Ury and Guy Miron, "Antisemitism: On the Meanings and Uses of a Contested Term," in *Antisemitism and the Politics of History*, ed. Scott Ury and Guy Miron (Brandeis University Press, 2024), 10; Yitzhak F. Baer, *Galut* (Schocken, 1947), 120; see too Yiftach Ofek, "Politics and Theology in the Historical Works of Yitzhak Baer," *Religions* 13, no. 6 (2022): 537.

14. The best current guide to what it was to be Jewish in antiquity is probably Shaye Cohen. See his "'Anti-Semitism' in Antiquity: The Problem of Definition," in *History and Hate: The Dimensions of Anti-Semitism*, ed. David Berger (Jewish Publication Society, 1986), 43–49; also his entertaining "'Those Who Say They Are Jews and Are Not': How Do You Know a Jew in Antiquity When You See One?," in *Diasporas in Antiquity*, ed. Shaye Cohen and Ernest Frerichs (Brown University Press, 2020), 1–46.

15. Carlo Ginzburg, "Postface," in *The Medieval Roots of Antisemitism*, ed. Jonathan Adams and Cordelia Hess (Routledge, 2018), 428–29; Simon Rawidowicz, "Israel, the Ever-Dying People," in *Israel, the Ever-Dying People and Other Essays*, ed. Benjamin Ravid (Associated University Presses, 1986), 53.

16. David Nirenberg, *Anti-Judaism: The Western Tradition* (W. W. Norton, 2013).

17. David Engel, "The Concept of Antisemitism in the Historical Scholarship of Amos Funkenstein," *Jewish Social Studies* 6, no. 1 (Autumn 1999): 111–129, here 118.

18. On continuities from medieval times, see Adams and Hess, *Medieval Roots of Antisemitism*; Magda Teter, *Blood Libel: On the Trail of an Antisemitic Myth* (Harvard University Press, 2020).

19. Horkheimer cited by Philip Spencer, "European Marxism and the Question of Antisemitism," *European Societies* 14, no. 2 (2012), 275–294, here 280; Salo Baron, foreword to *Essays on Antisemitism*, ed. Koppel S. Pinson (Conference on Jewish Relations, 1942), vii; Hannah Arendt, *The Origins of Totalitarianism* (Harcourt Brace Jovanovich, 1973), viii (preface to the first edition).

20. Sergio DellaPergola, "Jews in the European Community: Sociodemographic Trends and Challenges," *The American Jewish Year Book* 93 (1993): 25–82.

21. Joseph Jacobs, "Statistics," *Jewish Encyclopedia*, 1906, jewishencyclopedia.com /articles/13992-statistics; Leon Shapiro, "World Jewish Population," *American Jewish Year Book* 52 (1951): 195–200; Pew Research Center, "The Future

of World Religions: Population Growth Projections, 2010–2050," Apr. 2, 2015, pewresearch.org/religion/2015/04/02/religious.

22. W. E. B. Du Bois, review of *Essays on Antisemitism*, ed. Koppel S. Pinson, and *Jews in a Gentile World*, ed. Isacque Graeber and Steuart Henderson Britt, in *Annals of the American Academy of Political and Social Science* 223 (Sept. 1942): 199–200.

CHAPTER 2: EMANCIPATION AND ITS ENEMIES: 1880–1914

1. Amos Funkenstein, *Perceptions of Jewish History* (University of California Press, 1993), 324; cf. Theodor Herzl, *Der Judenstaat* (Jüdischer Verlag, 1920), 20.
2. Arthur Hertzberg, ed., *The Zionist Idea: A Historical Analysis and Reader* (Jewish Publication Society, 1997), 21.
3. David Sorkin, *Jewish Emancipation: A History Across Five Centuries* (Princeton University Press, 2019), 2.
4. Heine cited by Jacob Katz, "The Term 'Jewish Emancipation': Its Origin and Historical Impact," in *Studies in Nineteenth-Century Jewish Intellectual History*, ed. Alexander Altmann (Harvard University Press, 1964), 1–27, here 21.
5. Cited in N. M. Gelber, "The Intervention of German Jews at the Berlin Congress 1878," *Leo Baeck Institute Year Book* 5, no. 1 (Jan. 1960): 221–48, here 221–22; Max Kohler, "Educational Reforms in Europe in Their Relation to Jewish Emancipation, 1778–1919," *Publications of the American Jewish Historical Society* 28 (1922): 83–132.
6. On Italy, see Shira Klein, *Italy's Jews: From Emancipation to Fascism* (Cambridge University Press, 2017), ch. 1.
7. P.-J. Proudhon, *Carnets* (Dec. 26, 1847) (M. Rivière, 1960); Enzo Traverso, *The Marxists and the Jewish Question: The History of a Debate (1843–1943)* (Humanities Press, 1994), 13–25.
8. P. Mendes-Flohr, "The Emancipation of European Jewry: Why Was It Not Self-Evident?," *Studia Rosenthaliana* 30, no. 1 (1996): 7–20, here 15; Christopher Clark, *Revolutionary Spring: Europe Aflame and the Fight for a New World, 1848–1849* (Crown, 2023), 444–57.
9. Clark, *Revolutionary Spring*.
10. Clark, *Revolutionary Spring*, 445; Michael Stanislawski, *A Murder in Lemberg: Politics, Religion, and Violence in Modern Jewish History* (Princeton University Press, 2007).

11. Kohler, "Educational Reforms in Europe," 85; memoirs of Rabbi Lifschitz cited in Abigail Green, "Old Networks, New Connections: The Emergence of the Jewish International," in *Religious Internationals in the Modern World*, ed. Abigail Green and Vincent Viaene (Palgrave Macmillan, 2012), 53–81, here 63.

12. Clark, *Revolutionary Spring*, 455–62.

13. Ivan Davidson Kalmar, "Moorish Style: Orientalism, the Jews, and Synagogue Architecture," *Jewish Social Studies* 7, no. 3 (Spring/Summer 2001): 68–100; L. Scott Lerner, "Narrating Over the Ghetto of Rome," *Jewish Social Studies* 8, nos. 2/3 (Winter/Spring 2002): 1–38.

14. Otto Glagau, foreword to *Der Börsen-und-Gründungs-Schwindel in Berlin* (P. Frohberg, 1876).

15. Peter Pulzer, *The Rise of Political Anti-Semitism in Germany and Austria*, rev. ed. (Harvard University Press, 1988), 49.

16. James F. Harris, *The People Speak! Anti-Semitism and Emancipation in Nineteenth-Century Bavaria* (University of Michigan Press, 1994).

17. Moshe Zimmermann, "Two Generations in the History of German Antisemitism: The Letters of Theodor Fritsch to Wilhelm Marr," *Leo Baeck Institute Year Book* 23, no. 1 (1978): 89–99, here 97.

18. Frederick Busi, *The Pope of Antisemitism: The Career and Legacy of Edouard-Adolphe Drumont* (University Press of America, 1986), 43–45.

19. Cited in Thomas P. Anderson, "Édouard Drumont and the Origins of Modern Anti-Semitism," *Catholic Historical Review* 53, no. 1 (Apr. 1967), 28–42, here 33.

20. Philip Nord, *Paris Shopkeepers and the Politics of Resentment* (Princeton University Press, 1986), chs. 7–9; Stephen Wilson, "The Antisemitic Riots of 1898 in France," *Historical Journal* 16, no. 4 (Dec. 1973): 789–806.

21. Robert Byrnes, "Antisemitism in France Before the Dreyfus Affair," *Jewish Social Studies* 11, no. 1 (Jan. 1949): 49–68; Steven Schwarzschild, "The Marquis de Mores, the Story of a Failure (1858–1896)," *Jewish Social Studies* 22, no. 1 (Jan. 1960): 3–26; Raphaël Viau, *Vingt ans de l'antisémitisme, 1889–1909* (Paris, 1910), 344.

22. Robert Michael, *A History of Catholic Antisemitism: The Dark Side of the Church* (Palgrave Macmillan, 2008), 107–10, here 108; Robert Wistrich, "Karl Lueger and the Ambiguities of Viennese Antisemitism," *Jewish Social Studies* 45, nos. 3/4 (Summer/Autumn, 1983): 251–62, here 251, 253, 255.

23. Pulzer, *Rise of Political Anti-Semitism*, 150–58.

24. Deborah Cohen, "Who Was Who? Race and Jews in Turn-of-the-Century Britain," *Journal of British Studies* 41, no. 4 (Oct. 2002): 460–83, here 470; also

the magisterial David Feldman, *Englishmen and Jews: Social Relations and Political Culture, 1840–1914* (Yale University Press, 1994); Kevin Haddick Flynn, "The Limerick Pogrom, 1904," *History, Ireland* 12, no. 2 (Summer 2004): 31–33; "Letter Shows First Dictionary Editor Thought 'Anti-Semite' Wouldn't Be Used," *Times of Israel*, May 4, 2020.

25. John Röhl, *The Kaiser and His Court* (Cambridge University Press, 1996), 205, 211.

26. Dietz Bering, *The Stigma of Names: Antisemitism in German Daily Life, 1812–1933* (University of Michigan Press, 1992), 94–98.

27. Daniel Unowsky, "The 1898 Anti-Jewish Violence in Habsburg Galicia," in *Pogroms: A Documentary History*, ed. Eugene M. Avrutin and Elissa Bemporad (Oxford University Press, 2021), 46–69.

28. Irena Grosfeld et al., "Middleman Minorities and Ethnic Violence: Anti-Jewish Pogroms in the Russian Empire," *Review of Economic Studies* 87, no. 1 (Jan. 2020): 289–342.

29. Steven J. Zipperstein, *Pogrom: Kishinev and the Tilt of History* (Liveright, 2018).

30. See Steven J. Zipperstein, "Fateless: The Beilis Trial a Century Later," *Jewish Review of Books* (Winter 2015).

31. Julia Huston Nguyen, "Jewish Americans: Securing Rights and Responsibility to Others," May 30, 2024, EDSITEment!, edsitement.neh.gov/closer -readings/jewish-americans-securing-rights-and-responsibility-others.

32. Abigail Green, "Nationalism and the 'Jewish International': Religious Internationalism in Europe and the Middle East c.1840–c.1880," *Comparative Studies in Society and History* 50, no. 2 (Apr. 2008): 535–58; and Green and Viaene, eds., *Religious Internationals in the Modern World*.

CHAPTER 3: ANTISEMITISM ON THE RISE: 1914-33

1. Israel Cohen, "The Reign of Antisemitism," *New Statesman and Nation*, July 23, 1932, 96–97.

2. The classic study is Derek Penslar, *Jews and the Military* (Princeton University Press, 2013), esp. ch. 5; on the remarkable figure of Hertz, see Nicolas Mariot, "Social Encounters in the French Trenches," *French Politics, Culture and Society* 36, no. 2 (Summer 2018): 1–27.

3. Alan Kramer, *Dynamic of Destruction: Culture and Mass Killing in the First World War* (Oxford University Press, 2007).

4. Joshua Sanborn, *Imperial Apocalypse: The Great War and the Destruction of the*

Russian Empire (Oxford University Press, 2014); William W. Hagen, *Anti-Jewish Violence in Poland, 1914–1920* (Cambridge University Press, 2018), 75–86.

5. Eugene Kulischer, *Europe on the Move: War and Population Changes, 1917–1947* (Columbia University Press, 1948), 31–32, 109.

6. Wolf cited in Mark Levene, *War, Jews, and the New Europe: The Diplomacy of Lucien Wolf, 1914–1919* (Oxford University Press, 1992), 48.

7. Levene, *War, Jews, and the New Europe*, 51, 59.

8. Levene, *War, Jews, and the New Europe*, 95.

9. Israel Finestein, "Lucien Wolf (1857–1930): A Study in Ambivalence," *Jewish Historical Studies* 35 (1996–98): 239–54, here 251; Levene, *War, Jews, and the New Europe*, 110.

10. Levene, *War, Jews, and the New Europe*, 175, 195–96.

11. Jeffrey Veidlinger, *In the Midst of Civilized Europe: The Pogroms of 1918–1921 and the Onset of the Holocaust* (Metropolitan Books, 2021); Abraham Rechtman, *The Lost World of Russia's Jews: Ethnography and Folklore in the Pale of Settlement* (Indiana University Press, 2021), 6; Aviel Roshwald, *Ethnic Nationalism and the Fall of Empires: Central Europe, Russia and the Middle East, 1914–1923* (Routledge, 2002).

12. Herman Bernstein, "The Polish-Jewish Pact to End Antisemitism," *Current History* 23, no. 1 (Oct. 1925): 77–81; Laura Engelstein, *The Resistible Rise of Antisemitism* (Brandeis University Press, 2020), 79.

13. David Fraser, *Nazi Antisemitism and Jewish Legal Self-Defense: The Turn to Law in Liberal Democracies, 1932–39* (Routledge, 2023), esp. 38–41.

14. Michael Hagemeister, *The Perennial Conspiracy Theory: Reflections on the History of "The Protocols of the Elders of Zion"* (Routledge, 2021), ch. 1.

15. Brian Crim, "'Our Most Serious Enemy': The Specter of Judeo-Bolshevism in the German Military Community, 1914–1923," *Central European History* 44, no. 4 (Dec. 2011): 624–41, here 627.

16. Thomas Weber, *Hitler's First War: Adolf Hitler, the Men of the List Regiment, and the First World War* (Oxford University Press, 2010), 215; Weber, *Becoming Hitler: the Making of a Nazi* (Basic Books, 2017), ch. 1; Michael Brenner, *In Hitler's Munich: Jews, the Revolution and the Rise of Nazism* (Princeton University Press, 2022), 147.

17. "Hitlers 'grundlegende' Rede über den Antisemitismus," *Vierteljahrshefte für Zeitgeschichte* 16 (1968): 390–420; Oded Heilbronner, "German or Nazi Antisemitism?," in *The Historiography of the Holocaust*, ed. Dan Stone (Palgrave Macmillan, 2004), 9–23; Weber, *Becoming Hitler*, 167–70.

18. Brenner, *In Hitler's Munich*, 48.

19. Paul Hanebrink, "Transnational Culture War: Christianity, Nation, and the Judeo-Bolshevik Myth in Hungary, 1890–1920," *Journal of Modern History* 80, no. 1 (Mar. 2008): 55–80; Paul Hanebrink, *A Specter Haunting Europe: The Myth of Judeo-Bolshevism* (Belknap Press of Harvard University Press, 2018).

CHAPTER 4: ANTISEMITISM AS WORLD POWER: 1933–45

1. John Emerich Edward Dalberg-Acton, *The History of Freedom and Other Essays* (London, 1907), 12.
2. Alon Confino, *A World Without Jews: The Nazi Imagination from Persecution to Genocide* (Yale University Press, 2014), 183.
3. On the ambivalences of Jews and Fascism, see Alexander Stille, *Benevolence and Betrayal: Five Italian Jewish Families Under Fascism* (Picador, 1991); on Betar and the Revisionists, see Colin Shindler, "Models for the Radicals: Nationalism and the Origins of the Israeli Right," *Revue Européenne des études hébraïques* 11 (2005): 63–83.
4. Hermann Beck, "Between the Dictates of Conscience and Political Expediency: Hitler's Conservative Alliance Partner and Antisemitism During the Nazi Seizure of Power," *Journal of Contemporary History* 41, no. 4 (2006): 611–40; Hermann Beck, *Before the Holocaust: Antisemitic Violence and the Reaction of German Elites and Institutions During the Nazi Takeover* (Oxford University Press, 2022). Also see Noel Cary, "Antisemitism, Everyday Life and the Devastation of Public Morals in Nazi Germany" (review), *Central European History* 35, no. 4 (2002): 551–89.
5. Lawrence Stokes, "The German People and the Destruction of the European Jews," *Central European History* 6, no. 2 (1973): 167–90.
6. Bernard Dov Weinryb, *Jewish Emancipation Under Attack: Its Legal Recession Until the Present War* (American Jewish Committee, 1942), 7.
7. Oscar Janowsky, *People at Bay: The Jewish Problem in East-Central Europe* (Oxford University Press, 1938), 127.
8. Leon Volovici, *Nationalist Ideology and Antisemitism: The Case of Romanian Intellectuals in the 1930s* (Pergamon, 1991), 116, 121–22, 125; Mihail Sebastian, *For Two Thousand Years* (Other Press, 2017), 215.
9. Victor Klemperer, *The Language of the Third Reich: LTI—Lingua Tertii Imperii; A Philologist's Notebook* ("The Jewish War") (Bloomsbury Academic, 2021), 178.
10. Bela Vago, *The Shadow of the Swastika: The Rise of Fascism and Antisemitism in*

the Danube Basin, 1936–39 (Saxon House for the Institute of Jewish Affairs, 1975), 58, 69, 103.

11. Vago, *Shadow of the Swastika*, 394–95; Shmuel Almog, ed., *Antisemitism Through the Ages* (Pergamon, 1988), 340.

12. Confino, *World Without Jews*.

13. "Stenographic Report for a Portion of the Interministerial Meeting on the Jewish Question," Nov. 12, 1938, German History in Documents and Images, ghdi.ghi-dc.org/pdf/eng/English34.pdf.

14. G. K. Chesterton, *The New Jerusalem* (Hodder & Stoughton, 1920), 264–65.

15. William W. Hagen, "Before the 'Final Solution': Toward a Comparative Analysis of Political Anti-Semitism in Interwar Germany and Poland," *Journal of Modern History* 68, no. 2 (June 1996): 351–81.

16. Data from Eugene Kulischer, *Europe on the Move: War and Population Changes, 1917–1947* (Columbia University Press, 1948), 191–92.

17. Christopher Browning, "Hitler, Antisemitism, and the Final Solution," *Antisemitism Studies* 7, no. 1 (Spring 2023): 80–99, here 84.

18. "Pax Romanizing," *Time*, Dec. 31, 1934; see also the observations in Oded Heilbronner, "Großraum Europa: The Nazi Concept of 'Greater European Space' in Recent Literature" (review article), *English Historical Review* 136, no. 583 (Dec. 2021): 1574–94, at 1592–93.

19. Hitler speech, Sportspalast, Berlin, Sept. 30, 1942 at https://www.jewishvirtual library.org/adolf-hitler-address-at-the-opening-of-the-winter-relief-campaign -september-1942; Florent Brayard, *La "solution finale de la question juive"* (Fayard, 2023), 154; the general question of the European diplomacy of the Final Solution itself is well covered in Dan Stone, *The Holocaust: An Unfinished History* (Pelican, 2023), ch. 5.

20. Christopher Browning, *The Final Solution and the German Foreign Office* (Holmes & Meier, 1978), 83.

21. The question of secrecy and its emergence in the course of the war is brilliantly discussed by Florent Brayard, *Auschwitz, enquête sur un complot nazi* (Éditions Points, 2023), 442–49; the question of photography is discussed in detail in Fabian Schmidt and Alexander Olive Zöller, *Images criminelles sous nazisme* (Association française de recherche sur l'histoire du cinéma, 2024).

22. Lorna Waddington, "The Anti-Komintern and Nazi Anti-Bolshevik Propaganda in the 1930s," *Journal of Contemporary History* 42, no. 4 (2007): 573–94; Hanno Plass and Bill Templer, "Der Welt-Dienst: International Anti-Semitic Propaganda," *Jewish Quarterly Review* 103, no. 4 (Fall 2013): 503–22; Martin Kristoffer Hamre, "'Nationalists of All Countries, Unite!' Hans Keller and

Nazi Internationalism in the 1930s," *Contemporary European History* 33, no. 2 (2024): 477–96; Dirk Rupnow, "'The Antisemite Internationale': The Exporting of Anti-Jewish Scholarship and Propaganda by the Third Reich," in *A New Nationalist Europe Under Hitler*, ed. Johannes Dafinger and Dieter Pohl (Routledge, 2018), 259–70.

23. Bruno Blau, "The Jewish Population of Germany, 1939–1945," *Jewish Social Studies* 12, no. 2 (Apr. 1950): 161–72.

24. Bettina Stangneth, *Eichmann Before Jerusalem: The Unexamined Life of a Mass Murderer* (Alfed A. Knopf, 2014), 49–55; Raphael Lemkin, *Axis Rule in Occupied Europe: Laws of Occupation, Analysis of Government, Proposals for Redress* (Carnegie Endowment for International Peace, 1944); Koppel Pinson, "Antisemitism in the Post-War World," *Jewish Social Studies* 7, no. 2 (Apr. 1945): 99–118, here 99.

25. "Statement on Atrocities," October 1943 at https://avalon.law.yale.edu/wwii/moscow.asp.

26. S. W. D. Rowson, "Some Private International Law Problems Arising out of European Racial Legislation, 1933–1945," *Modern Law Review* 10, no. 4 (Oct. 1947): 345–62, and texts of various armistice agreements at the Yale Avalon Law Project. Also see S. W. D. Rowson, "The Abolition of Nazi and Fascist Anti-Jewish Legislation by British Military Administrations of the Second World War," *Jewish Yearbook of International Law* 1 (1948): 261–68. On Rowson, see Rotem Giladi, "Shabtai Rosenne: The Transformation of Sefton Rowson" in *The Law of Strangers*, ed. James Loeffler and Moria Paz (Cambridge University Press, 2019), 221–48, and the response in the same volume by Philippe Sands.

27. James Parkes, *The Emergence of the Jewish Problem, 1878–1939* (Oxford University Press, 1946), 230.

CHAPTER 5: AFTERMATH: COLD WAR EUROPE

1. Dittmer, Lowell, "The German NPD," *Comparative Politics* 2, No. 1 (Oct. 1969): 79–110, here 98.

2. Martin Conway, *Western Europe's Democratic Age, 1945–1973* (Princeton University Press, 2020), 72–75.

3. Alexander S. Kohanski, "Germany," *American Jewish Year Book* 47 (1945–46): 375–76; Geraldine Rosenfield, "Germany" and "Austria," *American Jewish Year Book* 48 (1946–47): 314–19; Boris Sapir, "Germany and Austria," *American Jewish Year Book* 49 (1947–48): 373.

4. Nathan Reich, "The Year in Retrospect," *American Jewish Year Book* 50 (1948–49): 114.

5. "NPD Antisemitism," *Patterns of Prejudice* 1, no. 1 (1967): 9.

6. "Western Germany," *American Jewish Year Book* 56 (1955): 366; "Growing Antisemitism: The Rightwing International," *Patterns of Prejudice* (1967): 9–11; Pauline Picco, "Extrême droite et antisémitisme en Italie. L'exemple du Centro Studi Ordine Nuovo (1955–1971)," *Laboratoire italien* 11 (2011): 17–52. The best general account is Jean-Yves Camus and Nicolas Lebourg, *Far-Right Politics in Europe* (Harvard University Press, 2017).

7. Bardèche cited in Martin Conway, *Western Europe's Democratic Age, 1945–1968* (Princeton University Press, 2020), 74; Jean-Pierre Rioux, review of *La tentative néo-fasciste en France de 1944 à 1965*, by Joseph Algazy, *Vingtième siecle* 5 (1985): 199–200.

8. Richard Vinen, "The End of an Ideology? Right-Wing Antisemitism in France, 1944–1970," *Historical Journal* 37, no. 2 (1994): 365–88, here 365.

9. Vinen, "End of an Ideology?," 376–81.

10. Decree cited in Elissa Bemporad, "Empowerment, Defiance, and Demise: Jews and the Blood Libel Specter Under Stalinism," *Jewish History* 26, nos. 3/4 (Dec. 2012): 343–61, here 345; Jan Rybak, *Everyday Zionism in East-Central Europe: Nation-Building in War and Revolution, 1914–1920* (Oxford University Press, 2020), 273; Brendan McGeever, *Antisemitism and the Russian Revolution* (Cambridge University Press, 2019).

11. Bemporad, "Empowerment, Defiance, and Demise"; Elissa Bemporad, "Behavior Unbecoming a Communist: Jewish Religious Practice in Soviet Minsk," *Jewish Social Studies* 14, no. 2 (Winter 2008): 1–31. Yuri Slezkine, *The Jewish Century* (Princeton University Press, 2004), 242–49. Thanks to Maria Stepanova for discussing these issues with me.

12. William Korey, "The Origins and Development of Soviet Antisemitism," *Slavic Review* 31, no. 1 (Mar. 1972): 111–35; Yohanan Petrovsky-Shtern, *Lenin's Jewish Question* (Yale University Press, 2010).

13. Victoria Khiterer, "Unwelcome Return Home: Jews, Antisemitism and the Housing Problem in Postwar Kyiv," *East European Holocaust Studies* 1, no. 1 (2023): 155–74.

14. Milovan Djilas, *Conversations with Stalin* (Harcourt Brace, 1963), 120.

15. Joshua Rubenstein and Vladimir Naumov, eds., *Stalin's Secret Pogrom: The Postwar Inquisition of the Jewish Anti-Fascist Committee*, trans. Laura Wolfson (Yale University Press, 2001), introduction; Allan L. Kagedan, "Revival, Reconstruction or Rejection: Soviet Jewry in the Postwar Years, 1944–48," in

Jews and Jewish Life in Russia and the Soviet Union, ed. Yaacov Ro'i (Frank Cass, 1995), 189–98; Allan L. Kagedan, *Soviet Zion: The Quest for a Russian Jewish Homeland* (St. Martin's, 1994).

16. Yaacov Ro'i, "Soviet Policy in the Middle East: The Case of Palestine During World War II," *Cahiers du monde russe et soviétique* 15, nos. 3/4 (July–Dec. 1974): 373–408; Matityahu Mintz, "Ben-Gurion and the Soviet Union's Involvement in the Effort to Establish a Jewish State in Palestine," *Journal of Israeli History* 26, no. 1 (2007): 67–78.

17. Rubenstein and Naumov, *Stalin's Secret Pogrom,* 39–41.

18. Rubenstein and Naumov, *Stalin's Secret Pogrom,* 281, 284.

19. Arkady Vaksberg, *Stalin Against the Jews* (New York: Knopf, 1994), 247–48; Bemporad, "Empowerment, Defiance, and Demise."

20. Alexander Lokshin, "The Doctors' Plot: The Non-Jewish Response," in *Jews and Jewish Life in Russia and the Soviet Union,* ed. Yaacov Ro'i (Frank Cass, 1995), 157–65, here 157, 161.

21. Mark Wischnitzer, *To Dwell in Safety: The Story of Jewish Migration Since 1800* (Jewish Publication Society of America, 1948), 266–67; figures from François Fejtö, *Les juifs et l'antisémitisme dans les pays communistes* (Plon, 1960), 60.

22. Robert Levy, *Ana Pauker: The Rise and Fall of a Jewish Communist* (University of California Press, 2001), 179.

23. Levy, *Ana Pauker,* 178, 203.

24. Levy, *Ana Pauker,* 219.

25. Benjamin Pinkus, *The Soviet Government and the Jews, 1948–1967* (Cambridge University Press, 1984), 104.

26. Yaacov Ro'i, *The Struggle for Soviet Jewish Emigration, 1948–1967* (Cambridge University Press, 1991).

27. Fejtö, *Les juifs et l'antisémitisme,* 215.

28. Dariusz Stola, "Anti-Zionism as a Multipurpose Policy Instrument: The Anti-Zionist Campaign in Poland, 1967–1968," *Journal of Israeli History* 25, no. 1 (2006): 75–201; Paul Lendvai, *Anti-Semitism Without Jews: Communist Eastern Europe* (Doubleday, 1971).

PART 2: ON THE BATTLEFIELD OF IDEAS

1. Europe includes the USSR. The Jewish population of Mandatory Palestine is shown as a darker circle within the total for the Middle East and North

Africa (MENA). This map is based on statistical data in Arthur Ruppin, *The Jews in the Modern World* (Macmillan and Co., 1934).

2. The Jewish population of the Middle East and North Africa excluding Israel today totals under 40,000. This map is based on statistical data in Sergio DellaPergola, "World Jewish Population, 2021," *American Jewish Year Book* (2021), 121.

CHAPTER 6: PRELUDE: THE UNITED STATES, ISRAEL, AND THE MIDDLE EAST: 1940s–1960s

1. Ben Halpern, "The Impact of Israel on American Jewish Ideologies," *Jewish Social Studies* 21, no. 1 (Jan. 1959): 62–81, here 65.

2. Lewis Namier, introduction to *The Jews in the Modern World*, by Arthur Ruppin (Macmillan, 1934), xxiii–xxiv.

3. Joseph Roth, "A Jew Emigrates to America," *The Wandering Jews*, trans. Michael Hofmann (W. W. Norton, 2001), 102.

4. Jacob Weinstein, "Antisemitism," in *The American Jew: A Composite Portrait*, ed. Oscar Janowsky (Harper & Brothers, 1942), 191; Milton Konvitz, "Intergroup Relations," in *The American Jew: A Reappraisal*, ed. Oscar Janowsky (Jewish Publication Society of America, 1964), 78–79; Leo Ribuffo, "Henry Ford and 'The International Jew,'" *American Jewish History* 69, no. 4 (June 1980): 437–77; Harold S. Wechsler, "The Rationale for Restriction: Ethnicity and College Admission in America, 1910–1980," *American Quarterly*, 36, no. 5 (Winter 1984), 643–67; Alan Brinkley, *Voices of Protest* (Vintage, 1982).

5. Leonard Dinnerstein, *Antisemitism in America* (Oxford University Press, 1995), chs. 5–7, here 145; Koppel Pinson, "Antisemitism in the Postwar World," *Jewish Social Studies* 7, no. 2 (Apr. 1945): 99–118; Susan Welch, "American Opinion Toward Jews During the Nazi Era," *Social Science Quarterly* 95, no. 3 (Sept. 2014): 615–35.

6. Arthur Liebman, *Jews and the Left* (Wiley, 1979), 588; Anne Sebba, *Ethel Rosenberg: A Cold War Tragedy* (Weidenfeld & Nicolson, 2021). Sinkoff, *From Left to Right*, 121.

7. Dinnerstein, *Antisemitism in America*, 150; Deborah Dash Moore, "Who Built New York? Jewish Builders in the Interwar Decades," *American Jewish History* 101, no. 3 (July 2017): 311–35; Marshall Sklare, "Jews, Ethnics, and the American City," *Commentary*, Apr. 1972.

8. Nate Bloom, "Woodstock: The Jewish Connection," *Jewish Standard*, Aug.

14, 2009; "Jewish Population in the U.S. Shifting Towards the Sun Belt," Jewish Telegraphic Agency, Feb. 14, 1979.

9. Dinnerstein, *Antisemitism in America*, 150, 170; "Freedom for Russian Jews, Less Antisemitism Predicted for Year 2000," Jewish Telegraphic Agency, Oct. 21, 1960, 4; Bert Gold cited in Marianne R. Sanua, *Let Us Prove Strong: The American Jewish Committee, 1945–2006* (Brandeis University Press, 2007), 197.

10. Dinnerstein, *Antisemitism in America*, 160; Weinstein, "Antisemitism," 202–3; Sinkoff, *From Left to Right*, 111–13; Murray Friedman, "John Slawson (1896–1989)," *American Jewish Year Book* 91 (1991), 555–58.

11. Peter Grose, *Israel in the Mind of America* (Schocken, 1984), 4–5.

12. Zvi Ganin, *An Uneasy Relationship: American Jewish Leadership and Israel, 1948–1957* (Syracuse University Press, 2005), 3–4; Naomi Cohen, *Not Free to Desist: The American Jewish Committee, 1906-1966* (Jewish Publication Society, 1972), 222.

13. Nathan Kurz, *Jewish Internationalism and Human Rights After the Holocaust* (Cambridge University Press, 2021), 26.

14. William Zukerman, *Voices of Dissent: Jewish Problems, 1948–1961* (Bookman Associates, 1964), 11–15, 31–36, 37–40.

15. Zukerman, *Voices of Dissent*, 31–36, 37–40, 64–70; on the campaign against him, Geoffrey Levin, *Our Palestine Question: Israel and American Jewish Dissent, 1948–1978* (Princeton University Press, 2023), 67–75. Also Marjorie N. Feld, *Threshold of Dissent: A History of American Jewish Critics of Zionism* (New York University Press, 2024); Doug Rossinow, "'The Edge of the Abyss': The Origins of the Israel Lobby, 1949–1954," *Modern American History* 1, no. 1 (2018): 23–43.

16. Judd Teller, "Zionism, Israel and American Jewry," in Janowsky, *The American Jew: A Reappraisal*, 317; Rossinow, "'The Edge of the Abyss,'" 28. For the crisis in American Zionism, see Zohar Segev, "American Zionists' Place in Israel After Statehood: From Involved Partners to Outside Supporters," *American Jewish History*, 93, no. 3 (Sept. 2007), 277–302.

17. Tal Elmaliach, "Beyond Mamlakhtiyut and Halutziyut: The Ben-Gurion–Blaustein Understanding in Light of Ben-Gurion's Theory of Revolution," *Israel Studies* 25, no. 3 (Fall 2020), 65–80; Ganin, *Uneasy Relationship*; Marc Dollinger, *Black Power, Jewish Politics: Reinventing the Alliance in the 1960s* (Brandeis University Press, 2018), 153.

18. Ganin, *Uneasy Relationship*, 36–37; "An Exchange of Views: American Jews and the State of Israel," *Israel Studies* 25, no. 3 (Fall 2020): 8–14.

19. Adam S. Ferziger, "Ben-Gurion and American Jewish Students at the Cusp of the Sixties: Between Solidarity and Persuasion," *Jewish Quarterly Review* 113, no. 2 (Spring 2023), 273–303.

20. Dollinger, *Black Power, Jewish Politics*, 154.

21. Ganin, *Uneasy Relationship*, 127, 146–48; Charles S. Liebman, "Diaspora Influence on Israel: The Ben-Gurion–Blaustein 'Exchange' and Its Aftermath," *Jewish Social Studies* 36, nos. 3/4 (July–Oct. 1974): 271–80.

22. Halpern, "Impact of Israel"; Dollinger, *Black Power, Jewish Politics*, 150.

23. Evyatar Friesel, "The Influence of American Zionism on the American Jewish Community, 1900–1950," *American Jewish History* 75, no. 2 (Dec. 1985): 130–48, here 146; Henry Feingold, *Jewish Power in America: Myth and Reality* (Transaction Publishers, 2008), 68.

24. Marshall Sklare, "Lakeville and Israel: The Six-Day War and Its Aftermath," *Midstream* (Oct. 1968): 1–18; on the fascinating figure of Sklare see Jonathan D. Sarna, "Marshall Sklare (1921–1992)," *Proceedings of the American Academy for Jewish Research* 58 (1992): 33–35. Sklare has been described as "the progenitor of an entire Jewish identity industry complex": Jonathan Krasner, "On the Origins and Persistence of the Jewish Identity Industry in Jewish Education," in Jon Levisohn and Ari Kelman, eds., *Beyond Jewish Identity: Rethinking Concepts and Imagining Alternatives* (Academic Studies Press, 2019), 52.

25. UJA data in Martin Raffel, "History of Israel Advocacy," in *Jewish Polity and American Civil Society*, ed. Alan Mittleman et al. (Rowman & Littlefield, 2002), 117; Lawrence Grossman, "Transformation Through Crisis: The American Jewish Committee and the Six-Day War," *American Jewish History* 86, no. 1 (Mar. 1998): 27–54, here 49–51.

26. Arnold Forster and Benjamin Epstein, *Cross Currents* (Doubleday, 1956), 14; ADL and National Council of Churches, *Current Problems of Anti-Semitism: Proceedings of a Conference* (New York, 1962).

27. Cited in Elie Podeh, "Demonizing the Other: Israeli Perceptions of Nasser and Nasserism," in *Rethinking Nasserism: Revolution and Historical Memory in Modern Egypt*, ed. Elie Podeh and Onn Winckler (University Press of Florida, 2004), 72–79, here 78.

28. Nahum Goldmann, *The Jewish Paradox* (Weidenfeld & Nicolson, 1978), 99.

29. Peretz Bernstein cited in Todd Endelman and Zvi Gitelman, eds., *The Posen Library of Jewish Culture and Civilization*, vol. 8, *Crisis and Creativity Between World Wars, 1918–1939* (Yale University Press, 2020), 54; V. Jabotinsky, "The Iron Wall" (1923); Arthur Ruppin, *The Jews in the Modern World* (Macmillan, 1934), 258; Anita Shapira, "Israeli Perceptions of Anti-Semitism and Anti-Zionism," in *Anti-Semitism and Anti-Zionism in Historical Perspective: Convergence and Divergence*, ed. Jeffrey Herf (Routledge, 2007), 228–50, here 230–31.

30. Amnon Raz-Krakotzkin, "Exile within Sovereignty: Critique of the 'Negation of Exile' within Israeli Culture," in Zvi Ben-Dor Benite, Stefanos Geroulanos and Nicole Jerr, eds., *The Scaffolding of Sovereignty: Global and Aesthetic Perspectives on the History of a Concept* (Columbia University Press, 2017), 393–420, here 411–413. A partial exception were the early Zionist Orientalists: See Jonathan Marc Gribetz, *Defining Neighbors: Religion, Race and the Early Zionist-Arab Encounter* (Princeton University Press, 2015); Yaron Peleg, *Orientalism and the Hebrew Imagination* (Cornell University Press, 2005).

31. Yosef Gorny, *Zionism and the Arabs, 1882–1948: A Study of Ideology* (Clarendon Press, 1987), 34–35, 43.

32. Adi Gordon, *Toward Nationalism's End: An Intellectual Biography of Hans Kohn* (Brandeis University Press, 2017), 145–50.

33. Evyatar Friesel, "It All Depends on the Point of View: David Ben-Gurion in the 1940s," *Journal of Israeli History* 26, no. 1 (2007): 79–89, a review of vol. 4 of *David's Zeal*, Shabtai Teveth's multivolume biography of Ben-Gurion; for Weizmann, see Gorny, *Zionism and the Arabs*, 204, 246; Ruppin, *Jews in the Modern World*.

34. Two excellent recent guides through the maze are Daniel J. Schroeter, "'Islamic Antisemitism' in Historical Discourse," *American Historical Review* 123, no. 4 (Oct. 2018): 1172–89, and Dario Miccoli, "The Jews of the Middle East and North Africa: A Historiographic Debate," *Middle Eastern Studies* 56, no. 3 (2020): 511–20.

35. Jonathan Frankel, "'Ritual Murder' in the Modern Era: The Damascus Affair of 1840," *Jewish Social Studies* 3, no. 2 (Winter 1997): 1–16. Anti-Christian violence was also connected to the intensification of European imperialism in the Ottoman lands: See Eugene Rogan, *The Damascus Events: The 1860 Massacre and the Making of the Modern Middle East* (Basic Books, 2024).

36. René Wildangel, "More Than the Mufti: Other Arab-Palestinian Voices on Nazi Germany 1933–1945, and Their Postwar Narrations," in *Arab Responses to Fascism and Nazism: Attraction and Repulsion*, ed. Israel Gershoni (University of Texas Press, 2014), 101–27.

37. Wildangel, "More than the Mufti," 122. See too the essays in the collection introduced by Ulrike Freitag and Israel Gershoni, "The Politics of Memory: The Necessity for Historical Investigation into Arab Responses to Fascism and Nazism," *Geschichte und Gesellschaft* 37, no. 3 (July–Sept. 2011): 311–31; on the Palestinian leadership, the classic work is Rashid Khalidi, *The Iron Cage: The Story of the Palestinian Struggle for Statehood* (M. E. Sharpe, 2006).

38. Benny Morris, *The Birth of the Palestinian Refugee Problem, 1947–1949*

(Cambridge University Press, 1988); Avi Shlaim, "The Debate About 1948," *International Journal of Middle Eastern Studies* 27, no. 3 (1995): 287–304; "Intelligence Brief from 1948 Hidden for Decades Indicates Jewish Fighters' Actions Were the Major Cause of Arab Displacement, Not Calls from Arab Leadership," Akevot Institute, akevot.org.il/en/article/intelligence-brief-from-1948-hidden-for-decades-indicates-jewish-fighters-actions-were-the-major-cause-of-arab-displacement-not-calls-from-arab-leadership; Benny Morris, "The Causes and Character of the Arab Exodus from Palestine: The Israel Defence Forces Intelligence Branch Analysis of June 1948," *Middle Eastern Studies* 22, no. 1 (Jan. 1986): 5–19.

39. Esther Webman, ed., *The Global Impact of "The Protocols of the Elders of Zion": A Century-Old Myth* (Routledge, 2018), ch. 11; Michael Hagemeister, *The Perennial Conspiracy Theory: Reflections on the History of "The Protocols of the Elders of Zion"* (Routledge, 2021).

40. Gilbert Achcar, *Les Arabes et la Shoah: La guerre israélo-arabe des récits* (Actes Sud, 2009); on Iran, see Meir Litvak, "The Islamic Republic of Iran and the Holocaust: Anti-Semitism and Anti-Zionism," in Herf, *Anti-Semitism and Anti-Zionism in Historical Perspective*, 250–69; Imam Khomeini, *Governance of the Jurist: Islamic Government* (Tehran, 2008 ed., original ed. 1970), 114.

41. A good discussion of Sayegh is in Geoffrey Levin, *Our Palestine Question: Israel and American Jewish Dissent, 1948–1978* (Yale University Press, 2023), 110–13 passim.

42. Levin, *Our Palestine Question*, 132; Zukerman, *Voices of Dissent*, 65.

43. See the fascinating new study by Jonathan Gribetz, *Reading Herzl in Beirut: The PLO's Effort to Know the Enemy* (Princeton University Press, 2024), ch. 6.

44. Nissim Rejwan, *Israel's Years of Bogus Grandeur: From the Six-Day War to the First Intifada* (University of Texas Press, 2006), 69–70.

45. Rejwan, *Israel's Years of Bogus Grandeur*, 133–34.

CHAPTER 7: A NEW ANTISEMITISM?
THE INTERNATIONAL ARENA

1. Antony Lerman, "Continuity and Change," *Jewish Quarterly* 31, nos. 3/4 (1984): 1–3, cited in Lerman, *The Making and Unmaking of a Zionist: A Personal and Political Journey* (Pluto Press, 2012), 76.

2. Howard Ehrlich, "The Swastika Epidemic of 1959–60: Anti-Semitism and Community Characteristics," *Social Problems* 9, no. 3 (Winter 1962): 264–72;

Sidney Liskofsky, "International Swastika Outbreak," *American Jewish Year Book* 62 (1961): 209–13.

3. US Department of State, *More Than a Century of Antisemitism: How Successive Occupants of the Kremlin Have Used Antisemitism to Spread Disinformation and Propaganda*, January 2004, 24, state.gov/wp-content/uploads/2024/01/GEC -Special-Report-More-than-a-Century-of-Antisemitism.pdf.

4. John Barron, *KGB: The Secret Work of Soviet Secret Agents* (Reader's Digest Press, 1972), 173–74; François Fejtö, *Les juifs et l'antisémitisme dans les pays communistes* (Plon, 1960), 171–72; Thomas Rid, *Active Measures: The Secret History of Disinformation and Political Warfare* (Farrar, Straus & Giroux, 2020), 131–32.

5. UN General Assembly, Third Committee, 20th Session, 132th Meeting, Official Records, 20 Oct. 1965: UN Doc. A/C.3/S.R.1312; Liskofsky, "International Swastika Outbreak," 209–13; Nathan Kurz, *Jewish Internationalism and Human Rights After the Holocaust* (Cambridge University Press, 2021), 117–20.

6. Kurz, *Jewish Internationalism*, 134.

7. Zeineddine cited in UN General Assembly, Ad Hoc Committee on Palestine, 13th Meeting, October 14, 1947: Summary Records, 80–81, un.org/unispal /document/ad-hoc-committee-on-the-palestine-question-summary-record-13 -14-october-1947; 1964 PLO Charter, web.archive.org/web/20101130144018 /http://www.un.int/wcm/content/site/palestine/pid/12363; Fayez Sayegh, "Zionist Colonialism in Palestine," *Settler Colonialism Studies* 2, no. 1 (2012): 206–25.

8. "Elimination of All Forms of Racial Discrimination: Zionism as Racism," Resolution Adopted by the General Assembly, 10 Nov. 1975, www.un.org /unispal/document/auto-insert-181963.

9. Leonard Dinnerstein, "Is There a New Anti-Semitism in the United States?," *Society* 41, no. 2 (Jan. 2004): 53–58]; Jerome Chanes, "What's 'New'—and What's Not—About the New Antisemitism?," *Jewish Political Studies Review* 16, nos. 1/2 (Spring 2004): 111–24; Nathan Perlmutter and Ruth Ann Perlmutter, *The Real Antisemitism in America* (Arbor House, 1982), 281; Neil Kressel, "How to Interpret American Poll Data on Jews, Israel and Antisemitism," in *Antisemitism in North America: New World, Old Hate*, ed. Steven K. Baum et al. (Brill, 2016), 12.

10. Henry L. Feingold, "Finding a Conceptual Framework for the Study of American Antisemitism," *Jewish Social Studies* 47, nos. 3/4 (Summer-Autumn 1985), 313; Chanes, "What's 'New'?," 113.

11. Edward S. Shapiro, "The Cognitive Dissonance of American Jews," *Culture and Society* 49 (2012): 547–52. For more on this, see Jeffrey E. Cohen, "Perceptions of Anti-Semitism Among American Jews, 2000–05: A Survey Analysis," *Political Psychology* 31, no. 1 (Feb. 2010): 85–107; Kressel, "How to Interpret American Poll Data," 5–6.

12. Henry L. Feingold, "The Continued Vitality of the American Jewish Committee at 80," *American Jewish Year Book* 87 (1987), 341; Arnold Forster, *Square One* (D. I. Fine, 1989), 302–4; Chanes, "What's 'New'?," 114; Harry Wallmarch, "Appreciation: Arnold Forster, ADL Leader and Israel Advocate," *Jerusalem Post*, Mar. 14, 2010; Arnold Forster and Benjamin Epstein, *The New Anti-Semitism* (McGraw-Hill, 1974), 1, 3, 5, 7–8, 324.

13. Forster, *Square One*, 302–3.

14. Forster and Epstein, *New Anti-Semitism* 128–49.

15. Eric L. Goldstein, *The Price of Whiteness: Jews, Race and American Identity* (Princeton University Press, 2006), 84.

16. Charles Seguin and David Rigby, "National Crimes: A New National Data Set of Lynchings in the United States, 1883–1941," *Socius* 5 (2019): 1–9; James Baldwin and Budd Schulberg, "Dialogue in Black and White," *Playboy*, Dec. 1966, cited in David Leeming, *James Baldwin: A Biography* (Arcade, 2015), 274.

17. Leonard Rogoff, "Is the Jew White? The Racial Place of the Southern Jew," *American Jewish History* 85, no. 3 (Sept. 1997): 195–230, here 195, 203.

18. Philip S. Foner, "Black-Jewish Relations in the Opening Years of the Twentieth Century," *Phylon* 36, no. 4 (1975): 359–67, here 360, 364–65.

19. Foner, "Black-Jewish Relations"; Goldstein, *Price of Whiteness*, 69, 81; Max Kohler, "The Jews and the American Anti-Slavery Movement," *Publication of the American Jewish Historical Society* 5 (1897): 137–155; Richard Kreitner, *Fear No Pharoah* (Farrar, Straus and Giroux, 2025).

20. Howard N. Rabinowitz, "Nativism, Bigotry and Anti-Semitism in the South," *American Jewish History* 77, no. 3 (Mar. 1988): 437–451; Seth Forman, "The Unbearable Whiteness of Being Jewish: Desegregation in the South and the Crisis of Jewish Liberalism," *American Jewish History* 85, no. 2 (June 1997): 121–142, here 124; Hasia Diner, *In the Almost Promised Land: Jews and Blacks, 1915–1935* (Greenwood Press, 1977).

21. Harvard Sitkoff, *Toward Freedom Land: The Long Struggle for Racial Equality in America* (University Press of Kentucky, 2010), 147–74; W. E. B Du Bois, "The Negro and the Warsaw Ghetto," *Jewish Life* 6, no. 7 (May 1952): 14–15; AJC cited in Forman, "The Unbearable Whiteness of Being Jewish," 128; also generally, David Feldman, "A History of Prejudice," *The Ideas Letter*, Sept. 19, 2024.

22. Forman, "The Unbearable Whiteness of Being Jewish," 134–35; Frederick Simonelli, "The American Nazi Party, 1958–1967," *The Historian* 57, no. 3 (Spring 1995): 553–566; Pierre Birnbaum, *Tears of History: The Rise of Political Antisemitism in the United States* (Columbia University Press, 2023), 115–123.

23. Cornel West, *Race Matters* (Beacon Press, 1993), 71.

24. Dawidowicz in Sinkoff, *From Left to Right*, 122; Silberman cited in Marianne Sanua, *Let Us Prove Strong: The American Jewish Committee, 1945–2006* (American Jewish Committee, 2007), 184.

25. Marjorie N. Feld, *The Threshold of Dissent: A History of American Jewish Critics of Zionism* (New York University Press, 2024), ch. 3; M. R. Fischbach, "The New Left and the Arab-Israel Conflict in the U.S.," *Journal of Palestine Studies* 49, no. 3 (Spring 2020): 7–12.

26. Harold Cruse, *The Crisis of the Negro Intellectual* (William Morrow and Co., 1967), 480.

27. Hugh Davis Graham, "The Origins of Affirmative Action: Civil Rights and the Regulatory State," *Annals of the American Academy of Political and Social Science* 523 (Sept. 1992): 50–62.

28. Albert Mindlin, "The Designation of Race or Color on Forms," *Public Administration Review* 26, no. 2 (June 1966): 110–18, here 111; on the politics of technological innovation, see Jason Ludwig, "Politics—Not Tech—Can Save Black Jobs from AI," *Public Books*, Feb. 22, 2024. Key work in this area has been done by Michael F. McGovern, "Justice in Numbers: Statistics and the Transformation of Civil Rights," Ph.D. dissertation, History of Science, Princeton University, 2023. My thanks to Dan Bouk for all his help.

29. US Commission on Civil Rights, "To Know or Not to Know: Collection and Use of Racial and Ethnic Data in Federal Assistance Programs," Feb. 1973; Statistical Policy Directive No. 15, May 1978, www2.census.gov/about /ombraceethnicityitwg/1978-statistical-policy-handbook.pdf.

30. *Crisis at Columbia: Report of the Fact-Finding Commission Appointed to Investigate the Disturbances at Columbia University in April and May 1968* (Vintage Books, 1968), 14; Goldstein, *Price of Whiteness*, 227.

31. Eric Goldstein, "Contesting the Categories: Jews and Government Racial Classification in the United States," *Jewish History* 19, no. 1 (2005): 79–107.

32. Goldstein, "Contesting the Categories," 102.

33. Nathan Glazer, *Affirmative Discrimination* (Basic Books, 1975).

34. Baldwin and Schulberg, "Dialogue in Black and White," 135; James Baldwin, "Negroes Are Anti-Semitic Because They're Anti-White," *New York Times*, Apr. 9, 1967.

35. Shaul Magid, *Meir Kahane: The Public Life and Political Thought of an American Jewish Radical* (Princeton University Press, 2021), 82–85.

36. Peter Novick, *The Holocaust in American Life* (Houghton Mifflin, 1999), 121–23.

37. Sanua, *Let Us Prove Strong*, 351.

38. Amy Kaplan, *Our American Israel: The Story of an Entangled Alliance* (Harvard University Press, 2018), 179–80.

39. Sinkoff, *From Left to Right*, 250 seq.; Evyatar Friesel, *The Days and the Seasons: Memoirs* (Wayne State University Press, 1996), 185–86.

40. Tom W. Smith, "A Review: The Holocaust Denial Controversy," *Public Opinion Quarterly* 59, no. 2 (Summer 1995): 269–95.

41. Philip Gleason, "Identifying Identity: A Semantic History," *Journal of American History* 69, no. 4 (Mar. 1983): 910–931, esp. 929–31; Jonathan Krasner, "On the Origins and Persistence of the Jewish Identity Industry in Jewish Education," in Jon Levisohn and Ari Kelman, eds., *Beyond Jewish Identity: Rethinking Concepts and Imagining Alternatives* (Academic Studies Press, 2019), 36–64.

42. Nathan Glazer, "Jewish Loyalties," *Wilson Quarterly* 5, no. 4 (Autumn 1981): 134–45; Pew Research Center, "A Portrait of Jewish Americans," Oct. 1, 2013.

43. Yuri Slezkine, *The Jewish Century* (Princeton University Press, 2004), 351–52.

44. Dinnerstein, "Is There a New Anti-Semitism?," 53–58.

45. Glazer, "Jewish Loyalties," 134–45; Charles Silberman, *A Certain People: American Jews and Their Lives Today* (Summit, 1985); Silberman is quoted in *Newsweek* in a discussion of his findings. On the impact of American identity politics on American Jewish attachment to Israel, see Derek Penslar, *Zionism: An Emotional State* (Rutgers University Press, 2023), 205; Marc Dollinger, *Quest for Inclusion: Jews and Liberalism in Modern America* (Princeton University Press, 2000), 215–21; also Feingold, "Finding a Conceptual Framework," 313–26, here 325.

46. On Pollard, see Martin Raffel, "History of Israel Advocacy," in *Jewish Polity and American Civil Society*, ed. Alan Mittleman et al. (Rowman & Littlefield, 2002), 128–31; Peter Medding, "The New Jewish Politics in the United States," in *The Quest for Utopia: Jewish Political Ideas and Institutions Through the Ages*, ed. Zvi Gitelman (M. E. Sharpe, 1992); 119–55, here 127–28; "Sumner Shapiro, Long-Serving Director of Naval Intelligence," *Washington Post*, Nov. 16, 2006.

47. Jacob David Herzog, *A People That Dwells Alone: Speeches and Writings of Yaacov Herzog* (Weidenfeld & Nicolson, 1975), 48–53.

48. Ilan Peleg, ed., *Victimhood Discourse in Contemporary Israel* (Lexington Books, 2019), 3–4; Shmuel Rosner, "Israel and a Hostile World," *New York Times*, Oct. 8, 2014; Paul Scham, "'A Nation That Dwells Alone': Israeli Religious Nationalism in the 21st Century," *Israel Studies* 23, no. 3 (Fall 2018): 207–15.

49. Forster, *Square One*, 244.

50. E. J. Hobsbawm, "Ethnicity and Nationalism in Europe Today," *Anthropology Today* 8, no. 1 (Feb. 1992): 3–8; Olga Litvak, "The God of History," in *The Social Scientific Study of Jewry: Sources, Approaches, Debates*, ed. Uzi Rebhun (Oxford University Press, 2014), 290–302; Michael Brenner, *Prophets of the Past: Interpreters of Jewish History* (Princeton University Press, 2010), 184–85; Avner Ben-Zaken, "The Father, the Son (Bibi) and the Spirit of Catastrophe," *Haaretz*, May 24, 2015; Michael Berkowitz, "Robert S. Wistrich and European Jewish History: Straddling the Public and Scholarly Spheres," *Journal of Modern History* 70, no. 1 (Mar. 1998), 119–36.

51. Ettinger cited by Antony Lerman, *Whatever Happened to Antisemitism? Redefinition and the Myth of the "Collective Jew"* (Pluto Press, 2022), 49; Scott Ury, "Strange Bedfellows? Anti-Semitism, Zionism, and the Fate of 'the Jews,'" *American Historical Review* 123, no. 4 (Oct. 2018): 1151–71.

52. Asaf Turgeman and Gal Hadari, "'Arab Anti-Semitism Debate': The Birth of New Anti-Semitism in Public and Academic Discourse in Israel," *Journal of Modern Jewish Studies* 14, no. 3 (2015): 501–19; Lerman, *Making and Unmaking of a Zionist*, 77.

53. Yehoshafat Harkabi, "On Arab Antisemitism Once More," in *Antisemitism Through the Ages*, ed. Shmuel Almog (Pergamon, 1988), 239; Harkabi recollected by Rashid Khalidi, interviewed by Tariq Ali, in "The Neck and the Sword," *New Left Review* 147 (May–July 2024): 5–38; Ami Pedahzur and Yael Yishai, "Hatred by Hated People: Xenophobia in Israel," *Studies in Conflict and Terrorism* 22, no. 2 (1999): 101–17. My thanks to Adam Shatz for conversations on this point.

54. Dov Waxman, *The Pursuit of Peace and the Crisis of Israeli Identity* (Palgrave Macmillan, 2006), 28–29; Anita Shapira, "Israeli Perceptions of Anti-Semitism and Anti-Zionism," in *Anti-Semitism and Anti-Zionism in Historical Perspective: Convergence and Divergence*, ed. Jeffrey Herf (Routledge, 2007), 242–43.

55. Carlo Ginzburg, "Postface," in *The Medieval Roots of Antisemitism*, ed. Jonathan Adams and Cordelia Hess (Routledge, 2018), 433.

56. Magid, *Meir Kahane*, 129–35.

57. Pierre Vidal-Naquet, "Theses on Revisionism" (1985), in *Assassins of Memory*,

trans. Jeffrey Mehlman (Columbia University Press, 1992); Novick, *Holocaust*, 161; Tom Segev, *The Seventh Million: The Israelis and the Holocaust* (Farrar, Straus and Giroux, 2019), 400–401; Amos Oz, "Better a Living Judeo-Nazi Than a Dead Saint," *Journal of Palestine Studies* 12, no. 3 (Spring 1983): 202–9.

58. Yael Aronoff, "Israeli Prime Ministers: Transforming the Victimhood Discourse," in *Victimhood Discourse in Contemporary Israel*, ed. Ilan Peleg (Lexington Books, 2019), 37–57; Waxman, *Pursuit of Peace*, 128.

59. Pedahzur and Yishai, "Hatred by Hated People," 111, 115; Weiss cited in Hanna Herzog et al., "Racism and the Politics of Signification: Israeli Public Discourse on Racism Towards Palestinian Citizens," *Ethnic and Racial Studies* 31, no. 6 (2008): 1091–1109, here 1104.

60. Data from Sivan Hirsch-Hoefler and Cas Mudde, *The Israeli Settler Movement: Assessing and Explaining Social Movement Success* (Cambridge University Press, 2021). On soccer, see "Israeli Soccer Fans Attacked in Incident Linked to Antisemitism in Amsterdam," *USA Today*, Nov. 8, 2024. Few made the connection with an earlier incident that had taken place in the center of Athens, in which a group of Maccabi fans beat up a Pakistani man: See "Opadoi edrasan anenochlitoi sto kentro tis Athinas," *Efimeris Syntakton*, Mar. 7, 2024. For the background, see Rami Younis, "Israel's Most Racist Soccer Club Isn't Shouting 'Death to Arabs,'" *+972 Magazine*, Apr. 27, 2016; "Inside Beitar Jerusalem, One of the World's Most Racist Soccer Clubs," *Haaretz*, July 4, 2022; Larry Derfner, "When an Israeli Soccer Game Looks Like a Klan Rally," *+972 Magazine*, Nov. 2, 2012.

61. Jacob Marcus, "Background for the History of American Jewry," in *The American Jew: A Reappraisal*, ed. Oscar Janowsky (Jewish Publication Society of America, 1964), 23–24.

62. J. J. Goldberg, *Jewish Power: Inside the American Jewish Establishment* (Basic Books, 1996), 7; Medding, "The 'New Jewish Politics' in the United States."

63. Shaul Kelner, *A Cold War Exodus: How American Activists Mobilized to Free Soviet Jews* (New York University Press, 2024), 9.

64. Dollinger, *Quest for Inclusion*, 221–22.

65. Marc Dollinger, *Black Power, Jewish Politics: Reinventing the Alliance in the 1960s* (Brandeis University Press, 2018).

66. Kurz, *Jewish Internationalism*, 140–63, here 158; Benjamin Nathans, *To the Success of Our Hopeless Cause: The Many Lives of the Soviet Dissident Movement* (Princeton University Press, 2024), on the complex interconnections between the Soviet Jewry movement and Soviet dissidence, including the role of Natan Sharansky.

67. Theodore H. Friedgut, "Soviet Anti-Zionism: Origins, Forms and Development," in Robert S. Wistrich, ed., *Anti-Zionism and Antisemitism in the Contemporary World*, ed. Robert S. Wistrich (Macmillan, 1990), 26–45, here 41–42; Mark Tolts, "A Half Century of Jewish Emigration from the Former Soviet Union: Demographic Aspects," paper presented at the Project for Russian and Eurasian Jewry, Davis Center for Russian and Eurasian Studies, Harvard University, November 20, 2019, now available in *Migration from the Newly Independent States*, ed. Mikhail Denisenko et al. (Springer Nature, 2020), 323–44. Jewish population statistics are a contested field. See Sergio DellaPergola, "World Jewish Population, 2020," *The American Jewish Year Book* 120 (2020): 273–370.

CHAPTER 8: WORD WEAPONS

1. Lewis Carroll, *Alice's Adventures in Wonderland* and *Through the Looking-Glass* (Oxford University Press, 2009), 190.
2. Saul Dubow, "Apartheid in South Africa and Israel/Palestine: A Case of Convergent Evolution?," *Palestine/Israel Review* 1, no. 2 (2024): 257–88.
3. On Zionism among American Jews today, see Dov Waxman, *Trouble in the Tribe: The American Jewish Conflict over Israel* (Princeton University Press, 2016), 28–29; on Israel, see Pew Research Center Report, "Israel's Divided Society," Mar. 8, 2016; Reinhart in a letter to *The Times* cited in Rory Miller, *Divided Against Zion: Anti-Zionist Opposition in Britain to a Jewish State in Palestine, 1945–48* (Frank Cass, 2000), 144. The literature on Zionism is huge. The best place to start is Michael Stanislawski, *Zionism: A Very Short Introduction* (Oxford University Press, 2017); also Noam Pianko, *Zionism and the Roads Not Taken: Rawidowicz, Kaplan, Kohn* (Indiana University Press, 2010). Here the discussion concerns the intellectual arguments for and against identifying Zionism with racism. The quite distinct question of whether such an equating of the two should be prohibited is raised in the next chapter.
4. US Department of State, "Report on Global Antisemitism," Jan. 5, 2005, at https://2001-2009.state.gov/g/drl/rls/40258.htm.
5. Craig S. Smith, "Free Speech and Hate Speech: French Ruling Roils the Waters," *New York Times*, June 27, 2005.
6. Brian Klug, "The Myth of the New Anti-Semitism," *The Nation*, Dec. 2, 2004; Leon Wieseltier, "Hitler Is Dead," *New Republic*, May 27, 2002.
7. W. Bergmann, "Xenophobia and Antisemitism After the Unification of Germany," *Patterns of Prejudice* 28, no. 1 (1994): 67–80, here 69.

8. The older right-wing demonization of Israel and Zionism is described in Pierre Birnbaum, "The French Radical Right: From Anti-Semitic Zionism to Anti-Semitic Anti-Zionism," in *Anti-Semitism and Anti-Zionism in Historical Perspective: Convergence and Divergence*, ed. Jeffrey Herf (Routledge, 2006), 145–59. On the National Front in France, see Alexandre Bande et al., eds., *Histoire politique de l'antisémitisme en France: de 1967 à nos jours* (Robert Laffont, 2024), esp. 68–69. On the general point of sanitization, see Tony Judt, *Postwar: A History of Europe Since 1945* (Penguin Press, 2005).

9. Reza Zia-Ebrahimi, "When the Elders of Zion Relocated to Eurabia," *Patterns of Prejudice* 52, no. 4 (2018): 314–37; see also Adi Schwartz, "The Protocols of the Elders of Brussels," *Haaretz*, June 20, 2006; Andrew Brown, "The Myth of Eurabia: How a Far-Right Conspiracy Theory Went Mainstream," *Guardian*, Aug. 16, 2019.

10. "Israel's Diaspora Affairs Minister Chikli Says Le Pen as French President "Excellent for Israel," *Haaretz*, July 1, 2024; "Romania Accuses Israel of Election Interference After Netanyahu Minister's Call with Pro-Nazi Candidate," *Haaretz*, Nov. 30, 2024; "The New Pro-Israeli Clothes of Europe's Far Right," *Le Monde*, May 31, 2024; https://united-jed.org/combating-antisemitism/; "Israel Invites Europe's Far Right to Conference 'Combating Antisemitism,'" *Haaretz*, Mar. 13, 2025; "Ex-ADL Head Slams Successor for Sharing Stage at Israel Antisemitism Confab with Europe's Far Right," *Haaretz*, Mar. 16, 2025.

11. David Feldman, "Jeremy Corbyn, 'Imperialism' and Labour's Antisemitism Problem," *History Workshop*, June 12, 2019, at https://www.historyworkshop .org.uk/anti-racism/imperialism-and-labours-antisemitism-problem/; see also on the Labour background: Jeremy Corbyn, "What I'm Doing to Banish Anti-Semitism from the Labour Party," *The Standard*, Apr. 24, 2018. The larger subject is well discussed by Owen Jones, *This Land: The Struggle for the Left* (Allen Lane, 2020), ch. 7.

12. Auschwitz visitor numbers: auschwitz.org/en/visiting/attendance.

13. C. M. Baker, "Challenges of 'The Jewish People': Promises and Perils of Collective Identities," in *Antisemitism, Islamophobia and the Politics of Definition*, ed. David Feldman and Marc Volovici (Palgrave Macmillan, 2023), 94–97; see too the useful discussion in Doris Bergen, "Studying the Holocaust: Is History Commemoration?" in *The Holocaust and Historical Methodology*, ed. Dan Stone (Berghahn, 2012), 158–177.

14. Antony Lerman, "Sense on Antisemitism," *Prospect*, August 19, 2002; Romano Prodi, "Against Anti-Semitism: For a Union of Diversity," speech, Brussels,

Feb. 19, 2004, at https://ec.europa.eu/commission/presscorner/detail/en/ SPEECH_04_85.

15. Lerman, "Sense on Antisemitism"; Arthur Hertzberg, "Is Anti-Semitism Dying Out?," *New York Review of Books*, June 24, 1993.

16. James B. Jacobs and Kimberly A. Potter, "Hate Crimes: A Critical Perspective," *Crime and Justice* 22 (1997): 1–50, here 13–15.

17. Jacobs and Potter, "Hate Crimes," 13–14; the dual-mission problem is explored in Alex Kane and Jacob Hutt, "How the ADL's Israel Advocacy Undermines Its Civil Rights Work," *Jewish Currents* (Spring 2021). Jim Sleeper, reviewing Jacobs and Potter's 1998 *Hate Crimes: Criminal Law and Identity Politics* (Oxford University Press). For a discussion of hate crimes and antisemitism, see Paul Iganski, ed., *The Hate Debate: Should Hate Be Punished as a Crime?* (Profile Books, 2002).

18. Antony Lerman, *Whatever Happened to Antisemitism? Redefinition and the Myth of the "Collective Jew"* (Pluto Press, 2022), 91–92.

19. Lerman, *Whatever Happened to Antisemitism?*, 94.

20. Based on Jacob Aasland Ravndal et al., "RTV Trend Report 2022: Right-Wing Terrorism and Violence in Western Europe 1990–2021," sv.uio.no/c -rex/english/publications/c-rex-reports/2022/rtv_trend_report_2022.pdf; Global Project Against Hate and Extremism, "Generation Identity," https:// globalextremism.org/reports/generation-identity/; Lerman, *Whatever Happened to Antisemitism?*, 98–99.

21. Lerman, *Whatever Happened to Antisemitism?*, 84; for background, see Hertzberg, "Is Anti-Semitism Dying Out?"; a good survey is Martin Raffel, "History of Israel Advocacy," in *Jewish Polity and American Civil Society*, ed. Alan Mittleman et al. (Rowman & Littlefield, 2002), 103–81.

22. Lerman, *Whatever Happened to Antisemitism?*, 176; Michael Galchinsky, *Jews and Human Rights: Dancing at Three Weddings* (Rowman & Littlefield, 2008), 121–22; Marianne Sanua, *Let Us Prove Strong: The American Jewish Committee, 1945–2006* (Brandeis University Press, 2007), 345.

23. "A 101-Year-Old Nazi Is Convicted: Late Justice Is Still Justice," Simon Wiesenthal Center, July 5, 2022, https://swcjerusalem.org/2022/07/05/a-101 -year-old-nazi-is-convicted-late-justice-is-still-justice/; also Rashid Khalidi, "The Case of the Mamilla Cemetery: Delegitimization or Desecration?," Center for Palestine Studies, Columbia University, https://palestine.mei .columbia.edu/event-extras/2017/5/22/the-case-of-the-mamilla-cemetery -delgitimization-or-desecration; "Fundraising the Rabbi Hier Way," *Jewish Journal*, Nov. 16, 2007.

24. Raffel, "History of Israel Advocacy," 166–181; Waxman, *Trouble in the Tribe*, passim; Edward Tivnan, *The Lobby: Jewish Political Power and American Foreign Policy* (Simon and Schuster, 1987).

25. Weinstein, "On Combating Antisemitism"; Natan Sharansky, "3D Test of Antisemitism: Demonization, Delegitimation, Double-Standards," *Jewish Political Studies Review* 16, nos. 3/4 (Fall 2004); Sharansky's Soviet-era activities are touched on in Benjamin Nathans, *To the Success of Our Hopeless Cause: The Many Lives of the Soviet Dissident Movement* (Princeton University Press, 2024); a good journalistic treatment that includes his Israeli political activities is "Natan Sharansky: Act III, Scene I," *Moment*, July–August 2012, at https://momentmag.com/natan-sharansky-act-iii-scene-i-2/.

26. Colin Powell, "Remarks at the Conference on Antisemitism of the Organization for Security and Co-operation in Europe," Apr. 28, 2004, at https://2001-2009.state.gov/secretary/former/powell/remarks/31885.htm.

27. Stephen Roth Institute for the Study of Contemporary Antisemitism and Racism, *Antisemitism Worldwide, 2004* (Tel Aviv University, 2006), 24.

28. Lerman, *Whatever Happened to Antisemitism?*, 70–73.

29. On Dinur, see David Myers, "History as Ideology: The Case of Ben Zion Dinur, Zionist Historian 'Par Excellence,'" *Modern Judaism* 8, no. 2 (May 1988): 167–93; text of the 1953 Martyrs' and Heroes Remembrance (Yad Vashem) Law 5713-1953, yadvashem.org/about/yad-vashem-law.html; see also Dina Porat, *Israeli Society, the Holocaust and Its Survivors* (Vallentine Mitchell, 2008), 347.

30. Simon Rawidowicz, "Israel, the Ever-Dying People," in *Israel, the Ever-Dying People and Other Essays*, ed. Benjamin Ravid (Associated University Presses, 1986), 192–203; for Rawidowicz more generally, see Pianko, *Zionism and the Roads Not Taken*, 6–69; David Myers, *Between Jew and Arab: The Lost Voice of Simon Rawidowicz* (Brandeis University Press, 2008). Yoram Shachar, "Jefferson Goes East: The American Origins of the Israeli Declaration of Independence," *Theoretical Inquiries in Law* 10, no. 2 (July 2009): 589–618; Martin Kramer, "Why Israel Is Called Israel and Not Judea," *Mosaic* (June 2021); on Ben-Gurion and Yiddish, see Zach Golden, "How Yiddish Became a 'Foreign Language' in Israel Despite Having Been Spoken There Since the 1400s," *Forward*, Sept. 11, 2023.

31. On the debate, a place to start is the works of Yaacov Yadgar, notably *Israel's Jewish Identity Crisis* (Cambridge University Press, 2020), and "The Great Sin of Today Is the 'Politicization' of Our Judaism, the Great Need, the 'Judaization' of Our Politics: Leon Roth and the Possibilities of a Jewish Critique of

Zionist Politics," *Journal of Modern Jewish Studies* 22, no. 4 (2023): 412–37; also Michael Brenner, *In Search of Israel: The History of an Idea* (Princeton University Press, 2018), esp. ch. 4. On the ultra-Orthodox critique, see Porat, *Israeli Society*, 367–70. Teitelbaum cited by David Myers, "Can There Be a Principled Anti-Zionism? On the Nexus Between Anti-Historicism and Anti-Zionism in Modern Jewish Thought," in Herf, *Anti-Semitism and Anti-Zionism in Historical Perspective*, 20–38, here 29.

32. Baker, "Challenges of 'The Jewish People,'" 102–3; Noam Pianko, *Jewish Peoplehood: An American Innovation* (Rutgers University Press, 2015); "Natan Sharansky: Act III, Scene I."

33. Stroock cited in Marc Dollinger, *Black Power, Jewish Politics: Reinventing the Alliance in the 1960s* (Brandeis University Press, 2018), 155; Netanyahu cited in Baker, "Challenges of 'The Jewish People,'" 104–5.

34. Diana Pinto, "Israel Poses a Serious Dilemma for Europe's Jews," *Haaretz*, Feb. 14, 2013; Gershom Gorenberg, "A Jew of No Religion," *American Prospect*, Oct. 19, 2011; Baker, "Challenges of 'The Jewish People,'" 89–90.

35. Martin Jay, "Ariel Sharon and the Rise of the New Anti-Semitism," *Salmagundi* 137/138 (Winter–Spring 2003): 12–29, here 25.

CHAPTER 9: THE VERY NATURE OF THE THING

1. Raymond Williams, *Keywords: A Vocabulary of Culture and Society* (Oxford University Press, 1985), 16.

2. Thomas Wilson, *The Rule of Reason, Conteinyng the Arte of Logique, Set Forth in Englishe* (London, 1551): "Of a Diffinition." On Wilson, see Albert J. Schmidt, "Thomas Wilson, Tudor Scholar-Statesman," *Huntington Library Quarterly* 20, no. 3 (May 1957): 205–18.

3. Ben Halpern, "What Is Antisemitism?," *Modern Judaism* 1, no. 3 (Dec. 1981): 251–62; Feingold, "Finding a Conceptual Framework for the Study of American Antisemitism," *Jewish Social Studies*, 313; David Engel, "Away from a Definition of Antisemitism: An Essay in the Semantics of Historical Description," in *Rethinking European Jewish History*, ed. Jeremy Cohen and Moshe Rosman (Oxford University Press, 2008), 30–53.

4. Antony Lerman, *Whatever Happened to Antisemitism? Redefinition and the Myth of the "Collective Jew"* (Pluto Press, 2022), 127–29; Kenneth Stern, *The Conflict over the Conflict: The Israel/Palestine Campus Debate* (University of Toronto Press, 2020), 149–51.

5. Dina Porat, "What Makes an Anti-Semite?," *Haaretz*, Jan. 28, 2007.

6. Williams, *Keywords*, 16–17; David Feldman and Marc Volovici, "'The Pure Essence of Things': Contingency, Controversy and the Struggle to Define Antisemitism and Islamophobia," in *Antisemitism, Islamophobia and the Politics of Definition*, ed. David Feldman and Marc Volovici (Palgrave Macmillan, 2023), 3–19; Frederick Harrison cited in Antony Anghie, *Imperialism, Sovereignty and the Making of International Law* (Cambridge University Press, 2004), 51.

7. Mark Weitzman, "The IHRA Working Definition of Antisemitism," in *Comprehending and Confronting Antisemitism*, ed. Armin Lange et al. (De Gruyter, 2020), 463–74; Jamie Stern-Weiner, "The Politics of a Definition: How the IHRA Working Definition of Antisemitism Is Being Misrepresented," Free Speech on Israel, April 2021, freespeechonisrael.org.uk/wp-content/uploads/2021/04/The-Politics-of-a-Definition.pdf.

8. A good discussion is Derek Penslar, "Who's Afraid of Defining Antisemitism?," *Antisemitism Studies* 6, no. 1 (Spring 2022): 133–45; also Jan Deckers and Jonathan Coulter, "What Is Wrong with the International Holocaust Remembrance Alliance's Definition of Antisemitism?," *Res Publica* 28, no. 4 (2022): 733–52; George Orwell, *Politics and the English Language* (Bodleian Library, Oxford, 2022), 43.

9. Peter Beattie, "Anti-Semitism and Opposition to Israeli Government Policies: The Roles of Prejudice and Information," *Ethnic and Racial Studies* 40, no. 15 (2017): 2749–67.

10. Lerman, *Whatever Happened to Antisemitism?*, 118.

11. Rupert Emerson, "Self-Determination," *Proceedings of the American Society of International Law at Its Annual Meeting* 60 (Apr. 28–30, 1966): 135–41, here 136; cf. Yeshayahu Leibowitz, *Judaism, Human Values, and the Jewish State* (Harvard University Press, 1992), 241.

12. Cited in Jean Améry, "Virtuous Antisemitism" (1969), in *Essays on Antisemitism, Anti-Zionism, and the Left* (Indiana University Press, 2021), 38–39.

13. Statement to the Knesset by Prime Minister Begin upon the Presentation of His Government, June 20, 1977, gov.il/en/pages/1-statement-to-the-knesset-by-pm-begin-20-june-1977.

14. Jerusalem Declaration on Antisemitism, https://jerusalemdeclaration.org; "The Nexus Document," The Nexus Project, https://nexusproject.us/nexus-resources/the-nexus-document/; The Nexus Document states: "Antisemitism consists of anti-Jewish beliefs, attitudes, actions or systemic conditions. It includes negative beliefs and feelings about Jews, hostile behavior directed against Jews (because they are Jews), and conditions that discriminate against

Jews and significantly impede their ability to participate as equals in political, religious, cultural, economic, or social life." The Jerusalem Declaration states that "Antisemitism is discrimination, prejudice, hostility or violence against Jews as Jews (or Jewish institutions as Jewish)."

15. Jerusalem Declaration on Antisemitism, https://jerusalemdeclaration.org/.
16. Stern, *Conflict over the Conflict*, 171.
17. Data cited by Neve Gordon, "Antisemitism and Zionism: The Internal Operations of the IHRA Definition," *Middle East Critique* 33, no. 3 (Mar. 2024): 345–60.
18. Aparna Gopalan, "The Hindu Nationalists Using the Pro-Israel Playbook," *Jewish Currents*, June 28, 2023; Azad Essa, *Hostile Homelands: The New Alliance Between India and Israel* (Pluto Press, 2023).

CHAPTER 10: HUNTING THE WRONG ELEPHANT

1. Irving Greenberg, "Jewish Survival and the College Campus," *Judaism* 17, no. 3 (Summer 1968): 259–81, here 260.
2. Avraham Burg, "Germany Provides a Kosher Stamp for the Israeli Occupation," *Haaretz*, July 26, 2022.
3. David Rozado, Musa al-Gharbi, and Jamin Halberstadt, "Prevalence of Prejudice-Denoting Words in News Media Discourse: A Chronological Analysis," *Social Science Computer Review* 41, no. 1 (2023): 99–122.
4. Irving Greenberg, "Jewish Survival and the College Campus," *Judaism* 17, no. 3 (Summer 1968), 259–81, here 260; also Frederic Cople Jaher, "The Search for the Ultimate *Shiksa*," *American Quarterly* 35, no. 5 (Winter 1983), 518–42.
5. Bret Stephens on Maoists: "'It Is Facing a Campaign of Annihilation': Three Columnists on Trump's War Against Academia," *New York Times*, March 15, 2025; on what the generational misreading of university culture gets wrong, see Musa al-Gharbi, "Misunderstanding Antisemitism in America," *Slow Boring*, Jan. 11, 2024.
6. "Business Titans Privately Urged NYC Mayor to Use Police on Columbia Protestors," *Washington Post*, May 17, 2024; on the predominance of young women in the encampments, see Hilary Hallett and Rebecca Kobrin, "Notes from the Encampment," unpublished manuscript. My thanks to the authors for their help. Eighty-one of the 91 students suspended after the first wave of police arrests were female; on the generation gap, see Becka A. Alper, "How

U.S. Jews Are Experiencing the Israel-Hamas War," Pew Research Center, Apr. 2, 2024, and Jordan Muchnick and Elaine Kamarck, "The Generation Gap in Opinions Toward Israel," Nov. 9, 2023, brookings.edu/articles/the-generation-gap-in-opinions-toward-israel.

7. Deborah E. Lipstadt, "How to Study Anti-Semitism," *Forward*, June 15, 2011; ISGAP board of advisers, isgap.org/isgap-advisory-board; Aiden Pink, "Think Tank Failed to Disclose Six-Figure Grant from Israeli Government," *Forward*, Aug. 31, 2020; Pink, "U.S. Pro-Israel Groups Failed to Disclose Grants from Israeli Government," *Forward*, Aug. 31, 2020. On Vaknin-Gil's efforts, see Benjamin Weinthal, "Sima Vaknin-Gill: A Former Brigadier-General's Battle Against BDS," *Jerusalem Post*, Sep. 20, 2017, jpost.com/international/a-former-brigadier-generals-battle-against-bds-sima-vaknin-gill-504686#google_vignette; on Israeli influence operations, see Derek B. Johnson, "Israeli Influence Operation Highlights Global Disinformation Industry," *CyberScoop*, June 5, 2024; Sheera Frenkel, "Israel Secretly Targets U.S. Lawmakers with Influence Campaign on Gaza War," *New York Times*, June 5, 2024.

8. Kenneth Stern, *The Conflict over the Conflict: The Israel/Palestine Campus Debate* (University of Toronto Press, 2020), 154–61; Rex Weiner, "Line Between Anti-Israel and Anti-Semitic Protests Splits AJC," *Forward*, Aug. 16, 2011.

9. Zach Montague, "Campus Protest Investigations Hang over Schools as New Academic Year Begins," *New York Times*, Oct. 5, 2024; Lila Levi, "Politicizing Antisemitism Amidst Today's Educational Culture Wars," University of Miami Law School, 2024, repository.law.miami.edu/fac_articles/1198.

10. PEN America, "The Wrong Way to Fight Campus Antisemitism," Apr. 15, 2024.

11. For background, see "Middle East Group Wants Anti-Defamation League to Disown List," *New York Times*, Jan. 30, 1985; Joel Beinin, "The New American McCarthyism: Policing Thought About the Middle East," *Race and Class* 46, no. 1 (2004): 101–15; more recently: James Bamford, "Who Is Funding Canary Mission? Inside the Doxxing Operation Targeting Anti-Zionist Students and Professors," *Nation*, Dec. 22, 2023; Gabriella Borter et al., "Name and Shame: Pro-Israel Website Ramps Up Attacks on Pro-Palestinian Student Protesters," Reuters, May 11, 2024; "Jewish Groups Targeted Columbia Grad Mahmoud Khalil, then ICE Arrested Him," *Forward*, Mar. 10, 2025.

12. Nahum Goldmann, "The Present Chance for Mideast Peace," *Worldview* 23, no. 3 (Mar. 1980), 11–13; Rachel Burnett, "I'm a Recent Jewish Grad from a University the ADL Deems to Be 'Failing' at Campus Antisemitism. Their 'Grade' Is Misleading," *Forward*, July 12, 2024; Lauren Haines, "I'm a Jewish

College Student. I Wish External Activists Were Promoting Education, Not Confrontation," *Forward*, Apr. 11, 2024.

13. Brian Klug, "The Myth of the New Antisemitism," *Nation*, Jan. 15, 2004; Antony Lerman, "Fictive Anti-Zionism: Third World, Arab and Muslim Variations," in *Anti-Zionism and Antisemitism in the Contemporary World*, ed. Robert S. Wistrich (Macmillan, 1990), 121–39; David Myers, "Can There Be a Principled Anti-Zionism?," in *Anti-Semitism and Anti-Zionism in Historical Perspective: Convergence and Divergence*, ed. Jeffrey Herf (Routledge, 2007), 31.

14. Antony Lerman, *Whatever Happened to Antisemitism? Redefinition and the Myth of the "Collective Jew"* (Pluto Press, 2022), 166–67; Hugo Gye and Jane Merrick, "Honeymoon Ends with Fuel Payouts and Arms Sales to Israel," *The Independent*, Sept. 7, 2024; James Loeffler, "Anti-Zionism," in S. Goldberg et al., eds., *Key Concepts in the Study of Antisemitism* (Palgrave, 2021), 39–51.

15. Jacques Derrida, "Autoimmunity: Real and Symbolic Suicides," trans. Pascale-Anne Brault and Michael B. Naas, in *Philosophy in a Time of Terror: Dialogues with Jürgen Habermas and Jacques Derrida*, ed. Giovanna Borradori (University of Chicago Press, 2003), 103–04; Jan Deckers and Jonathan Coulter, "What Is Wrong with the International Holocaust Remembrance Alliance's Definition of Antisemitism?," *Res Publica* 28, no. 4 (2022): 733–52; Rebecca Ruth Gould, "Legal Form and Legal Legitimacy: The IHRA Definition of Antisemitism as a Case Study in Censored Speech," *Law, Culture and the Humanities* 18, no. 1 (Feb. 2022): 153–86; PEN America, "The Wrong Way to Fight Campus Antisemitism," Apr. 15, 2024.

16. "Labour Adopts IHRA Definition in Full," *Guardian*, Sept. 4, 2018; the best analysis is Ben Gidley et al., "Labour and Antisemitism: A Crisis Misunderstood," *Political Quarterly* 91, no. 2 (Apr.–June 2020): 413–21. Also see Owen Jones, *This Land: The Struggle for the Left* (Penguin UK, 2020), ch. 7.

17. Hebh Jamal, "IHRA Definition Is Silencing Palestine Advocacy Across Europe, Says Report," *+972 Magazine*, June 7, 2023.

18. Felix Berenskötter and Mor Mitrani, "Is It Friendship? An Analysis of Contemporary German-Israeli Relations," *International Studies Quarterly* 66 (2022): 1–13; Daniel Marwecki, *Germany and Israel: Whitewashing and Statebuilding* (Oxford University Press, 2020); Peter Kuras, "The Strange Logic of Germany's Antisemitism Bureaucrats," *Jewish Currents*, July 18, 2023.

19. Thorsten Brenner, "'Reason of State': Germany's Support for Israel and Its Limits," *Agenda Publica*, Dec. 11, 2023; Kuras, "Strange Logic."

20. Cited in Irit Dekel and Esra Öyzürek, "The Logic of the Fight Against

Antisemitism in Germany in Three Cultural Shifts," *Patterns of Prejudice* 56, nos. 2/3 (2022): 157–87.

21. Kuras, "Strange Logic"; also see Hebh Jamal, "Germany's Anti-Palestinian Censorship Turns on Jews," *+972 Magazine*, Apr. 4, 2023; "Germany Passes Controversial Antisemitism Resolution," Deutsche Welle, Nov. 6, 2024; Itay Mashiach, "In Germany, a Witch Hunt Is Raging Against Critics of Israel. Cultural Leaders Have Had Enough," *Haaretz*, Dec. 10, 2020.

22. Simon Wiesenthal Center, "Global Anti-Semitism 2021 Top Ten," https://www.wiesenthal.com/assets/pdf/global_anti-semitism_2021_top_ten.pdf; Cnaan Liphshiz, "EU Slams Simon Wiesenthal Center, Says Its Annual Anti-semitism List Goes Too Far," *Times of Israel*, Jan. 11, 2022.

23. Shira Miron, "In the Fraught Debate over Antisemitism in Germany, Jews Are Just a Pawn in a Larger Battle," *Haaretz*, Jan. 11, 2025.

24. Irit Dekel, "Philosemitism in Contemporary German Media," *Media, Culture and Society* 44, no.4 (May 2022): 746–63. Ian Buruma, "Israel's Flirtation with Anti-Semites," *Project Syndicate*, May 8, 2023; Daniel Cohen, *Good Jews: Philosemitism Since the Holocaust* (Cambridge University Press, 2025); Christopher Clark, *The Politics of Conversion* (Oxford, 1995), 281. There is a large literature on philosemitism: See Jonathan Karp and Adam Sutcliffe, *Philosemitism in History* (Cambridge University Press, 2011); Pierre-André Taguieff, *Sortir de l'antisémitisme?: Le philosémitisme en question* (Odile Jacob, 2022). Also A. Dirk Moses, "The German Catechism," *Geschichte des gegenwart*, May 23, 2021.

25. Sophie Hurwitz, "Why Does Biden Keep Making the Same Dangerous Comment About Jews?," *Nation*, Mar. 6, 2024; Ben Samuels, "Biden: Without Israel, Every Jew in the World Would Be at Risk," *Haaretz*, July 16, 2024; Martin Jay, "Ariel Sharon and the Rise of the New Antisemitism," *Salmagundi* 137/138 (Winter–Spring 2003): 12–29.

26. "In the Knesset, ADL Chief Admits Failure to Extinguish the Post-Oct. 7 'Inferno of Antisemitism,' Calls for New Strategies," European Jewish Press, Jan. 7, 2025, https://ejewishphilanthropy.com/in-the-knesset-adl-chief-admits-group-has-failed-to-combat-antisemitism-calls-for-new-strategies/; Charles Herbert Stember, *Jews in the Mind of America* (Basic Books, 1964), 233, cited by Dennis Wrong, "The Psychology of Prejudice and the Future of Anti-Semitism in America," *European Journal of Sociology* 6, no. 2 (1965): 311–28, here 311; Runnymede Trust, "Our Statement on Rising Antisemitism and Islamophobia," Feb. 19, 2024.

27. Masood Farivar, "'Backlash Effect': Why the Middle East Conflict Triggers

Hate Crimes in the U.S.," Voice of America, Nov. 2, 2023; European Commission Against Racism and Intolerance (Council of Europe), "Annual Report on ECRI's Activities Covering the Period January 1 to December 31, 2023," 10–11, rm.coe.int/annual-report-on-ecri-s-activities-covering-the-period-from -1-january-/1680b0505d.

28. David Feldman, Ben Gidley and Brendan McGeever, *Facing Antisemitism: The Struggle for Safety and Solidarity* (Runnymede Trust, January 2025), https://www.runnymedetrust.org/publications/facing-antisemitism-the -struggle-for-safety-and-solidarity; Graham Wright et al., *Antisemitism on Campus: Understanding Hostility to Jews and Israel* (Cohen Center for Modern Jewish Studies, 2024), brandeis.edu/cmjs/research/antisemitism/antisemitism -on-campus.html; Eitan Hersch and Laura Royden, "Antisemitic Attitudes Across the Ideological Spectrum," *Political Research Quarterly* 76, no. 2 (2023), 697–711; Arno Rosenfeld, "Separating Anti-Zionists from Antisemites on Campus," *Forward*, Aug. 27, 2024.

29. For a cultural conservative approach to the antisemitism question, see "Project Esther: A National Strategy to Combat Antisemitism," Oct. 7, 2024, Heritage Foundation at https://www.heritage.org/progressivism/report /project-esther-national-strategy-combat-antisemitism; and for its dubious underpinnings, "Internal Project Esther Documents Describe Conspiracy of Jewish Masterminds Seeking to Dismantle Western Values," *Forward*, Dec. 6, 2024; Republican Staff Report, Committee on Education and the Workforce, US House of Representatives, "Antisemitism on College Campuses Exposed," Oct. 31, 2024, 78.

30. Steven Beller, "Israel and its Elephants: Problems of Definition, Narration and Analogy in Discussing Antisemitism," *Antisemitism Studies* 8, no. 2 (Fall 2024), 278–83, here 272.

31. Pew Research Center, "The Future of World Religions: Population Growth Projections, 2010–2050," Apr. 2, 2015.

32. Sergio dellaPergola, "World Jewish Population, 2021," *American Jewish Year Book* 121 (2021), 313–412.

33. On Cohn, see Shira Robinson, *Citizen Strangers: Palestinians and the Birth of Israel's Liberal Settler State* (Stanford University Press, 2013), 99.

34. Haim Cohn, "Antisemitism, Zionism and the State of Israel," in *Present-Day Antisemitism: Proceedings of the Eighth International Seminar of the Study Circle on World Jewry Under the Auspices of the President of Israel, Chaim Herzog, Jerusalem, 29–31 December 1985*, ed. Yehuda Bauer (Jerusalem, 1988), 329–35. Also cited by Lerman, *Whatever Happened to Antisemitism?*, 64.

EPILOGUE: WHAT I SAW

1. See Ethan Bronner, "Why 'Greater Israel' Never Came to Be," *New York Times*, Aug. 14, 2005, for the older use of the slogan; see also Nadav Shelef, "From 'Both Banks of the Jordan' to the 'Whole Land of Israel': Ideological Change in Revisionist Zionism," *Israel Studies* 9, no. 1 (Spring 2004): 125–48. I tried to convey my sense of the mood on campus at the time in: "The Week That Shook Columbia," *Financial Times*, Apr. 27, 2024, and "A Diary of the Tumultuous Days at Columbia," *Kathimerini*, May 10, 2024.

2. Lee C. Bollinger, *In Search of an Open Mind* (Columbia University Press, 2025), 261.

3. Amira McKee, "DA to Drop Hate Crime Charges Against Former Student Accused of Assaulting Israeli Student with Stick," *Columbia Spectator*, June 20, 2024; cf. https://president.columbia.edu/sites/default/files/content /Announcements/Report-2-Task-Force-on-Antisemitism.pdf.

4. For the exchange on Ashkenormativity, see Representative Jim Banks to Columbia University President Shafik, congress.gov/committees/video/house -education-and-the-workforce/hsed00/31Eu-xEZKzQ at 1:51:41; cf. Sarah Benor, "I'm a Jewish Linguist, and I Think 'Ashkenormativity' Is a Perfectly Fine Word," *Jerusalem Post*, May 3, 2024. Ashkenormativity refers to the idea that Ashkenazi Jews are privileged over Mizrahi and Sephardi Jews in Israeli society.

5. On collective victimhood, see Ilan Peleg, ed., *Victimhood Discourse in Contemporary Israel* (Lexington Books, 2019). On grieving for both sides, politics, and the workings of the "grief machine," see the exchange between Joshua Liefer and Gabriel Winant in *Dissent*: Liefer, "Toward a Humane Left," *Dissent*, Oct. 12, 2023, and Winant, "On Mourning and Statehood: A Response to Joshua Leifer," *Dissent*, Oct. 13, 2023.

6. Antony Lerman, "The Politics of Antisemitism," *Jewish Quarterly* 32, no. 1 (1985), cited in Lerman, *The Making and Unmaking of a Zionist: A Personal and Political Journey* (Pluto Press, 2012), 77; Pope Francis, *Fratelli Tutti*, at https://www.vatican.va/content/francesco/en/encyclicals/documents/papa-francesco_20201003_enciclica-fratelli-tutti.html#_ftn2; Victor Klemperer, *The Language of the Third Reich: LTI— Lingua Tertii Imperii; A Philologist's Notebook* (Bloomsbury Academic, 2021 ed.), 1.

INDEX

Page numbers in *italics* indicate illustrative material.